ULTIMAYA 1.0

ULTIMAYA 1.0

The Trouble with the Wishes
of Leopold Stokes

A novel

Saniel Bonder

Human Sun Media
Sonoma, California

ULTIMAYA 1.0

Version 1.0.1 December 2011

 Published by
Human Sun Media

Cover design by Gaelyn Larrick, www.artservingspirit.com

Back cover photo by Al Porter

Interior design and layout by Deborah Perdue, www.illuminationgraphics.com

Orders and information:
info@sanielandlinda.com
toll-free U.S. 1.877.783.3873

ISBN 978-0-9753532-5-7

Early praise for

ULTIMAYA 1.0:

The Trouble with the Wishes of Leopold Stokes

"The Matrix meets *Alice in Wonderland* in *Ultimaya 1.0,* which takes us way, way down the rabbit hole. Saniel Bonder serves up a rollicking good read in which deep metaphysical insights are married with gritty Southern dialogue, fascinating twists of fate, and perspective-bending scenes generated by a more-than-mischievous computer program, all leaving the reader wondering what ground we can actually stand on. The journey of spiritual liberation has rarely been explored with this much panache. I highly recommend this book!"

> ~ Stephen Dinan, CEO, The Shift Network, author, *Radical Spirit*

"Ultimaya 1.0 is thrilling, unlike anything I've ever encountered before. A carnival ride into the face of God."

> ~ Louise Herschelle, MFT (Marriage and Family Therapist)

"What a wild rumpus of a novel! I sometimes wished I could've just reached into the pages and shaken small town Carolina banker Leopold Stokes to help him wise up—but his lessons here are really lessons for all of us. We're all far too familiar with the disastrous consequences of unrestrained greed that nearly destroyed our economy in recent years. It helps that Saniel Bonder is a gifted writer with a sense of humor and a folksy Southern touch, as well as a lot of heart and deep wisdom. I recommend *Ultimaya 1.0* as required reading for every banker, trader, financier, corporate executive, economist, regulator, and entrepreneur on the planet. Read it and see why for yourself!"

> ~ Monika Mitchell, author, *Conversations with Wall Street,*
> CEO, Good Business International, named Standout Company
> of the Year in 2010 by the Washington Post Leadership Playlist

"Every texture of this brilliant yarn of life feels amazingly real. Bonder's style is fluid and engaging; his characters and dialogue deliver a sense of fun and energy throughout. And Leopold Stokes' wild adventure draws you in, touches the heart, and leaves you wondering—what is it to live consciously in our strange and challenging world today?"
~ Gena Netten, former Brand & Marketing Manager,
Educational Testing Service

"The story was part thrill ride with twists and turns and part nostalgic tech journey back to the days when DOS was new. I enjoyed it very much."
~ Mike Hatfield, CEO, Cyan Optics

"*Ultimaya 1.0* is a compelling novel that is highly imaginative and rich with astute insights. This daring tale has everything—adventure, mystery, romance, wisdom, tantalizing twists and turns, and truly memorable characters. It is sure to inspire and entertain you!"
~ Susanne West, Professor of Psychology, John F. Kennedy
University, author, *Soul Care for Caregivers*

"*Ultimaya 1.0* is a worthy and admirable plunge into some extremely deep territory, written both with unusual flair and uncommon spiritual savvy. Its colloquial yet engagingly nuanced texture and flow give us ground for the launching of the protagonist, Leopold Stokes, into a reality-unlocking adventure (one that we all, sooner or later, will have to take). The description of his journey, both inner and outer, is wonderfully compelling reading; there is something (including between the lines) there we can't directly get at with language, but Saniel's way of telling it brings that 'something' into richly tangible focus. *Ultimaya 1.0* doesn't explain the Mystery, but deepens our intimacy with It. Sit back, relax into the story, fasten your seatbelt, and keep your eyes as open as possible as the rollercoaster crests its first big hill and starts to really fly... Highly recommended!"
~ Robert Augustus Masters, Ph.D., author,
Spiritual Bypassing and *Transformation Through Intimacy*

Dedicated to the memory
and living spirit of
my late father,
Murray Bonder

And for everyone who's trying
to become happy
by fulfilling wishes
and making dreams come true

"I give people what they want
so they will begin to want
what I want to give them."

~ Shirdi Sai Baba, miracle-working saint
of early 20th century India

Contents

TROUBLE

Leopold Stokes knew he was in trouble. Trouble was, he didn't know what kind of trouble he was really in. He thought he knew. But he didn't really know.

It had all begun the night before. It was a cold evening in December 1992, long enough before Christmas that Leo still couldn't be bothered to think about it. He was at the table and Nan, as usual, was ragging him mercilessly with her pet naggation about his persisting singleness and obvious need for female companionship of his own age. She, of course, was only speaking to him because of her loyalty to his parents and their dear solemn memory. It had nothing to do with her own concerns. For all she cared, he could go solitarily to his grave—that was his business. But his momma had always been aggrieved over his failure to marry and have a family. Now that she was gone, well, she, Nan, felt she really had no choice but to continue to press the issue, even though she was not even family, she was really only a friend of the family. As Leo well knew—and Nan never failed to acknowledge at this point in her speech—she had only come to live with them lo these many years ago due to his momma and daddy's kindness at a time of severe trials in Nan's own life.

But Nan had been there at his momma's passing. And his momma's virtually last words, according to Nan, had been her plea to Nan to continue to remind, that was the exact term, *remind* her dear Leo to please find a wife and have some children. How else, his momma had

worried, could Leo carry on the fine Stokes name that his poor daddy—
and his granddaddy too—had labored so long and hard to bring to
distinction there in Cotton County? (Leo always wondered about that
phrase of Nan's, "*vur*-choo-ul-lay last words"; if those weren't his
mother's actual last words, then what exactly were?)

Well, right in the midst of Nan's diatribe, Leo surprised even himself.
He had by now virtually memorized her speech (there it was again, "*vur*-
choo-ul-lay;" she said it so often and with such emphasis that he now,
to his annoyance, found himself using it even in silent ruminations). He
could recite her rant more or less *verbatim,* could interrupt her at any
point and carry on without a hitch, and in fact often did so, rather politely
of course, with downcast eyes—not wanting to mock her too much
because that would really wind her up. And Nan would listen to every
word, nod emphatically, and then, as if she had not given him the same
shrill speech two thousand times, crow in response, "*That* is *precisely*
what I was about to declare!"

But this time, instead of mimicking her, with both hands Leo yanked
up the large, nearly empty casserole dish, lifted it two full feet into the air,
and then let it drop, so that it smacked onto the solid mahogany dinner
table with a tremendous whack. The whole table shook so hard that the
slightly melted Jell-O sloshed over the edges of its bowl, and the remains
then came to a tremulous rest in the bowl's innards, as if still quaking in
fear of Leo's next potentially violent act.

Leo resisted the urge to grin and looked from the jiggling Jell-O to Nan.
She too was tremulous—thin little mouth agape, narrow-set blue eyes
stunned wide open, one pallid and blue-veined little hand frozen motionless
on her gray bun, where it had been tucking in stray wisps when the crockery
crashed to the table. This was a new and totally unforeseen event in Nan's
universe, and she was duly astonished. Knowing her resiliency in the—
what did she call it—"give and take of life's hick'ry switches," Leo leaped
into speech before she could gather her wits and start talking again. He
looked her square in the eye and—pausing for just an instant to register

her obvious discomfort under his glare, for she'd never anticipated he might silence her with such a look—he delivered his admonition with a deep metallic grind of threatening authority, so that each syllable was like a tank rumbling up to the border of the shrill little solitary spinster's nation of Nan and taking dead aim right between her beady blue eyes.

"Nan...shut...your...gol-...dang...*mouth!*"

The "goldang," which he'd added only to strengthen his point, sped right past her. Leo had the strange sense of the word missing its target and landing, mute and harmless, on the kitchen floor beyond her right shoulder, like a dud Iraqi Scud missile in the recent Gulf War. The thought made him want to laugh, but he suppressed it, didn't even let his lips twitch into a grin. He did make a mental note to reserve what she called "shocking sinful speech of the Devil" for her less mind-shattered moments. Then he waited.

After a time, Nan closed her mouth and rather modestly—he even suspected submissively—turned her eyes away and down from his implacable gaze.

And after a few more crucial moments, for she could have gone either way, it was his turn to begin to feel a sense of astonishment, accompanied by elation.

It had worked. Nan wasn't saying so much as a single word.

They both returned to their meals. Leo forced himself to breathe calmly, like nothing had happened. Nan didn't look up. She didn't even ask him to pass anything from his side of the table. Leo knew very well that on an ordinary night she would have gobbled down the entire bowl of black-eyed peas, and part of the standard evening lecture would have been a stern disquisition on the necessity of his eating his collard greens—"if you want to protect a body against heart disease in old age, a necessity you have never faced up to, not since I was young and purty and you were dressed in short pants, little man." Tonight, mercifully, the lecture was cancelled, and Leo enjoyed the leisure of wondering for a few moments how she ever pieced together a connection between collards and cholesterol.

He glanced around the room a bit, seeing that some of the pine paneling was just slightly warping off the wallboard, and that the old red and blue Oriental rug that covered most of the oak floor was going threadbare in places. No surprise, he thought, remembering that his mother had had that rug in this dining room since his boyhood. Simultaneously he realized that during most of his meals with Nan these days he felt so set upon that he barely looked up from his plate to register anything around them. It occurred to him that he should replace the plain white ceiling fixture with something, well, something a little more modern, and that he should ask Nan to get some flowers for the center of the table (plastic ones would be okay, as long as they looked real). It would be good to have a new houseplant or two for the white-painted brick flooring in front of the unused fireplace and chimney, which were likewise of white brick. And maybe he ought to find a new painting for the mantelpiece, a colorful Matisse print perhaps; the stern photo of Abner Stokes Sr., his grandfather, might well deserve retirement, at least from such prominent display. Leo felt a pleasant surge of energy to change things. Indeed, he felt like it had been ten years since he had last even looked at the room.

Nan, meanwhile, averted her eyes for the rest of their dinner together. She ate in uncharacteristic birdlike nibbles, and soon retreated in silence to the kitchen and the dishes. She seemed so cowed that Leo almost began to feel sorry for her.

But then she began talking to him again, not with words, but nonetheless out loud. As Leo sat savoring his Maxwell House, he heard her begin to clang each finished plate and utensil into the dish drainer. With every one, it seemed, Nan put more force into her protest, so that he began to fear the dishes would break, or that she would hurt herself on a knife. He sighed, removed his orange paper napkin from his lap, and strode to the open kitchen door.

"All right, Nan...I'm sorry I yelled at you and used foul language."

She did not look up. She was just then rinsing a large porcelain serving tray, and she held it up with both hands while looking for an open slot in the drainer. Then she smashed the tray into its slot so hard that several forks and knives bounced out of the silverware container and clattered onto the floor. Nan didn't even look at them but only turned to clean her next victim, the big casserole dish.

Leo sighed again, this time aloud. "Come on, Nan, no hard feelings. Stop smashing that poor dinnerware around and talk to me again."

No response. Nan continued to bend into the casserole dish, scrubbing it with the piece of steel wool as if to scrape the enamel right off. Leo knew what was coming next; it too would be crashed into the dish drainer, as would everything else left in the sink. Nan had been grievously wronged and he would be paying for it as long as she could find dishes to scrub that evening. Given her resourcefulness in such affairs, she'd likely find ways to keep him paying dearly a good deal on into the night. There was no room in the little two-bedroom brick house for him to get far enough away from the noise to be able to ignore her. And Leo knew very well that Nan knew very well that he decidedly did not like going out at night. He had no nighttime socializing friends to speak of. Ashlin had no bars, no nightspots, at least not with sufficient class for him to frequent—though he would never have dreamed of going to such a place anyway, at least not there in town. The library closed each evening promptly at six. And there was no way he was going to give in and call Constance, who was probably on duty at the hospital anyway.

Nan had him.

For an instant Leo wondered why his second command had not worked. He had told her to stop smacking the plates around, he had even told her to talk to him again. *What about the program? What about Ultimaya 1.0?* But in that instant the casserole dish came down onto the counter with a shocking crash, and Leo entirely forgot his grumbling wonderings.

In a flash he felt himself being overwhelmed by the kind of rage that his old friend since high school, Charley Bass, used to call "the Leo-nuclear weapon" or, for short, "the L-bomb." He could feel the blood rushing to and reddening his already red neck and face, and the act of compressing his lips to keep from shouting somehow seemed to make his eyes bulge out—Charley had teased him about how his face and eyes got as red as his hair—and he knew he wouldn't be able to hold it in. Even under ordinary circumstances he sometimes felt his thickset, strong body was as rigid as a brick chimney. And though he was incapable of radiating emotional warmth of a tender kind, when an explosion of anger started churning in his guts, Leopold Stokes could neither control nor contain the internal fires. Raging words and acts would burst out of him like smoke spewing into a room through faulty flues and cracked mortar. No matter how hard he tried to restrain himself, it never did any good.

Like right now.

Without a word, Leo smashed his fist into the kitchen door so hard that the door cracked back against the wall and then stood shaking on its hinges, reverberating. Leo looked in fury at Nan.

She had already picked up the frying pan and was scrubbing away, her back toward him and her head bent over the sink.

Leo glanced down at his bloody and bruised knuckles, which hurt so bad he had to fight back tears. He had a sudden sense of himself as a stick of dynamite with a half-inch fuse. His ears felt hot enough to blister; he knew he'd better get out of that room fast. But as he turned to go, he could not resist shrieking: "Nan, goldang it—if you don't want to talk to me, then WHY DON'T YOU JUST SPONTANEOUSLY COMBUST!"

What happened next was something Leopold Stokes would not likely forget for the rest of his life. Just as he was about to stomp off, he noticed that Nan had stopped moving. She stood stock still in front of the sink. Then, with a clatter, the frying pan slid out of her left hand onto the dishes stacked underneath it. Her right hand still clutched the steel wool as she turned toward him, nothing moving except her feet and legs, the rest of her body frozen like a statue.

Leo felt the blood drain out of his face and neck. "Nan?"

She seemed not to hear him. In fact, she seemed oblivious to everything, even though her eyes were wide open and staring straight through Leo's. Her gaze was so bizarre that he felt like a cornered creature. Despite his discomfort, he could not avert his eyes until something began to happen in her clenched right hand that distracted him.

The ball of steel wool in her hand appeared to be enveloped by a strange, bluish green light. As Leo looked on dumbfounded, strands of it began glowing orange and dissolving, until—with an almost silent *poof!*—the whole ball of steel wool burst into incandescent flame and then floated away in shreds of ash.

Leo hardly had time to register all that before he noticed that now the same bluish green light had extended up Nan's arm and was enveloping her whole body. His mouth dropped open and he let out a gargled croak as it hit him what was about to happen. He reached for her with his undamaged hand in a desperate effort to somehow prevent what was coming, but then there was another, almost entirely silent— but this time monstrous—flash of light and heat that knocked him back through the dining room doorway and threw him flat on his back.

For a moment, Leo lay there disoriented. Then he remembered what was happening and sprang to his feet. The entire front of his body felt hot and singed, as if he'd been in front of a blast furnace. Trembling, he groped his way to the doorway again. It dawned on him that the room was so full of—what? Smoke? Soot? Ash? Whatever it might be, there was so much of it flying around, he could not see.

"Nan?"

The particles of ash were settling to the floor. Dark gray soot coated the walls all around the kitchen, including the dining room door and the refrigerator door, even obscuring all of Nan's little scribbled yellow post-it warnings to him not to eat her private foods in the fridge.

"Jesus…what? What's—Nan! Where are you?"

There was no answer. Leo struggled to make himself look at the floor where she'd been standing.

There was nothing there—except one little black old-lady's shoe, kind of shapely and not too stodgy looking now that Nan wasn't standing in it, with the brand name "P. W. Minor & Son" ash-dusted but still visible on the insole. The shoe was standing upright exactly where her right foot had been planted the moment before the explosion.

Leo gulped, croaked aloud, and began to shout. He threw himself to the floor, his hands outstretched so that both of them grasped the shoe without moving it, his face and whole body flat on the linoleum. Tears began streaming from his eyes, and he began to moan aloud.

"Aagh! *AAAAAAGGGGGHHHHH!!!*...Oh God, I'm sorry. I'm sorry. I'm sorry, God! NAAAAANNNN!! I didn't mean it, Nan! I didn't want to hurt you! You get on my nerves, but I didn't mean for you to die! Nan! Where are you? God A'mighty, this can't be true! Aagh! *AAAAAGGGGHHHH!*"

Suddenly, a thought struck Leo like a laser beam in his brain. He was quiet for a moment, the stillness broken only by his sobs and the snufflings of his nose. Then, still without moving, he said out loud, real loud, with all the ardent hope and need of his being:

"Oh God, if you exist—I know you exist—dear God, Lord of my soul, have mercy on me. Have mercy on me, Lord. I did not really mean for Nan to die. I did not mean to set her on fire. That was horrible, Lord. I mean, it was *horrible!* I would not wish that on anyone. I *will* not wish that on anyone. Never again. NEVER!!"

Leo paused. With a weird, oily sensation of being caught in the act, he felt he must have sounded like Burt Reynolds in the movie *The End,* bargaining with God when he thought he was drowning. Leo redoubled his efforts to be sincere, so that he was practically shouting:

"So *please* don't let Nan die. If there is any way under the sun—under the moon and the stars—that You can bring Nan back to life, I swear Lord, I swear it on my mother's grave, on the Bible, on everything I hold true and sacred, I swear it on the foreclosure notice I'm holding on that little country Baptist church—Lord, I will rip that notice up tomorrow morning, I'll go down to the office and do it tonight! I'll pay their rent myself for three months—but dear God, Lord of Hosts, Father of our blessed Savior, Jesus, yes, holy Jesus, You too, I beg You: Please, please, PLEEEAASE bring old Nan back to life. Don't leave her dead, and me here to try to live my life now that I have made this terrible thing come to pass. I beg You, Father. I beg You, Jesus. I beg You. I beg You. I beg You!"

Leo could think of nothing else to add to his prayer. Despite his desperation, it still left him cool and a little queasy. And, as he lay there, his nose and face flattened on the linoleum, his outstretched hands cradling Nan's one remaining shoe, he couldn't help wondering: horrific as this moment was, what was the point of making such supplications at all?

After all, Leopold Stokes never had been more than a Sunday, preen-and-pray Christian. He'd been baptized, but it meant little to him. He just never could detect any "hand of God in human events," no matter how hard he looked. So his point of view was, why bother with something that's inconsequential—whether it exists or not?

In their teens, he and Charley Bass, who at the time was reading European existentialist philosophy, used to tease some of their more zealously devout friends. One of them was a card-carrying fire 'n brimstone Baptist boy named Job Hawkins. (Leo could never fathom that somebody had actually named their own flesh-and-blood kid "Job," right out of Judges or wherever it was—Job!) Whenever Job would fulminate to Charley about how certain it was, due to his incessant blasphemy against God and other sins, that he, Charley, would be crisped in hell on Judgment Day, Charley and Leo used to sing him a little ditty of Charley's composition. They'd stand side by side, hands folded before their chests in mock prayer, and ground it out *basso profundo* like monks working the low end of a Gregorian chant.

"What in hell could God possibly be? Where in God could hell possibly be?"

"Who in the world could possibly give definitive answers to such infinite questions?"

And then, finally, just to poke at their fundamentalist friend a little closer to the fundament:

"And who but the Devil could possibly believe the things Job does to his little sister?"

During Charley's more overtly spiritual days, in the late '60s and early '70s, Leo used to argue with him now and again about God and the import of Charley's mystical (but, to Leo's way of thinking, sheerly pharmacological and wacko) experiences. In a funny, wistful sort of way, just as he'd earlier envied Charley's devil-may-care wildness, Leo now envied Charley's daring loss of face among their friends, the renegade glamour of his "altered states of consciousness," the romantic halo of his sudden sincere ardor for God. "St. Charley of the Harley," he sometimes teased him; but to Leo, he was a kind of venerably pious James Dean. Leo himself always felt so, well, constricted, so burdened with patrilineal expectation, that he would not or could not allow himself the freedom to explore life with such abandon.

He never let on to Charley how he felt, though. And, as if in compensation for his uncomfortable hidden sympathies, Leo always made sure to snort all the more cynically during their conversations about religion and such.

Neither of them had ever won a single one of those debates. Eventually, at least to some degree, Charley had become sour and rather silent about the whole matter. So Leo, disinclined to pursue the subject further on his own (and secretly fearing he'd get nowhere anyway), had persisted in his conclusion that God was at best inconsequential in human affairs.

In the pragmatic Stokes tradition, however, he did appreciate the virtue of consequential matters, even if they were illusions or mere appearances. His father, Abner Stokes Jr., hadn't really cared for spiritual things either. But he'd gone to church religiously every Sunday, primarily to keep good standing in the community and only secondarily—or so he told Leo—to placate Leo's mother, Agnes, who was always conspiring with Nan to secure the salvation of her husband's immortal soul.

As far as Leo could surmise, Nan and their minister reckoned that, when the accident happened, Abner Stokes was just barely, if at all, in the doorway of the elect. Thus, upon inheriting his father's role as the upstanding owner of the principal local bank, Leo figured he'd best begin attending church services regularly simply to serve as the local cornerstone he knew he was expected to be.

He could tell it made a difference. People noticed Leo. His being at church every Sunday helped them trust him. And everybody from sharecroppers to cotton planters to J. N. Pippin with his Cadillac-Olds dealership made it a point to bow his head with just a bit of a nod when he walked into Leo's office at Cotton County Regional Bank looking for advice or a little munificent sympathy.

"Leopold Stokes! What in tarnation are you doing on that floor? Let go of my foot, young man!"

Leo looked up, blinking through his drying tears.

It was Nan!

For the second time that night, his mouth dropped wide open. "Nan! You're back! You're alive! Oh God, I can't believe it! I just cannot believe it!"

Nan was standing with the ball of steel wool in her right fist, the heel of her palm resting on her hip so as to keep the wet wool away from her apron. The casserole dish, still not cleaned, was in her left hand. Leo looked at her hands and arms, then her head, then down her whole body, right to her feet. She was all there. Nan was fine!

"I said to you, Leopold Stokes, let go of my foot! I mean it!"

Leo sprang back, letting go of her shoe and raising himself up to sit on the floor with his legs underneath him. He was weeping again, inwardly thanking God and Jesus and whoever else had answered his prayers, and making a mental note to find some way to refinance the mortgage on that little church. His body was shaking with gratitude.

Nan turned back to the sink, muttering, "Never been so mortified in all my born days!" She continued with her dishes.

Leo just sat on the floor, sniffing with joy. First he noticed that there was not a trace of soot or ash anywhere in sight. Then he noticed Nan wasn't smashing dishes into the drainer anymore. He wondered how long he'd been lying there on the floor, lost in thought. It could've been fifteen minutes, or only five seconds; he had no idea.

"Nan?"

"What do you want from me now?"

"What happened before you noticed me, lying there on the linoleum—"

"Holding my foot like some kind of devil-worshipping sex pervert? I cannot imagine what is going on with you, Leopold Stokes!"

"Yeah...yeah...I know that, Nan. I mean, I'm sorry, okay? I don't think I can explain it exactly—but, Nan, what happened right before that?"

"I don't know! All I know is I heard you smashing your fist into that dining room door for some fool reason. I turned around to ask you what in the world you were doing, boy, and you just stood there and looked at me like I was a ghost or something, and the next thing I knew you'd thrown yourself on the floor and grabbed me by the shoe!"

Nan eyed him suspiciously. "Are you all right, Leopold? I tell you what, seems to me this is just one more sure sign you are wanting a woman of proper age and disposition to provide you with feminine companionship. And I'll tell you this too: if you ever take such liberties with my person again, Leopold Stokes, well, no never mind what I told your momma, I will have to find myself another place to call my home!

"And at my age! Can you imagine that? That would be a true scandal in this little county seat, and I don't think a man in your position would be wanting such a thing to come to pass. Can you imagine what Constance Cunningham would say to that? I wonder how long you could continue to take her attention for granted—"

Nan carried on with her harangue, oblivious, as she scrubbed away at the forks and knives. Leo grinned, wiped his nose with the cuff of a shirtsleeve, and rose to his feet.

"Good night, Nan."

She was still talking to herself, or whoever, and did not notice as Leo beamed at her with more love than he'd probably felt for her since he was in actual fact dressed in short pants. Smiling, he then turned and walked through the dining room toward his bedroom to retire.

"Make a Wish!"

Leo lay awake long into the night. Sleep was out of the question. He had the distinct sensation that his brain was steaming under fierce pressure, like a chunk of beef in a double boiler. He had to get a grip on what had just happened. If it was possible.

His trouble, he realized as he pieced things together, had not begun that night at dinner. It had begun a few hours earlier, that afternoon. He'd come home early after his regular Wednesday afternoon golf game with J. N. Pippin, owner of the town's Cadillac-Olds dealership, and Jeremiah Michaelson, the local superior court judge. Though it was a bright, sunny day, the wintry temperature and wind chill had gotten to them by the thirteenth hole. They'd settled up on their bets—Pippin and Michaelson as usual razzing Leo about his unwillingness to play for more than small change—and at four o'clock in the afternoon Leo found himself at home with nothing to do before dinner. So he'd decided to sit down and fiddle a bit with his new computer.

Leo had been so impressed by the innovations and the savings in time, not to mention wages, that computerizing had brought to the bank over quite a few years now, that he had decided to get a little portable, a laptop, to use at home and on his occasional business trips to the state capital. Of course the "business trip" business was really just an excuse. Fact was, he had liked the looks on the tellers' and junior officers' faces when he happened to bring a friend's laptop to the bank one day, carrying it in a fine gray case with a shoulder strap. In that instant he had decided to get one just like it, except better, but also cheaper.

So he'd called his old friend Charley Bass, who now owned the biggest computer retail chain in the state, based in the capital. Charley had questioned Leo a bit about his needs and had recommended a new, svelte, lightweight yet heavy-duty machine, a Texas Instruments 3000WinSX. Charley'd run a babble of numbers and technical specifications past Leo at superspeed; Leo could only gather the machine not only had some kind of software called "Windows" built in, but it was actually built for and upon this Windows "platform."

Finally, Leo had raised a hand and said, "Charley, you know me. I am not about to buy some new top-of-the-line machine that I have to pay big for. Just give me something a little older, a little easier, a little slower, a little heavier—something that works. Maybe I'll jump into or out of your 'Windows' later on. I want the easy stuff right now. And I want a bargain."

Charley had sighed and chuckled. Then, together, they decided it would be good for Leo to get a Toshiba T3100e/40—Charley commenting, "Now I reckon in about a year, mebbe two, you'll be up and running real good, and you'll want to trade this old baby in. But it'll do for starters. Pretty quick for a 286, reliable, a stalwart 40 megabyte hard drive; hell, you'll be able to record a whole library of data on this thing, old bud!"

Leo had gone down on Tuesday, after Charley took a couple of hours to install all the necessary software for him to do some spreadsheets and also word processing—mainly for correspondence. He wasn't really interested in the machine for number-crunching. If that was all he wanted, he could just use the big mainframe computer down at the bank. Besides, running spreadsheets was exactly the kind of work he hired other people to do. No, no. Leopold Stokes took home his gray slate Toshiba laptop with another intention entirely.

Strangely enough, he didn't quite know what that intention was. Leo just knew he had to have that computer, and he was going to do something with it that would change his life. He had no idea what. He did know he didn't want anyone else to know about it. Not even Constance, or Charley, and certainly not Nan. And he wanted to be able to do it whenever he pleased. Whatever *it* was going to be!

So, as near as Leo could reckon, lying in bed at 2:00 a.m. with his brain still cooking, his troubles had really begun right here in his bedroom when he first fired up the computer and checked out the menu Charley had set up for him. Everything was there just as they'd agreed, and it all looked just like it had when Charley'd demonstrated it for him—the Lotus program and various accounting programs following along underneath it on the list, the WordPerfect 5.1 word processing program, the MCI Pro Comm program for telecommunications, MS/DOS, and a couple of other internal analysis programs so he could stay on top of what the computer had in it. He already couldn't remember what those internal programs were, and he knew he'd have to call Charley just to get reminded.

Leo had decided to jump into WordPerfect immediately, just to play around a little. He moved the cursor onto the WordPerfect line and, with his right little finger, hit the shift key. In the same instant, he blurted, "Oops"—he realized he'd meant to hit the enter key, which would have activated WordPerfect.

Leo had worked on enough computers at the office to know that this was a common enough mistake. Though he shared every computer duffer's dread of hitting a wrong key and getting hopelessly lost in the machine's meta-programming, he was pretty certain that this particular flub should not have caused any serious problems. Pressing shift, after all, should only produce capital letters. At worst, or so he thought, it should have just not done anything.

But that's not what had happened. Not at all.

Instead the cursor jumped to the top of the menu. And there, Leo noticed, was a program he'd never heard of before and had certainly not ordered. And he could have sworn, later, that the name of the program lit up with several bright colors as he looked at the menu: Ultimaya 1.0.

"Ultimaya 1.0? What the heck is that?" Leo mumbled aloud. Then he figured he'd better call Charley about it, just in case by using the software he might get charged for it even if he didn't want to keep it. Or maybe he'd screwed something up by hitting shift instead of enter. So he left the main menu on the screen and dialed Charley Bass.

"What's up, Leo?"

Leo told Charley what he'd stumbled upon.

"'Ultimaya 1.0!' Damn, Leo, I've never heard of any such program. Don't have a clue to what that is or how it got on your machine. Hitting shift instead of enter doesn't explain it, that's for sure. Have you checked it out?"

"No, Charley, I thought I'd better not, in case if I used it and didn't want it, they could charge me for it anyway."

"Who's 'they,' Leo? *I* sold you all those programs and installed every last one of 'em. And I haven't got the slightest idea what that thing is or where it's come from. You haven't paid a penny for it, and I sure as hell wouldn't charge you for something I never had to begin with. So don't worry about money." Charley chuckled. "You skinflint rascal. Y'ain't changed a bit in thirty years, you know that, buddy?"

Charley laughed out loud. Leo laughed a little and cleared his throat.

Charley went on: "Anyhow, all that being the way it is, you could bring it back on down here and I'll check to make sure this Ultimaya thing isn't a virus. But I'm pretty up to date on what's out there and I never heard of anything at all by that name."

Charley paused, then continued. "Nah. You don't need the hassle of another trip to Raleigh. The computer's brand new. You don't have anything on it yet, and it's not networked in to your big equipment at the bank. There's no way a virus could've crawled in there. Or if it did, well, you're under warranty. If it's messed up somehow, I'll replace it.

"So if I was you, Leo, I'd just leap on in there and check out this Ultimaya program before you do anything else. What's the harm, know what I mean? Somehow this strange little number must've gotten piggybacked into one of the programs I did sell you and installed on

Tuesday. So it's yours. But I can't picture what it might be. Tell you what—give me a call after you take a look, okay? I am definitely interested to hear about this one. Never heard of such a thing!"

As he hung up the phone, Leo felt—well, he felt weird. He could not figure it out. It was the strangest thing—contemplating opening the Ultimaya 1.0 program was like facing up to his father when he was a boy, or like the first time he'd had sex, at age twenty-three, or…he wasn't sure why he was so queasy about it, but there it was.

Leo sat at the desk in the alcove of his bedroom, staring at the menu on his computer screen. The cursor was on the Ultimaya 1.0 line. All he had to do was hit enter. Yet he could not move. He just sat staring at the screen, bewildered and a little angry at himself for getting so flustered, while the sun sank below the tops of the nearby pines and the wintry day drew to a close. He was vaguely aware of the picture window to his right— one of the few things he'd done to this house since inheriting it, along with Nan in it and her slew of non-renovate-able memories in every corner, was to enlarge his old bedroom window so he could have a nice view of the yard and the pines bordering the Jenkins' lot just next door. He was also vaguely aware of his solitary bed and nightstand to his left, his old fine handcrafted High Point rocker, the knotty pine dresser and mirror on the other side of the room, both of which he'd had since he was a boy, the old throw rug and now-threadbare armchair. The whole environment was becoming indiscernible and dark in his peripheral vision as he gazed at the computer screen, somehow mesmerized by the name "Ultimaya 1.0" and paralyzed by hesitation, or maybe plain old fear.

At last he was startled by Nan's call from the kitchen: "Leopold Stokes! Dinner will be ready promptly in twenty minutes! Just reminding you, hear me?"

Leo's right hand shot forward and he hit the enter key just as the feeling flashed through him that if he only had ten minutes or so to check out the curious program—since he did have to wash and straighten up a bit for dinner—he couldn't very well get too involved.

There! It was done. The main menu disappeared, and Leo felt a thrill as the computer began its internal machinations to access the new program and display before him the mystery of Ultimaya 1.0.

At least, that was what he thought was going to happen. But after the typical internal whirring he'd grown accustomed to hearing other computers do, the machine went dead silent, its screen pitch black—or whatever color closest to black it got there in the twilight.

For a moment, Leo again thought something had gone wrong. Did he choose the wrong program on the menu? No—he knew that wasn't it. He considered trying to get back to the main menu and starting again, but then he realized he didn't know how to get back again, unless it'd be by turning the machine off entirely.

Just when he was ready to conclude that was what he should do, a message flashed on the screen in white letters:

"No—everything is fine. Do not tamper with the machine. Just...RELAX."

Then the screen went dark again.

All this had taken place without a sound.

Leo felt slightly embarrassed. He shrugged his shoulders and said aloud, hesitantly, drawing out each syllable, "O—K—." Then he took a couple of deep breaths and tried to relax. His solar plexus was completely tight. It was like he was having butterflies before a big meeting with one of the regulatory commissions. Not just nervous—he was real wound up, a lot tighter than usual.

Leopold Stokes felt tight all the time. It was a constant aggravation in his life, that sense of constriction. When he was a kid, he'd always felt it too, and had often imagined what it would be like to be squeezed to death by a big boa constrictor, or an eighty-foot anaconda, because it didn't seem to him that it would feel much different from how he always felt. Now, even as an adult, it was almost like he walked around expecting something like that to happen. In this moment, he was wound up like a spring, just about ready to explode physically—even though he felt inept and, well, virginal. Those embarrassing sensations and feelings of inadequacy heightened the tension in the spring he felt himself to be and kept anxiety condensing into his whole system like grain alcohol in a still.

By now Leo's room was completely dark. He could barely distinguish the computer screen from the rest of the alcove. Now and again, a car's headlights, passing on the street outside, threw a pale yellow beam onto his wall and the screen in front of him. Otherwise he was in a womb of deep grays and blacks with no clear shapes at all.

Then a thought boomed like thunder through his brain, drawing him bolt upright in his chair: "This confounded machine knew what was on my mind." He was amazed it had taken him so long to notice the obvious: *the program had just told him not to turn it off. It had told him to relax. It knew what was on his mind!*

No other thoughts could coalesce in his head. He stared at the screen, dark before him. And then, as he began to grope inwardly for some rationale to explain what had just occurred, several more sentences, white against black, flashed up on the screen one at a time before his eyes, the internal machinery of the computer still completely quiet: "Ultimaya 1.0 User Integration sequence completed."

"Huh?" Leo said aloud.

"Preliminary impulse vector scan completed."

"What in the world?" Leo murmured again, turning his ear to the machine, as if by trying to hear something inside it—even though it was still dead quiet—he would maybe comprehend the technical language.

"Ultimaya 1.0 fully operational with this User."

"'This User'...I think it's talking about me!" Leo sat back, a quizzical smile on his face. This was bizarre.

"Ultimaya 1.0 program operational only with this User. This program will self-destruct if other Users are interpolated into operations."

Then the screen went completely black again. Leo whistled through his teeth, "O—K—." He wasn't sure exactly what those few sentences of computer jargon meant, but he had a feeling he *did* know, and the familiar knot in his stomach got tighter.

The ordinary whirring of the computer began again, relieving him of at least some of his distress. Then the screen on his monitor exploded into a burst of colors, and just continued exploding before him. His room was by now otherwise pitch dark, so no other source of light dimmed the intensity of the display. His eyes were riveted on the monitor as a visual riot of blues and grays and greens, oranges, pinks, chartreuses and purples, whites and reds and lavenders fluted, streamed, gridded, and spiraled all around in ever flowing and changing shapes. It was all happening extremely fast. Not a thought crossed his mind, except a subliminal registering that the colors were becoming brighter in hue, the shapes were rounding and softening, and that as all of this went on he was unaccountably feeling more and more relaxed and relieved and, why, he was *happy*. He felt *good*. Just at the instant this feeling came to his awareness, there appeared on the screen, with all the dramatic visual flourish of the initial credits on a lavishly produced film, another communication, this time in an elaborate typescript instead of the functional lettering of the previous words and phrases.

> Welcome to…
> U L T I M A Y A 1.0
> The Ultimate in Interactive,
> User Integrated, Virtual Software …
> the One and Only Software Package
> That Fulfills …
> Y O U R …
> Deepest Wishes!

Leo's mouth was hanging open, his brow furrowed in amazement. The screen went awash again in a blaze of bright and tumultuous colors, just for an instant, and then another communication appeared, now in a functional black typeface against a soft, light gray background:

"Since you may not have much time for your first exploration of Ultimaya 1.0, and perhaps wish to put the power of this unique software package to an immediate test, why don't you simply—"

The screen went black, then white, then purple, and on the purple these words arose one at a time in gold: "Make...a...WISH!"

Leo let out a muffled laugh, almost a croak, and sat back in his seat, grinning. His brain began to race. "This is crazy!" he spluttered. "This is great! What in God's Creation is this thing? I don't believe this! Too dang wild—"

The screen went black, then white, then purple again. Then: "Don't think about it. Just DO IT!"

He laughed again. "All right! Okay! I will!" he said aloud. But suddenly Leo felt confused. How should he proceed? Should he just type something? Or say it?

The program flashed up these words: "To make your wish concrete and precise, simply type it onto the screen exactly as you want to communicate it."

"Okay...whatever you say, Mr. Ultimaya 1.0," Leo chortled under his breath. For a second, the bizarreness of this conversation broke upon him, so that he glanced all around the room to make sure no one else was watching or listening; then he laughed at himself. "Shoot, I'm setting here in my own dang bedroom, there's nobody here." He sat back in his chair and pondered for a few moments.

Then an idea hit him like a thunderbolt again, so that he sat straight up with a roar of laughter. "Ha! That's it! That's it! I can't believe it! That's it!" And he began typing in his wish.

"I wish that tonight for dinner I can have some peace and quiet. I wish that tonight I can somehow put Nan in her place so I can have a peaceful dinner without her nagging me about all and sundry and especially my goldang personal romantic life! I wish ..." He paused, puzzled, then typed, "Is this all one wish or am I asking too much?"

He sat back. The computer's hard drive whirred and the program responded: "This is all fine. A singular impulse in your dynamic wish-field is being articulated. Please continue."

"Good! You're dang right!" Leo said out loud. Then he finished his typing: "I wish that no matter what it takes for me to shut her up, I'll be ready and capable of the challenge, so that tonight, for a change, at the table she does what *I* want, not vice versa."

The program flashed: "This then is the full statement of your wish?"

Leo nodded, speaking to the screen, "Yessirree. That is it 'preciselay.'"

Nothing happened.

"Oh, right," he chuckled, and typed, "Yes."

The program responded. "Thank you very much. Wish processing begins. Please proceed with your affairs. Do not turn your computer off or perform any other keyboard operations."

Then, abruptly, the screen went black and the whirring of the computer's innards went stone dead again. Leo sat before the screen, a little bewildered. The sudden silence made him feel uneasy again. Not too much—just a tad.

"Leopold Stokes! Where in tarnation are you? This dinner is gittin' cold, young man!"

Nan's shrill voice made Leo jump, and he muttered, "I'm coming, I'm coming!" He almost leaped out of his chair, jostling his desk and the computer as he stood. Nervously, he checked to make sure the machine did not register any negative effects—but no, nothing changed. It wasn't making a sound.

Yet, as he turned toward his bathroom to go wash his face and hands, he had the distinct, unnerving feeling that whatever Ultimaya 1.0 was, it was at that moment very active indeed. Even very...conscious.

Rinsing his hands, he felt a surge of delayed anger. Dang it, if she would only stop calling him "young man" and "boy"—he was forty-two years old, for goodness sake!

And as he dried his hands with the towel, it occurred to him that maybe, just maybe, that very dinnertime Nan Creech would start doing exactly what *he* wanted.

Now that, Leo thought, would be a novelty. Yes, indeed!

THE CONNECTION

So that was how it had all started. Leo looked at his illuminated alarm clock. Three o'clock in the morning! He'd be a mess tomorrow at the bank. Oh, right—he had to remember to refinance that little Baptist church. "Too bad," he thought. "I did a mighty fine job of convincing those folks that not even God Almighty could work a second on that mortgage. Well, maybe they'll be all the more beholden..."

He lay back, stared at the dark ceiling, and realized he was not going to be able to fall asleep until he'd made some sense out of this madness. The room was silent but for the barest breeze, audibly tingling through the pines outside and ruffling his curtains inside. He looked over at his new laptop, still standing open on the desk. It wasn't making a sound. But he could feel that it was not by any means "off." It was like living with a large motionless snake coiled under his bed— made him nervous, to say the least.

Leo shook his head, trying to throw off that uneasy feeling. "No use complaining," he thought. "What happened, happened. But what did happen? What kinda weird fix am I in here, anyway?"

He rehearsed the events of the dinner again. "Right!" Now he made the connection. "I specifically—concretely and precisely—typed that at the table Nan should do what I want, and not vice versa. That was what I wanted, and that, sure as shooting, was what I got!

"But then, once Nan left the table, she was outside my specifically communicated 'dynamic wish-field' or whatever in God's Creation that weird program called it. And so I couldn't get her to—"

The hair on the back of Leo's neck rose up and he shuddered. It wasn't that simple. Not at all.

Because Nan was not at the table when—he hardly dared think of it—she combusted. And he, like it or not, had for certain wished it on her. He hadn't typed it into the program either. He'd just shouted it to her face, or actually, now that he remembered, to her back.

Leo did not want to think about that event again, but his mind kept jerking back to it, like a spooked kid near a neighbor's deathbed. He wondered where in the world the idea had come from. Such a fate was not something he'd consciously wished on Nan Creech before. It was not something he would consciously wish on anyone—even a murderer or a child molester. "Shoot," he chuckled, laughing at himself, "I wouldn't even wish that on someone who robbed my bank!"

No matter what he thought or reasoned, Leo could not shake the image of Nan about to…to…*incandesce.* That might not be a word, he mused, but it sure was an event. Or so he thought. When she came back to life, or back from wherever she'd been blown away to, Nan had no knowledge such a thing had even happened.

How could she possibly have not experienced what he so starkly saw her experiencing? Where was she when it happened? Or where was he?

It was all so bewildering it made him shudder. He wondered briefly what drug-induced hallucinations were like, and if this had been something like one of those. One thing was certain: one or the other of them, him or Nan, had just been zipped right out of reality into some kind of whole other dimension. "Shifted"—and "entered"—into a whole other world!

"What would Charley make of something like this?" Leo whispered. "I oughta call him and tell him about this, all right. He used to have hallucinations by the dozens in his glory days of synthetic nirvana! I'd like to see how he'd interpret this one."

Just then two things struck Leo simultaneously. First was the unpleasant observation that he was sitting up, shivering and muttering to himself in his darkened bedroom like a bag lady on a city sidewalk on a wintry night. Second was the curious possibility, beckoning before his mind's eye, that maybe Charley was somehow *responsible for all this.*

That thought intrigued him. It'd been a long, long haul since the times when old C.B. III had pulled his sterling adolescent pranks, now fixed in the legend and lore of Ashlin High and North Carolina State University. The time in their high school sophomore year when, in broad daylight, while everyone was in the dining hall, he somehow managed to lead a full-grown Hereford bull in the front door, down the main hallway, and into the principal's office, where he tethered it to the desk of old Horton Stoner himself. Having fed it choice oats and hay all morning, Charley left a note on its feedbag saying, in letters cut from a newspaper and pasted to the note page, "What goes around comes around, Mr. Stoner, SIR!" The mess had taken some cleaning up, but he was grinning the whole time, and kept smiling the whole month of his suspension from the football team.

Then there was the time, two years later, when, rising to a drunken dare, Charley bet a thousand dollars he did not have against a consortium of their friends and then proceeded to win it by getting the gorgeous and somewhat wicked, or better to say uninhibited, Helen Folger, then still underage, to elope with him. That too took some cleaning up. Not so much the annulment—her father blew that one through the local court so fast you'd have thought it was wind. But disarming the threat of a statutory rape charge took the concerted efforts of practically everyone in Ashlin who knew old man Folger, including Charley's father. In fact, C.B. Jr. put so much time into it that he was still collecting payment for his intercession on Charley's behalf seven years later, when Charley turned twenty-five. No way Jr. was gonna let Number III off that hook!

And there was the time, during midterm exams in the dead howling iciness of January of their sophomore year at State, when Charley got word that some sorority was planning to deliver surprise home baked cookies to everyone cramming frantically in the main undergrad library. Just at the exact moment those spirit-lifting, bright-eyed, red-cheeked young ladies converged on the library entrances and started making their humanitarian rounds, Charley called the library's main office to warn the startled staff, in a harsh voice, that "cookie bombs" were about to go off all over the building. In that era—it was 1970, the year of Kent State and whatnot—there'd been a couple of apparently serious bomb threats even at a hog, tech, and textile school like State.

Charley'd meant it as a joke, of course, but the authorities didn't take it as anything of the sort. The entire building was evacuated four whole study-precious hours before closing time, and no one could return until the security squad pronounced it clean the following evening, when no one needed to use it because all the exams were over. This time, for his safety, since Charley had most of the school on his case, old man Bass arranged an instantaneous and open-ended leave of absence for his son. C.B. Jr. was fairly philosophical and pragmatic about it all. He just charged Charley his standard rates plus a 50 percent "aggravation fee," like he'd probably charge any other rich-kid reprobate who came his way.

During his night in jail, though, Charley'd turned about a dozen hard-bitten cons on to LSD; later, outside, they became steady customers. From his point of view, so he laughed later, it was a once-in-a-lifetime chance for "unique psychosocial exploration, combined with a unique psychofinancial opportunity." And it only took a month or six weeks for Charley to get back into the good graces of the university administrators, get reinstated, and carry on like nothing had happened.

Yes, Leo mused, in his time his old friend had been a legend. But all that had been years ago, when they were still just punks—or, at least, when Charley still was. Leo had never exactly permitted himself to do more than go along for the ride and hang out on the periphery of Charley's and some of the other guys' capers. For him, it was like he was walking an imaginary tightrope extending between maximum thrill and minimum risk of discovery, incarceration, family disgrace, fatherly disaster, motherly shame, Nan-erly excoriation, and so on. The compound threat kept him from ever walking very far or very fast out on that rope; lots of times he just looked on, or found out the next morning.

But then, over time, Charley had changed. It'd started with the summer he spent living at some ashram in the Southwest, that same year he'd cookie-bombed himself out of school for a while. He'd gone out there blustering about how he was "gonna get to the bottom of all this transcendental business" that he'd stumbled on through drugs and the so-called counterculture. But he'd come back pious as hell and fairly redolent with self-disciplined goodness. Odoriferous, in fact. The guy who'd once been the King of Crude, the Wizard of Wild, and the Crown Prince of Cynicism suddenly couldn't hack it when Leo so much as poked fun at his newly acquired penchant for Sanskrit. All Leo had to do was twang out "ashram" in deep cracker drawl, the way they'd jokingly talked together since they were thirteen, cranking out both *a*'s raspy and hard to make the word sound the way a real hick might voice it—and Charley would first fly off the handle in a blistering rage and then sulk for hours on end when he realized he'd blown his saintly poise.

All that Mr. Saintly Sinless stuff had been hard enough to take. But underneath, some kind of wind had gone out of Charley's sails. Over time, it became obvious to Leo and everybody else that the man had lost his fundamental steam. It was plain as day, though Charley wouldn't admit it. He'd just say he'd gotten "real sober about what it really takes"—whatever that meant.

From that point on, now more than twenty years ago, he'd kind of curled up on that whole religious side of himself. That was the end of his and Leo's God debates. Not that Charley returned to his previous irreverence. It was more like he just took his whole spiritual quest and submerged it into himself. He fell in love, had kids with Ginny in no time, built a huge computer business in the '70s and '80s, and outwardly had a fairly happy, certainly successful lot, at least until the relatively recent tragedies in his family.

But something had died in him way back. Leo knew it, and so, he suspected, did Charley. That lightness, that wildness, that devil-may-care daring fire-hose juice of his—it was gone, or, as far as Leo could tell, was all tightly channeled into his business and his personal life.

So it wasn't likely, not at all likely, that Charley had thrown this wild card software program into Leo's computer as a practical gag. This was no joke, for one thing. In fact, given what Charley'd been through in the last decade, what with Ginny and Josh and all, there was no way he'd play games with something as powerful and potentially dangerous as Ultimaya 1.0 had already proved itself to be.

Abruptly, Leo opened his eyes wide in the darkness. He'd managed to distract himself so much with reveries and reminiscences that he'd forgotten why he was up at this hour steam-thinking to begin with. The image of Nan's spontaneous combustion jolted into his mind's eye again.

He remembered reading in an old magazine somewhere how there were a number of cases of spontaneous combustion on record. One was a woman in a dance hall in England before the Second World War, a very famous case. She and her beau were just gliding away on the floor when suddenly, out of nowhere, this weird bluish-green light erupted from her body just like what had happened to Nan tonight. Then, as the whole room of proper English folks stood by and watched in utter shock and disbelief ("Especially her man," Leo thought, "you can imagine what that fella must've been feeling!"), her entire body was consumed by a terrific flash of light and heat. When it was over an instant later, there was nothing left of her but a scrap of bone and a fine ash on everybody else's tuxes and gowns!

This had actually happened. There had been other cases like it, more recently. Most often happening to people when they were alone. No identifiable common characteristics. Often old people. Some forensic speculations about a chemical predisposition based on certain medicines being taken, or perhaps cough syrup, that kind of thing. But with that level of sheer heat? The really strange thing was that nothing else in the room would burn, but door handles would be red-hot hours later and there'd be this fine oily soot all over the walls. One old lady's rocking chair that she'd been sitting in at the time of the combustion was completely unscorched, just very hot. The detectives investigating the case were able to tell she'd been sitting there only because—Leo grimaced, thinking about it—the largest bone of her left heel was all that was left of her, on the floor underneath the rocker.

Leo sat up in bed and shook his head, muttering again. "All right! Gotta stop all this meandering and figure this thing out. Stop beating around the proverbial bush and jump in instead. In any case, far's I know, none of those folks ever got wished to spontaneous combustion. And none of 'em ever got prayed back to life either!"

That thought stopped him.

Who had he prayed to?

He remembered mentioning Jesus. God. Something about "Whoever else" there might be.

Then an idea broke upon him, like sweat on the brow of a man going to the gallows. He sneaked a glance at the computer and then lay down and bundled his blankets around him, nearly covering his face.

The idea would not desist, however. It stayed with him without abating until he finally drifted into an anxious, restless sleep.

Maybe his "prayer" wasn't really a prayer. Maybe it was a "concrete and precise" statement from his "dynamic wish-field."

And maybe it wasn't God or Jesus who'd brought Nan back to life.

Maybe it was the same whoever or whatever that had arranged her instantaneous incineration.

Maybe it was...Ultimaya 1.0.

Freon

The next morning Leo rose earlier than usual, just after dawn. It was bright out, but still cool, and he dressed warmly. He hardly even looked in the direction of his Toshiba, still sitting with the screen raised high in the air. He didn't even allow himself to think about that machine. It was as if the merest acknowledgment of its existence held some dread portent for him that he was in no way ready to confront that day. He hurried from his room.

Nan was unusually cheery, and they shared quite a pleasant breakfast of pancakes, eggs, and bacon, with hominy grits on the side, orange juice before and coffee after. Then Leo rose, grabbed his overcoat and briefcase, and strode out the door, bidding Nan good-bye till that evening.

Closing the front door behind him, he made a fast visual scan of the neighborhood to make sure no one was out and about—and then Leopold Stokes sprinted at top speed to his eight-year old Lincoln parked in the drive, hurled himself into the seat, and burned rubber both backing out and then heading off down the maple-lined residential street.

Leo felt like a total madman; there was absolutely nothing he could do to stop himself. He couldn't remember ever taking off so wildly before in a car, even when he was in his teens. Back then, whenever they heard Charley screech away from the Stokes house, which was often, his daddy, old Abner Stokes, had inveighed upon Leo the economic waste of ruining good tires. But now Leo had to get as much distance between himself and that computer as he could, and fast. He could've cared less how much rubber he was burning.

There was no denying it: he was spooked. Something very, very odd was going on around him and, what was worse, inside him. And some ideas and plans he didn't like much but couldn't shake were starting to percolate in him.

Everyone at the bank was quick with the usual deferential pleasantries. For a few brief moments, Leo indulged in some deep, relaxing breaths and thought to himself, "Shoot, look at me—a grown man, chairman and CEO of a bank! Must've been something I ate last night—gotta talk to Nan about those black-eyed peas, or something anyway. I must've been hallucinating."

Renewed, he concentrated on organizing his desk and his day. He called his secretary, Mrs. Ernestine Elkins, and she dictated to him his already scheduled appointments. As he contemplated each one, he felt his familiar energy and decisiveness surging back.

Until, that is, Mrs. Elkins mentioned that at two in the afternoon he'd be seeing a delegation from the Strap Rock Baptist Church out in Eden Hollow.

That was the church he'd promised God or Whoever last night that he would refinance. And remembering that promise put Leo back in touch with everything else he was trying to put out of his mind. The instant effect of the recollection on his brain and his work, even on his body, was as if someone had taken a backhoe to his guts and at the same time dumped a quart of Freon into his cranium. The breath went out of his chest like air from a popped balloon and he crumpled back into his chair.

Now what was he going to do?

He sat tapping his Bic pen against his slicked back red hair, then tracing the line of his widow's peak with the cap. The feeling was oddly pleasurable, but his brain was oddly in pain. He could not rouse a single clear and authoritative thought. And, he did not fail to notice the old anxiety coiling again in his guts like a viper.

After nearly twenty minutes in this state, Leo knew what he'd better do, and fast. "Ernestine," he said over the intercom, "get me Charley Bass, will you? Thank you, ma'am." Leo knew Charley was no stranger to the stranger realms of human experience. Plus, he remembered the two of them talking a couple of times about spontaneous combustion, way back. He knew Charley was aware it was a documented fact, not just some sci-fi fantasy.

In a few moments, Mrs. Elkins put Charley through to him.

"What's up, Stokes? How's that new program of yours?"

"Well, Charley …" Those first two words, cracking so hard they barely got out of his mouth in recognizable sounds, belied the resolve that was now upon him. Leo coughed and cleared his throat.

"Well, Charley, I did get into the program. It was, well, quite an experience, yes it was. You're right, I'm pretty sure it's not a virus. But… well. I was wondering…you got some time today we can get together?"

"Leo, you're a good old bud, but hell, man, this place is jumping today. Why don't we try for tomorrow, maybe lunch or something?"

"Mm, well …" Leo pursed his lips. He didn't know what to say. There was a silence between them.

"Are you trying to tell me you need to talk this thing over today? Is that it? What the hell's going on?"

"Yup." Leo felt inexplicably very sad, almost on the verge of tears, and said no more. Over the phone, he sensed a powerful, silent emotion filling the space between Charley and him, like water rising in the submerged cabin of a sinking ship. He could not speak another word.

There was another long silence. Then Charley spoke. "Okay, buddy, come on down around, let's see…how about two?"

Leo looked at his calendar. He had the Strap Rock Baptists to meet right at two. But, he thought, no problem, Ernestine could put them off. For a split second he considered asking for a time even sooner, but then blurted out, "Yes!" The affirmation was so strong and loud, he embarrassed himself. "I mean, sure, that'd be just fine."

"And hey, don't forget to bring the computer so's I can get in there and monkey around with this thing."

Once again, Leo couldn't speak.

"Leo?"

"Charley...I'll tell you why later. But—I just can't."

"What do you mean, you *can't*?" Charley exhaled audibly. "All right, bud, whatever you say. Just come on down at two."

Leo was relieved. "Great. See you then, Charley...and thanks so much."

"No problem, Leo. Pleasure's mine."

Snakebite

eo asked Ernestine Elkins to handle the Strap Rock Baptist group, put them off for a day or two. She said she'd be happy to do so, it'd be no problem, and he knew that was true. Ernestine Elkins was a gem of a secretary, a stunning, happily married matron in her mid-fifties, and something of a human relations magician. He'd watched her at work time and again. People who'd likely fume at him about the slightest delay on some loan or other would be happy simply to get a chance to say to her, "Oh, that'll be just fine, Miz Elkins." Loan applicants would even be understanding, or at least quite gracious, upon receiving a call telling them their requests had been turned down—if the call was from Ernestine. So Leo knew she'd see to it that, tight as their financial deadlines were, the Strap Rock boys would cheerfully bide their time. And, after all, he was the one holding their note.

Leo put the rest of his afternoon affairs on back burners as quickly as he could before noon, shoving most of his papers back into the "In" file, and after wolfing down a tuna sandwich with a Coke at his desk, he took off. Ernestine knew to explain to everyone that he had an appointment with some legislators down in Raleigh.

He went out the back door of the bank, still feeling strange. Leo couldn't quite make out what was aggravating him. It wasn't just what had happened last night, or the Ultimaya 1.0 program. There was something about it all that was challenging him, exhilarating him, leaving him feeling both curious and combative. There was something else, though, and he didn't know what. Some kind of sadness?

Normally, Leo enjoyed the two-hour drive to Raleigh, south and east through the pine-covered hills of North Carolina's piedmont. There was no outward reason he shouldn't have enjoyed the drive this time either. The sun shimmered off the road and the pine needles all the way down. There wasn't a cloud in the sky. And he knew from when he'd been outside earlier that the temperature was the kind of bracing cool, with a touch of warmth in the direct sun, that he'd loved since his boyhood winters.

But Leo could not shake the ill feeling. The sense that someone had poured Freon or some other coolant into his brain did not abate even a little, and surely contributed to his discomfort. And disturbance. Where in God's Creation was a sensation like that coming from? No way it was black-eyed peas, or this morning's coffee.

For a bizarre moment, the idea turned around in Leo's head that maybe Nan was poisoning him! Then he laughed out loud. "Shoot," he thought, "I'm her whole reason for being alive, and we both know it." Her crusade to get him hitched was something he suspected she had programmed herself to continue, without permitting success, of course, until the day she would die.

He had a hunch that Nan's deepest unspoken wish would be to have Leo and Constance be married right next to her deathbed. She could look on approvingly and with all due pride, and then—in full view of as many of the townsfolk as could squeeze into the room, and if she had her way it'd be the main ballroom at the country club—she'd expire before their very eyes right after, or maybe just before, the preacher instructed him to kiss the bride.

No, no. No way this side of paradise that Nan Creech would ever dream of trying to do Leo any bodily harm. She had to have him around to yap at, to aggravate, to give her life a persnickety but sincere and well-meaning purpose.

It hadn't always been that way between him and Nan. He could remember how he felt about her when he was a boy. From about the age of eight, when she came to live with her lifelong friend Agnes Stokes and the Stokes family, until he was well into his teens, Leo'd had a crush on Nan that even his friends knew about, and at times teased him no end for. "Leo 'n Nan—settin' in a tree ..." It made him flush with embarrassment even now, recalling it thirty years later.

Because, he had to face it, their teasing had been right on target. In the days when he spent most of the time from the last spring frost to the first autumn one running barefoot in torn-off jeans with no shirt, glorying in the seasons of budding cotton and ripening tobacco, the feeling of fine, thick red clay mud squishing between his toes and the clean eternal fragrance of the pine woods all around Ashlin, there was Nan. She was young then, and pretty, really pretty. Her slender diminutive beauty—she must have been, what, in her early thirties when he was around eight or ten?—captivated him.

In fact, because of Nan, Leo substantially bypassed the age of arrogant disdain for everything and everyone female that most boys exult in from the time they get out of kindergarten, or thereabouts, until right around the onset of puberty.

Which had its, well, developmental complications. The boy Leo wasted no time on and felt no affection for any of the girls his own age, or for his mother, or for any other women. But Nan made him nervous and agitated. He could feel that her claim on his heart was cheating him out of some promised-land glory of boyhood that his friends all knew. It was almost like he was crippled, or like he had to wear glasses; he just couldn't work up the same macho disgust they reveled in, and that compromised his young boy's manhood.

He'd resolve not to let himself feel that way, not to let it go on any longer. All day at school, or out roaming with his friends in the woods and fields, playing football, baseball, or basketball in the seasons, shooting their BB rifles, riding their bikes wherever they wanted, or swimming, he was certain that day he'd be like stone no matter what Nan said, no matter how pretty her hair might be, or how rosy-cheeked her smile at dinner, no matter how much of her shape might beckon through her gown toward his glance when she came out of the bathroom they shared along the hallway—but it never made any difference. The moment he slammed his way in through the backdoor screen, as soon as he heard her cheery, "Well, hey there, young Mr. Stokes," something would leap in his heart, or his belly, or somewhere. He'd flush, and it really made no difference whether he replied or pretended not to have heard. She had him. By the heart.

When Leo was a little older it dawned on him that, in some odd way, he had her, too. Nan had come to live with the Stokes family under a cloud of dark sorrow and trouble, which at the time the adults did not feel obliged to explain to Leo. The other boys spat out the usual kid rumors: she'd been a whore, had a child out of wedlock, had syphilis, had killed her husband. Leo would fiercely challenge all such spite and more than once pounded some young friend to the dirt for one or another mocking insult.

Only many years later did he learn that, in fact, Nan's young husband, Jed Creech, had died in a drunken brawl, shot by a drifter in a bar down near the capital. They had no children, but he'd left her a pile of debts she didn't know about till after his death. Because Nan and Agnes, Leo's mother, had been friends since their childhood, and because she had no other family and no way to handle her personal and financial disgrace, Agnes prevailed upon Abner to allow them to take her in for a time.

But Nan never left. And even though she was indeed still fairly young and very pretty for even a decade and more thereafter, Nan never accepted any man's invitation for a date or even so much as a stroll after church. Something had gone dead, or comatose, in Nan's heart, and she never allowed it to come back to life. So the only "man"—though he was still a cowlicked, redheaded boy—she ever allowed herself even the suggestion of flirtation with was Leo himself.

When he was ten, he loved it. When he was fifteen, he hated it. By the time he was twenty, she'd begun throwing him poison-tipped verbal barbs about "finding yourself a suitable gal, young Mr. Stokes." By the time he was thirty, he dreaded coming home, because he knew the lecture was coming. Once his folks had been killed in the accident—Abner had died instantly, but Agnes had held on three more days before expiring—Nan had been there at Agnes' deathbed to solemnly swear her eternal vigilance over Leo's marital estate. And that was the coup de grâce.

It really was a coup. After the wreck, Leo had felt so aggravated by Nan's proprietary relationship to his mother's hospital bed and room that he avoided going there often or for very long, even though Agnes had remained in critical condition the whole time. From then on, he'd felt guilty about not having been there for her himself. And, also from then on, Nan's mission in life was as fixed as if it had been graven on the courthouse steps—and it was just that obvious to everyone in the entire town too. Everybody knew of Nan Creech's eternal crusade to get Leopold Stokes married. And everyone knew she wouldn't have the slightest idea what to do with herself if she succeeded.

So that sunlit wintry day driving down to Raleigh, Leo knew there was no way he could ascribe his weird feeling to some nefarious scheme in Nan or chemicals in her cooking. Nan needed him healthy and strong as much as he did, maybe more.

Something else was going on. He just did not know what it was.

With a sense of foreboding then, but also a strange kind of antsiness, Leo pulled into a parking lot at one of the seemingly endless new malls on the north side of the state's capital city. He remembered from his youth when all that country around Raleigh had been pine forests and fields. It'd been a big deal when they put in the Crabtree Mall shopping center, in an area that now seemed relatively close to downtown. But today, between the shopping malls and the upscale residential developments, the suburban sprawl stretched for miles in every direction.

He didn't even know the name of the small and nondescript shopping center where Charley had his main store and offices; he just knew how to get there.

Leo drove his gray Lincoln around the back of the mall to an area outside Charley's offices and went directly into the building. One of the salespeople in the store recognized him.

"Afternoon, Mr. Stokes. Mr. Bass is right upstairs."

"Thank you kindly."

Leo clambered up the stairs to the second floor. Charley's secretary waved him in. He entered the large cool room from which Charley bemusedly masterminded his computer products empire. The décor, if you could use the word, might be called "techno-metallic"; Charley had little sense of how to maintain an attractive office environment. The furniture was drab gray metal desks and chairs he'd bought for a song at a military auction fifteen years before.

As usual, there were monitor screens, electronic chips and other computer parts, and other paraphernalia of the business all over the rug, the just barely bluer than gray tone of which was almost the only touch of color in the room. On the far wall, to the right of the main desk, sat a bookshelf with some of Charley's longtime favorites from what he used to call his "survival of the free-est" literature—titles from his eclectic selection of the world's spiritual and religious texts, most of which he kept in an extensive library at home.

And there, talking on the phone behind one of the room's several drab gray desks, was Charley Bass himself. "Charles Bass the Third," Nan called him; "C.B. Three" to most of Leo and Charley's childhood friends; "Mountain Man," often enough, to Leo himself.

Leo sat down in one of the chairs and affectionately regarded his old comrade. Charley was a bear of a guy, huge, with a big brown beard just starting to streak with gray. He hadn't had his hair cut much since the '60s. Never wore a suit; he was sitting there right now in casual brown slacks and a rumpled light-blue, short-sleeved Arrow, his white T-shirt visible at the neck. Never traded in his car until it collapsed and died on the road somewhere. Never took out a loan. Paid for everything in cash. Not much good to a banker! Charley didn't seem too concerned about his business, either, but somehow it just grew around him, and his attitude was, why fight it?

Charley had a reputation for being a little, well, "tetched," having done way more than his share of drugs during the heyday of that Tar Heel, still slightly antebellum version of the counterculture that had sprung up in the cosmopolitan parts of Carolina during the late '60s and early '70s. For not a few of their friends, the drug culture had added psychedelic pinwheels to the "stars 'n bars" of their still-cherished old Confederate flag.

Though Charley never had much of a taste for brew or booze, he'd been a real connoisseur of the psychoactive. But even then, and for sure now, as a businessman and as a man his integrity was unquestioned, even by competitors.

Charley was listening to someone on the other end of the line, and he raised a finger to Leo, indicating he'd be done in just a moment. Leo remembered his reveries about old C.B. III the evening before, when he'd been lying there with his nose plastered to the linoleum after Nan's explosive disappearance, and his further dark-of-night reminiscences sitting up in his bed.

Now he thought even further back, to the early days of their friendship in high school. Then, as later, Charley had always been the hell-raiser, the daredevil—Leo was always inhibited by propriety and his stodgy destiny at his father's bank. It amused him now to think that the whole time of Charley's wild explorations of sex and drugs, he, Leo, had stayed virginal and totally buttoned-down, yet their friendship had stayed strong the whole time. It was just one of those inexplicable connections that one has very few of in a lifetime. Leo felt a surge of gratitude to have a man like Charley to turn to at this time.

41

Charley hung up the phone and, eyeing Leo curiously, lit a Winston. Leo sniffed disdainfully as loudly as he could, though he knew it would do no good. He hated having to inhale cigarette smoke around Charley, but it was a price of the man's company.

Charley began gruffly. "All right, Stokes. I've put off a mighty sweet contract meeting to have this little conversation. What the hell is going on with you, buddy roe? You look like somebody drained your blood and replaced it with...I don't know, refrigerator coolant or something."

Leo was dumbfounded. How did Charley know that was exactly what he felt like? For a moment, he couldn't speak.

Charley waited for a reply, then rolled his eyes and sighed out loud.

"Old bud, as a banker you will surely appreciate my time is worth something like five hundred scoots an hour. On bad days. Real bad days." Charley leaned back and dragged on his Winston. "Now you know on some deep profound level I do not give a damn about money. But, just on principle, if I am in business, I like to do business. And in this moment, obviously, I am in business as your combination computer techie and counselor, your 'psycho-software therapist,' to coin a...well, I would not want to make a career of it, exactly. But here we are. So—what's cooking?"

Leo smiled wanly. "Well, Charley, you know I've never been the one to get into strange doings. I mean, that's been your strong suit, not mine. But...uh...Lordy. I don't even know where to start."

Charley leaned forward. "That's easy. Just pick up right after our phone call yesterday. The first one, when you told me about this program—what'd you call it?"

"Ultimaya 1.0."

"Right. Ultimaya 1.0. Slick name. Okay, I encouraged you to jump on in and check it out. So what happened?"

Leo looked at his hands and, seeing he was wringing them, rested them on the arms of his chair. Once again an uncomfortable tension rose in his guts, chest, and throat.

"Whew," he breathed. "Okay." It bothered him that his voice was so high and cracked, but he pushed on. "Here's what happened. I'll just tell you the whole story. But you gotta just hear me out, huh? I mean, you start laughing or something, I don't reckon I'm going to be able to keep going."

Charley chuckled, then covered his mouth with his hand, puffing his cigarette at the same time. His eyes were dancing. "Hey, no problem. Even if I do laugh, I'm not laughing, okay? Though I gotta say this must be good, to have a stick like you in a stew like this."

Leo tried to grin, but his face felt like taut canvas around his mouth and cheekbones. He started telling Charley what happened when he first opened the Ultimaya 1.0 program. Charley just listened, nodding but not responding, until Leo described how the machine seemed to turn off shortly after the new program kicked into gear. Charley leaned forward again.

"Wait a minute. You said this thing was turned on but was making no sound at all?"

"Yeah. It was like it was shut off. I mean, dead silent."

"Hm." Charley blew a smoke ring, gazing over Leo's shoulder through the window. "I can sure as hell tell you this: there ain't no way that Toshiba computer can run any kind of software at all without humming at you pretty damn loud. I mean, there are some slick little numbers coming out now so quiet you hardly know they're on—like that Texas Instruments beaut I was trying to get you to buy. But that 3100 of yours is a real workout computer; it always sounds like it's earning its keep, y'know? And the hard drive cannot process software without sounding that way. It is plain-old, flat-out impossible for you not to hear at least *something* when that machine is on. I don't care what program it's running."

Leo felt a sudden strength, and it came out in his voice. "Charley, it went absolutely silent. I heard it, and then I stopped hearing it, but it kept on doing its thing. No two ways about it."

"Well, then, either you're having auditory hallucinations—and I don't know how that could happen, you never even smoked any weed and for all I know you don't even hear your own fantasies! I mean, no offense, old bud, but you are not exactly the, uh, how to say it, audiovisually imaginative type, right? So you're not having acid flashbacks or anything like that, that's for sure." Charley looked off again, then brought his gaze back to Leo, his eyes narrowing to slits. "Unless you did a little indulging back there in the grand old days of psychedelia that you just didn't happen to mention?"

Leo smiled. "Not a chance. You know that."

Charley nodded. "All right—so much for that possibility. I have to conclude, then, that either somebody has been monkeying around with your machine or something pretty strange is going on here. Go on."

Leo proceeded to relate all the events of the previous evening. Charley roared with laughter at Leo's descriptions of how he had come to program in his main wish for the night, and at what happened when Leo and Nan were sitting at the table. But when Leo began, embarrassed that his voice was cracking again, to tell about what happened in the kitchen, Charley was riveted to his words. And when Leo described his futile attempt to reach out to Nan after watching the steel wool spontaneously incinerate in her hand, Charley shouted, "You gotta be kidding me! Leo, are you out of your mind or what?"

Leo said he was not lying. It was all actual, factual truth. Swear to God.

Then he described Nan's spontaneous combustion.

The story astounded Charley enough that he forgot the lit cigarette between his fingers. It burned down so far it started to singe him. He winced and hastily stamped it out in an ashtray already loaded with Winston butts, not missing a word coming out of Leo's mouth.

When Leo finished his account, he looked at Charley and laughed. "Hey, C.B. III, not wanting to plagiarize ..." He slowed down and finished his comment gently, "but you have the look of a man who just had his blood replaced by Freon!"

It was true. Charley's face looked gray, and both moist and pasty, like drying mud on sheetrock. At first he could only bring himself to murmur,

"Hm," in response.

They sat in silence.

Charley was deep in thought; Leo could see that. He felt another sudden surge of gratitude. To be able to come to someone who was able to hear out his whole tale and not just arbitrarily conclude he was nuts—what a gift!

Finally, Charley spoke, with an air of solemn authority. "Well, well, well, Mr. Stokes. I have to say this is one of the most—not the only, mind you, and not necessarily *the* most, 'cause I've heard some pretty amazing yarns in my time, told like they were the gospel truth—but this is without a doubt one of the most outrageous stories I ever heard in my life."

He raised his eyebrows and spoke wide-eyed. "This is amazing! I mean, you're talking about one hell of an 'interactive' program, if you know what I mean!"

Leo shook his head. "No, I don't. What's that?"

"Well, pretty simple, it's a program that interacts with the user. But this is going way beyond everything I know about on the market. Even in development. Even in anyone's doodles on a napkin! *Way* beyond. This thing is in a class all by itself."

Charley pulled out another Winston and lit up.

"I'll give you an angle on it," he said, blowing another smoke ring. "Nowadays one of the hottest things on the creative edge of the computer industry is what they call 'virtual reality.' People are creating new hardware and software—oh, you probably aren't hip to those terms yet, okay, new machinery, the hardware, and new programs, the software—that allow the user to experience all kinds of sensations in a way that 'virtually' duplicates physical and, for that matter, emotional and mental reality."

Charley took another long drag on his cigarette and then exhaled.

"Most of this stuff is still so far out from commercial, it costs a fortune for one rig. What I'm trying to say is, this is not stuff I'm ready to sell in Charley's Computer Stores across the southeast, if you get me.

Not yet by a long shot. It's hugely experimental, and not a little kinky—some of what these dudes are into is pretty strange—and in any case, it's too expensive. But even the best of it doesn't come anywhere close to what you're telling me this little number did on your Toshiba last night before dinner!"

"Well, during and after dinner too," Leo corrected him.

"All right, all right, that's not the point."

Charley puffed on his cigarette, then looked away from Leo, his eyes widening again. "Whoa now! I just tapped into what this sucker is all about!"

Leo was confused. "What are you talking about?"

"Jesus…this cannot be real. But it must be. That must be what this thing is all about, Leo, you crazy fool!"

"What, Charley?"

Charley looked straight at Leo, his eyes still bugging out. "Good buddy, it just hit me what 'Ultimaya' is. What it means."

"What do you mean 'what it means'? I didn't drive down here two solid hours and tell you this nutso story, Charley, to have you psychoanalyze the dang *meaning* of it!"

Charley had a wild and twisted grin on his face. "I don't mean what it means. I mean what it's *doing.*"

Leo felt exhausted, like there wasn't another drop of gas left in him. He rubbed his hands across his brow and face. "Would you just tell me what in tarnation you're talking about?"

Charley nodded and tamped out his cigarette. "Right. Exactly. I hear you. But if you want to do something about it, if you want to deal with it, you've got to have at least some operating notion of what it is and how it functions. And that's what I just maybe picked up on. The *name,* Leo, the *name.* 'Ultimaya.' You got a clue yet on the meaning of that name?"

Leo shook his head. "Not even a teeny tiny one."

"Well, I do. Started working on me the moment you first said it: Ultimaya."

46

He lit yet another Winston and got up to walk around the office as he spoke. "Here's the deal. What that name means, I suspect, is 'Ultimate Maya.' Now *maya* is a Sanskrit word—picked up on this in some of my Eastern explorations and other metaphysical reading. It's typically translated to mean the 'Female Force' or Divine Goddess of the universe, but in some kind of negative way. The power of temptation, illusion, of ignorance, bondage, sin, endless desire and craving, suffering, karma, and so on. The word literally means 'she who measures.' But it tends, see, to have all these negative connotations.

"There is, though, another way of looking at what this Force is all about. A value-free kind of perspective. It is—I recall the phrase well from this one book because it always stuck with me—'form-building power.'"

Charley looked at Leo, who raised his eyebrows and shook his head. He didn't have a clue where all this was heading. Charley continued.

"I don't know what else to say about it at the moment. Excepting that, this is what you just plugged yourself into somehow. A something or other that creates actual realities and even uncreates them, builds and unbuilds forms, according to what you really want. This is not virtual reality. This is no simulation. This is the real thing. Form-building power, Leo! Who knows how? I get the impression that if you want to, you can get into some very creative jamming with this thing."

Charley stopped walking and looked closely at Leo's face. Leo was sitting there with his brow knitted and mouth just slightly ajar. Charley snorted and laughed.

"And you can get into a whole stack of trouble too, if that's where you're headed. Come to think of it, that's in fact exactly where you've already been...so maybe it's your turn to talk again, Leo. Just where are you headed with this thing? What do you want to do with it? How are you gonna domesticate something that can breathe firestorms like the one that hit Nan and then destroy all the evidence in a millisecond?"

Charley didn't wait for Leo to try to respond.

"Or are you trying to say you don't want to domesticate it? You came in here looking like a ghost. What is it—you want me just to trash the whole program? Or even the whole computer, if you feel maybe this thing's got its tentacles digging away inside the hardware, so there's no way to get free of it except to obliterate the whole mess?" Charley flicked some ash off his cigarette. "Whaddya have to say?"

"That's what I came here mainly to talk to you about—what I want to do with this thing. Because I've got a lot I want to do with this thing."

Leo cleared his throat, embarrassed by the sudden energy of his confession. At the beginning of the conversation, he'd still been feeling strangely defeated and weird. He'd tried to maintain a convivial, even a kind of humble tone as they talked. But now he could feel the dealmaker, the strategist, the player in him coming to the fore. He was getting into the swing of this dialogue. He'd just blown Charley's mind sky-high—no small feat in the man's own office in broad daylight, and with no more chemical aid than the nicotine in Charley's perpetual Winstons.

In a flash, Leo knew his voice just now had the edge to it that it got sometimes during intense negotiations when he suddenly knew he was going to get what he wanted. He chided himself—he was too hot for this particular "deal."

Charley seemed to catch Leo's change of tone. Taking in everything Leo was saying, he'd gotten more and more animated and talkative himself. Now he stopped walking and talking. He looked at Leo with narrowed eyes and a wry smile. Then he ambled around to his chair and took his seat again.

Not a word was said. Charley lit himself another cigarette and smoked, looking away. Leo was looking right at him. He felt a little abashed. He also knew what he wanted.

"All right, Mountain Man. I don't want to beat around the bush. Both of our time is important. I don't need you to cheer me up or get me over the shock of this thing. It is what it is. Every ten or twenty years, a hurricane runs through the piedmont here and rips everything to shreds.

Now a lot of folks have never experienced anything like it, they weren't here last time, they don't have a point of reference to make sense of something that powerful and destructive. But there's nothing anyone can do about it. It is what it is. This program is the same way. Except maybe not just destructive—not necessarily at all, in fact."

Leo sat back. Charley was still looking away, but Leo knew he had his attention.

"Running my bank, I spend one heckuva lot of time figuring out variables and running probabilities. Some cotton farmer comes to me, I have to know his soil quality, his yield last year and in the past, his rep in the county as a solid, honest businessman; I have to know what the weather's predicted to be like for this season, what kind of machinery he's got and what shape it's in, how many hands he hires and how he pays and treats them, what the market's likely to be. I have to get my arms wrapped around the whole ball of wax so I can make the best educated estimate of how good this good ole boy's gonna do and what I can do to help him out and how likely I am to get a yield on my investment—"

Charley interrupted him. "Leo, you're beating around the bush. Get to the bottom line. What do you want, and what do you want from me? Two simple questions. Let's have it." His expression was unemotional.

Leo took a deep breath and looked his old friend square in the eye. "All right. Here's my idea. Tell me what you think."

He spent the next five minutes outlining certain inspirations and plans that had been running through his brain ever since he'd woken up that morning. Charley listened closely, never looking away from Leo's gaze. After Leo finished, there was a brief, tense silence. Charley spoke again.

"Leo, tell you what…you better let me look at that program."

Leo sighed and shrugged. "Sorry, my friend. No can do."

"Whaddya mean 'no can do'? Why the hell not?"

"Program instructions. If I try to bring you in, the program's gonna self-destruct."

Charley fumed. "How the hell do you know that?"

"It said so. And I'm not going to take that risk."

Charley pursed his lips, eyeing Leo coolly. "Know what? You're playing with fire. This sucker is bigger and meaner and a whole lot more sophisticated than your way of drawing a bead on cotton farmers! If I were you, I would not mess around with this mother. It's gonna burn your ass, man. Maybe not like it did Nan's last night—if that even actually happened, and if you aren't already in a wacko state of hallucinatory derangement—but you watch. I can feel it coming. You can put perfume on a pig, but it still stinks. What this thing has blown your way already, I say it stinks! You can wrap a bikini around a cottonmouth moccasin, too, but that mother's still gonna bite your ass bad, so bad you'll have to fight just to keep on breathing. And I say this thing is a snake! How far do you have to look? What more do you have to see?"

Leo shook his head, annoyed. "Come on, Charley. Where's your sense of adventure? For a guy who built a multimillion-dollar corporation, why do I get the feeling that, like we used to say when we were kids, 'you just ain't got no gumption'? Come on, man! This is like that line of cable you found out in the lumberyard that you set up with a cinch so you could fly down from the top of your treehouse to the ground in no time flat— except this ride's gonna be 50,000 times faster, more exciting, more fun; and who knows, maybe even something we can do some good with for this sad old world? But now, instead of me when we were kids, you're the scaredy-cat tippy-toeing back down the ladder, nice and safe.

"And you're giving me one message one minute, another the next. For a man who doesn't wanna pass value judgments on Maya, this great creative cosmic Mother you know so much about, don't you think the 'snakebite' bit is just a tad much? Where are we, in the Garden of Eden? Besides, it doesn't feel to me like I'm talking to a woman. Feels to me like Ultimaya 1.0 is more like a man, or masculine. I don't know—"

Charley exploded. "We're not dealing with human gender games, for Christ's sake! We're dealing with existence. We're not dealing with

50

adventure. We're not in a damn treehouse here. We're dealing with life and death. If not, then we're dealing with the fact that you have somehow managed overnight to go totally insane.

"Check the stats, buddy. In case you haven't noticed, Mother Nature—Father Time—whatever you wanna call It—kicks butt. Everybody dies, Leo! And they don't miraculously resurrect either, like Lazarus, Jesus, and hey—whaddya know—now good old Nan! Everybody struggles like mules and then, zap—*finito!* They sweat and suffer the whole time, sucking up every drop of love and pleasure and joy they can get, but it's never enough. Not really."

Too energized to sit still, Charley jumped out of his chair and smacked his open palm on the center of his chest. *"I'm no saint,* Leo! But I sure as hell have taken enough of a gander at Maya to notice this is no lifelong party here. I watched Ginny die of cancer in my arms. Remember? I saw my little boy dead on a beach, drowned. I know for a fact you ain't seen anything like that. I have a screenful of the whole picture here, so you can just cut the adventure crap. And try growing up. You're a little long in the tooth for sowing computer-generated wild oats. I'm also getting enough of a scan on that weirdo computer program of yours to see that however 'ultimate' it may be, whatever slice of the great form-building power it got a franchise on—and I don't have a clue on that, except it sounds like Software from Hell—I mean, this stuff you're sucking down through that Toshiba straw ain't cherry coke, you get me? This stuff gives acid kicks with every shot. Now, you lap up what it squirts at you long enough—well, I guaran-damn-tee you, you're gonna wake up one day choking down your own blood! And who knows who else's!"

Charley had pushed his chair aside and was standing behind his desk right in front of Leo. He drew himself up full mountain height. "Dig in, Stokes! Take a body count! Unless you truly are bonkers with hallucinations, this thing actually crisped a human being in two seconds just because you got pissed off and ordered her execution!"

Charley leaned halfway across the desk, his eyes practically bursting out of their sockets. He exhaled loudly through his mouth. When he spoke, his tone was quiet and deliberately calm, but there was a bristling edge underneath. "So let's bypass the 'value judgment' critique for just a moment, shall we?"

Now it was Leo who leaned forward. Resisting the urge to bolt upright and yell back at Charley, he rested his elbows on the broad desk and placed his hands one on top of the other, one of them palm down on the cold metal. He pushed closer in his chair, so that his face was less than two feet from his friend's. When he spoke, his tone, too, was calm and deliberate.

"Charley, I hear you. I 'preciate what you're saying. I do. And I respect your judgment. You know I do. I know life's given you plenty of bad along with the good. I don't deny what you went through, losing Ginny and then Josh, so now it's just you and Sarah. You're right. I can't possibly know what that's been like for you. But you wound up with some wisdom. And that's part of why I value your counsel. I will try to be very careful, dealing with this thing. That's why I came down here. I need your help."

He paused to let that admission sink in. Neither of them moved or averted his gaze. Leo continued. "I understand that, based on everything I've told you, you feel I'd be better off just junking the whole program. Getting rid of it, burning the computer—you've made it plain that if you were me, that's what you'd do. But you're not me, Charley. I am. And I'm the one who's plugged into this program. Not you. I don't know why, but that's the way it is. If you try to mess with it, it'll blow itself up in my computer somewhere. Of that I have zero doubt."

Leo moved back a few inches, to ease the pressure of the confrontation for them both.

"You help me out, on the other hand, and maybe we get to see what it can really do. Maybe we both benefit. Maybe other people too. Maybe we can tame it, work it, 'domesticate' it. Who knows where it came from, but it's a confounded computer program; it's not a dang earthquake. It's not some God-given force of nature. It's not a wild and deadly reptile. It did not come from hell and Satan. It's a man-made product running on a man-made machine, designed to be used to full advantage by human beings.

"Come on, Charley, think back. Remember the Job Hawkins chant: 'Who in the world can possibly give definitive answers to infinite questions?' And 'where in God could hell possibly be?' We're not talking about playing God. We're not talking about heaven and hell. We're talking about working with technology. Right here—on Earth.

"Now, C.B. III, you know software. You know hardware. You're a pro. You navigate the whitewater of your crazy industry like it was a farm pond in a dead calm. And you're the only man on Earth I can trust to help me deal with Ultimaya 1.0. For everybody's sake. Not just mine, and not even just yours and mine. Everybody's."

Leo leaned back in his chair. That was a very good stroke, reminding Charley that Ultimaya 1.0 was, after all, a computer program. And that this was for the greater good—that'd mean a lot to Charley. Leo knew his friend was not going to refuse him now.

"What's it gonna be, Mountain Man? You gonna help me out on this one, or not?"

Charley fumed, puffing hard on another Winston. "Hell, Leo. You're crazy. You've already seen what this sucker can do. You think you're gonna hold on to the hat of your—I quote—'deepest wishes,' so you can actually control this thing? You think you have such high and mighty desires that when what you really want comes true, it's gonna do the whole world some good? You *wish,* Stokes!" He laughed. "Naw. You don't wish anything of the sort. Correct my specs, if need be, but I ain't looking at no Mother Teresa here. No Carl Jung either. I'm looking at Leopold Stokes, stingiest cracker in Cotton County, Carolina. No, Leo, take my word for it. You're nuts. You sure as hell are trying to play God with this thing."

Charley sat down again and looked out the window. Then he turned back to Leo with a quizzical smile. The mood between them had shifted. He spoke softly, in almost conspiratorial tones. "Hey, Leo, just out of curiosity, back when we were in school, did you ever read Goethe's *Faust?*"

"Gertrude's *what?*"

Charley chuckled and looked away once more. "Ah...never mind. Don't matter none no how."

He smiled at Leo. "Well, what am I gonna do? Tell you no? Let you destroy yourself and God knows what and who else? Course not. Not old Charley Bass. No, I'm gonna *help you* destroy yourself, you madman."

Charley gazed at his friend with a lifetime's affection, shaking his head. "All right, here's my recommendation for what you do next. You can take it or leave it."

Leo smiled. "Thanks, I appreciate it."

Charley nodded. "Don't mention it. In fact, if I was you, I wouldn't mention any of this to anyone, anywhere. Now, if you want to get some kind of edge on this program, here's what you probably ought to do..."

In Charge

t was nightfall by the time Leo turned the old Lincoln into his driveway and parked. His body was exhausted, both from the events of the last day—yes, it had only been twenty-four hours since it had all begun—and from the strain of the four hours on the road and his intense conversation with Charley. Even so, he felt alert and awake. And wary.

As he opened the front door, it struck him: he could actually feel the presence of Ultimaya 1.0 emanating from the bedroom. It was like a living creature, and in no way a safe or merely benign one. A "snake," Charley had said. Except extremely cold and mechanical—no heart, no soul, not even any animal instinct of self-preservation. And to do what he now intended to do with it, Leo would have to be more than its equal in cunning and ruthlessness.

Tired as he was, he felt ready.

Once again, as at breakfast, Nan seemed uncharacteristically demure and sweet. She greeted Leo with a warm smile—"Bless your heart, you must be clean wore out, Leopold Stokes!"—and cheerily served him a fine, hot meal of Salisbury steak, carrots and potatoes, homemade biscuits, and a large fresh salad. She was so nice, Leo didn't know quite how to respond to her. Nan even seemed to forget her nightly diatribe; she hardly said a word, just making sure Leo got enough to eat.

In any case, much was on his mind, so he welcomed the opportunity not to have to be too sociable. He had deliberately washed in the guest bathroom just inside the foyer, so as not to enter his bedroom until he was ready to face the computer and its ever-alert program.

After eating, to return Nan's kindness, but also to put off the coming confrontation in his room, Leo helped with the dishes. Nan, he could tell, was genuinely touched. As he stood drying pots, Leo tried to remember the last time he'd helped out in the kitchen like this. He couldn't. So both he and Nan were acting like different folks with each other. Maybe this Ultimaya program really was a benign work of someone's genius, after all. He hadn't seen Nan so sweet and placid since his childhood.

Finally, the floor was swept and the last fork was in the silver drawer. Leo hung the apron he'd borrowed back up on the rack in the pantry and sighed deeply. Nan, sponging down the counter, looked up at him.

"You feeling all right, Leopold?"

"Yeah, Nan. No problem. I just guess I'll turn in early tonight."

"Well, sleep tight. Hope you feel better in the morning."

"Thanks. G'night."

Leo smiled at Nan, his face feeling a little rigid, and walked through the dining room toward his bedroom. He stopped for a moment at the door. That weird anxiety was coming over him again; he could feel his face flushing and sweat in his armpits. But there was no turning back now. He opened the door and walked into his room.

He looked over at the alcove. The computer monitor still stood straight up, as if beckoning to him, menacing and mesmerizing at once, like the hood of a cobra. A snake!

He shook his head sharply, thinking, "Leo, would you relax, dang it? It's a machine. A *machine!*"

Trying to maintain his composure, he took off his tie, dress shirt, and suit pants and put on an old baggy sweater and some casual slacks. It occurred to him that Nan had been here in the room with the computer when she was cleaning that morning. He wondered if she had felt anything. She hadn't said anything about it. He knew for sure she hadn't touched his computer. They had an agreement that she would never handle, clean, move, or read anything on his desk.

Then he wondered if the program had maybe in some weird way possessed her while she was cleaning. Could mere proximity to the machine increase susceptibility to the program?

"Nah," he thought. "Come on, Leo, you're getting paranoid."

But then it hit him that maybe, just maybe, the old Nan had forever disappeared in her spontaneous combustion last night, and the one who had now come back, all cheery and nice, was actually—he grimaced—a humanoid form, some kind of robot created by Ultimaya 1.0. That would certainly explain her sweetness and light. And, truth be told, this was the kind of Nan he'd had on his wish list for a mighty long time!

Could it be true? Was Nan's whole existence since last night only the fulfillment of his own deepest wishes? She'd been a little sharp with him when she reappeared and found him virtually ("VUR-choo-ul-lay") worshipping her shoe. But that was understandable. After all, she'd found him prostrated on the floor with her foot firmly ensconced in his sweaty, prayerful palms.

Leo shook his head sharply, trying to shake the whole train of thought. He muttered, "Good God A'mighty, I must be nuts, just like Charley said. This is loco. Nan is Nan. So she had a good day. Big deal. She is who she is. She'll be her old self tomorrow, or soon, or I don't make money off cotton! And of course the dang program hasn't gotten to her. It hasn't gotten to anybody. It hasn't gotten to me. It's a confounded computer program! It's not alive. It's not in charge. *I* am!"

Even as he ranted these affirmations in a shrill whisper, Leo could feel a tinge of concern. All that was very well, but he still had to face the program again. No point putting it off any longer.

He suddenly realized that he'd now been staring into the face of his own reflection in his mirror for a minute or more, riding the locomotive of thoughts and feelings in his own mind. He examined his image. He'd never quite liked his face—the redness of his complexion, that kind of bulldog squareness to his jaw, and now, these last few years, his hairline retreating from his widow's peak in a V formation. There wasn't anything particularly wrong about how he looked. There just wasn't anything particularly right about it, either.

Eyes a touch of icy blue. Reddish, nondescript eyebrows. Some lines on his forehead and around the eyes. A few acne scars from his teens. He'd never felt very handsome, always unsure around women. That was part of why he had stayed semi-committed, but only semi-so, to Constance all this time.

Well, maybe Ultimaya 1.0 would be changing his whole life's picture. Without another thought, Leo strode to the alcove, pulled out his chair, sat down, moved closer to his desk, and was about to hit the on switch of his computer when he remembered that the machine was already on, just in that strange hibernation created by Ultimaya 1.0. He tried hitting the enter key on his keyboard as Charley had suggested. It worked. The computer whirred and came back to life.

While the machine worked through its initial paces, with arcane computer language flashing across the monitor screen, Leo refreshed himself on his plan. Part of what made him a little uneasy was that, in their discussion of strategy, it had become clear to Charley that Leo did not know and couldn't readily learn enough about what Charley called the "nervous system" of the computer to be able to do any "end runs" on the Ultimaya 1.0 program.

Charley had tried at first to suggest a few such moves. But the more he explained them, the more confused Leo got. Finally, exasperated, Charley'd just said, "Look, Leo, old bud, I'm beginning to get a picture of why that program chose someone like you instead of someone like me. I could maybe outfox it. You can't. You're dog meat for that little number and, in some midnight-in-the-graveyard way, I think it knows it.

"So my gut tells me you're gonna have to take a much simpler and more direct approach. You try to get around the innards of that hard drive and such, you're just gonna get all confused, or brain-fried, and you're going to abort the program. Which, from my not-so-humble point of view, would be ideal. But that's not what you want, right, buddy roe?"

So they agreed that Leo would just try to play along with the program and get some information about it. That's what he was now prepared to do. And that's why he had to be cunning. He had no trump card, no strategic advantage he could rely on. Just his own mind. An old American folk tune his father had sometimes played on the stereo, "John Henry," came into his head out of nowhere:

John Henry said to his captain
"Now a man ain't nuthin' but a man
"But before I let your steam drill beat me down
"I'll die with my hammer in my hand, Lord Lord
"I'll die with my hammer in my hand."

"Ain't gonna let your steam drill beat me down, Ultimaya. No way!" Leo thought.

When the main menu came up on the screen, he saw that Ultimaya 1.0 was now a fixed item, right where it had appeared the day before, at the top of the list on MS-DOS. For a moment, he hesitated again, wondering if it was even possible for him to get into any other software program. "Just out of curiosity," he thought, and then hit the downward arrow key.

The cursor didn't move.

He hit several other keys, randomly.

The cursor still didn't move.

Leo breathed out with a low whistle, staring at the screen. "Whew, just like Charley said," he muttered. "It's got its tentacles into the hard drive itself. It's taken over." For a minute or two, he sat motionless. Then he thought, "Well, so be it," and hit enter to bring up the program.

This time there was no sudden apparent shutdown of the machinery. Everything whirred and beeped in a natural, ordinary way. Leo wondered if maybe none of that was necessary now. There was no on-screen acknowledgment of "User integration sequences" either.

Maybe that was because the program was already integrated with the User: himself!

That idea made him shudder. It kept him less than receptive to the fifty–sunset color display that ensued just as it had the night before. Then there was a pale blue, blank screen, then a vivid red one—and then, on white, these black words: "It's NOT GOING TO WORK."

Leo felt a bit startled. What the heck did that mean? But he wasn't about to be hornswoggled this time. He rapidly typed, "What's not going to work?"

The computer registered his question just below the statement it had brought up itself. Then Leo's question instantly disappeared. The sentence, "It's NOT GOING TO WORK," then magnified in size to fill the whole screen, the letters all ballooning and compressing one another crazily until hardly any white spaces remained between them, and then the sentence shrank back down to its original size.

Leo sighed, saying aloud, "Come on, don't stonewall me now. Cooperate, dang it! Give me some slack here!" Then he typed, "I request, in fact beg for the opportunity to ask Ultimaya 1.0 some questions about how it operates. This is my deepest wish tonight."

The computer whirred at a high frequency for a few seconds.

Then, one character at a time, starting from the end of what he had written and moving backward, Leo's request began to disappear from the screen. An audible click accompanied the sudden demise of each letter. Leo leaned forward, scrunching up his face, trying to figure out what was happening. "What the—?"

Suddenly, an anomaly appeared. The *s* in "wish" remained on the screen, exactly in place. The other letters before it, starting with the *i*, continued to click off the screen one at a time.

Fuming, Leo pushed his rollaway chair away from the desk with a violent shove that sent him whirling around in it. "Dang it! What in tarnation is this Godforsaken thing doing? I cannot *believe* this!" His chair came to rest with him facing the computer again, just in time for him to see another letter survive the disintegration of his request.

It was the *b* in "beg."

Leo rolled closer again, intent on seeing if any other letters would remain. Hardly any of the others were left. Click—*q* in "request" gone. Click—*e* gone. Click—*r* likewise. Click—space. Click—*I* vanished. No other letters remained on the screen except the two that had been spared.

The machine was silent, except for its usual low whirr.

Leo sat back in his chair. He was still annoyed, and now nonplussed to boot. "What in tarnation...gol*dang* it! What kinda stupid—"

Then he got it.

Leo's eyes bulged and he leaped out of his chair a full foot into the air, coming down standing like a fighter with both fists clenched, and shouting, "Goldang you! Don't you 'B-S' me! Where do you come off with that kinda talk? What kind of computer program are you? What in God's name are you, *period?* How dare you swear at me! How do you know what my deepest wishes are and ain't? *Jesus,* I cannot believe this is happening. I don't need you! I don't need what you can give! You're a confounded computer program! You ain't nobody! You got no power, and you sure as shootin' got no power over *me*—"

Suddenly, he stopped shouting. He stood glaring at the monitor, all white with a little black lowercase *b* near one side of the screen and a little black lowercase *s* skewed off on another line at the other side.

Leo let out a sigh and slumped into his chair again. He didn't say anything. But his mind was racing. "Leo, you dumb mule, you're losing it. Good Lord, how many years has it been since you got so flustered? And by a dang machine!

"What is going on with me? What in God's glorious Creation can I want so bad that this silly little computer program can get under my skin so dang good? I'm the one who gets people to blow their top and their cool in negotiations. Nobody—no man, and for dang sure no piece of confounded software—does that to me! I was just shouting at the top of my lungs at a derned lump of electronics. Am I losing it or what?"

He remembered that he was, after all, still sitting in his bedroom. Wondering if Nan had heard his outburst, he looked toward the door, listening for any sound from the rest of the house. But all was quiet. Nan had probably gone to bed already, and she was a sound sleeper, quick to fall into deep sleep. Besides, who knew if she was even Nan anymore?

Leo took a deep breath in and out, then chuckled, shaking his head. He looked at the computer again and spoke aloud, in quiet, measured, calm tones.

"All right. Good. I appreciate a worthy man across the table. You aren't a man, but that was good. Oh yeah, that was good. But you have to understand. I must know a little more about what you are and what you do before I'm going to be willing to play your game. So, Mr. Ultimaya 1.0, I reckon one way or the other you're just gonna have to give a little in this negotiation. Otherwise…well, I reckon I'll just turn you off and go to bed. What do you say to that?"

Leo sat silently, waiting. Nothing happened. The *b* and *s* still hung lopsidedly on the screen.

Then Leo snorted, rolling his eyes to the ceiling. "Oh, right," he said. "You don't get anything from me if I don't type it up. Right. Of course. You can pick up my arsonistic rages from the kitchen but no, no, you can't register good calm logic at a distance of two feet. Well, B-S to you too, Ultimaya 1.0! But all right, I'll type it in."

He began pecking away: "I most earnestly request that the Ultimaya 1.0 program give me some vital information on how it operates. I do not feel I can cheerfully and in good conscience continue—"

Leo paused, his fingers hovering over the keyboard. He shook his head slowly as he watched the letters disappearing again, but now silently and starting at the beginning of what he had written, rather than from the end. Finally, "continue" dissolved. The screen was blank again.

Leo pushed away once more from the desk. He leaned forward and put his elbows on his knees and his head in his hands. It had been a very long day. And now he was getting nowhere. He thought, "Heck, if I had any gumption at all, I'd just turn the dang thing off and haul it back to Charley first thing in the morning. Be done with it, period."

But Leo knew he was not going to do that. No way. Too much was possible. Too much was at stake. In all kinds of ways. He had to push on. Dang it! There must be some way to get into some kind of dialogue, to get some kind of agreement with this thing!

Suddenly, he sat straight up, wheeled to his desk again, and began typing, clicking the caps lock key and pounding every letter with intensity:

"LOOK. I ACCEPT YOUR PRESENCE IN MY LIFE. I WANT TO COOPERATE WITH YOU. I WANT YOU TO FULFILL MY DEEPEST WISHES, LIKE YOU SAY YOU CAN AND WILL. I BELIEVE THIS IS TRUE. BUT YOU HAVE GOT TO BELIEVE ME WHEN I SAY THAT I NEED YOU TO FULFILL AT LEAST ONE WISH OUT FRONT BEFORE I CAN GO ANY FURTHER. WILL YOU PLEASE CONSIDER MY REQUEST FROM THE BOTTOM OF MY HEART?"

The computer whirred loudly for a moment. Then these words appeared under Leo's request: "Please state your wish."

"Thank you!" Leo shouted. "Thank you, sir! All right!" Without stopping to think, he typed: "I want my wishes to be fulfilled. But I don't want anyone hurt, even temporarily, just because I get mad or something. Will you agree that no one will be hurt while you are fulfilling my wishes?"

The computer made strange sounds again. Then there was a silence. Leo felt odd, like some kind of ray was scanning him. At last a reply appeared onscreen: "People get hurt all the time. Even temporarily."

Leo bit his lower lip, thinking fiercely. He responded: "True. I understand. But at least promise me that no one close to me and no one who I ask for specific changes to happen to personally will get hurt in any basic or fundamental way while you are fulfilling my wishes. Or afterward."

He paused and considered whether he should add any more technical stipulations. He couldn't think of any. On the other hand, signature time was no moment to be having to figure out terms on any deal, especially one as crucial as this. He hadn't anticipated being pinned back to a wall the way he surely was right now. He wished he'd prepared a little better—he needed a dang lawyer to deal with this machine—yet who could've predicted how this so-called conversation would turn out?

Meanwhile the computer was responding: "The fulfillment of deep wishes in and for the User, like any other operation in the world of causes and effects, necessarily operates by certain laws. The Ultimaya 1.0 program, while extraordinarily capable of achieving remarkable effects, necessarily operates within the parameters dictated and governed by those laws."

There was a pause. Leo was gazing so intently at the computer monitor that he hardly breathed. Was that all?

A further reply appeared: "Nonetheless, Ultimaya 1.0 has integrated fully with the User and is consequently bound and determined to fulfill his deepest wishes, when they are truly and fully indicated. Therefore, an adjustment has been made. This adjustment will necessitate consequences of one kind or another in the future. But yes, this wish is granted."

"All right!" Leo whooped aloud, then he remembered Nan was sleeping. So he continued laughing and exclaiming at the same time in a kind of screeching whisper. "All right! Thank you! Thank you very goldang much!"

He then typed in the words, "I appreciate your kindness and accept your terms. Thank you."

The monitor went blank immediately, and new words appeared: "Do you have any further wishes this evening?"

Leo sighed. "What a day," he thought. "What a two days!" Suddenly, his body seemed to melt with signals of deep weariness, so that he felt he could lie down and not move a muscle for two weeks.

He typed, "No. Not tonight."

Underneath his words the program responded: "This is fine. Please leave the computer on as before." Instantly, the screen then went black, and the machine went into that strange silence it had maintained since last night.

Leopold Stokes rose from his chair and stretched, yawning. He had a bit of an uneasy feeling in his guts. After all, he hadn't accomplished a tenth of what he'd hoped to in his negotiation with Ultimaya 1.0.

In fact, he couldn't remember the last time he'd gotten so stomped while trying his best to work a deal to his own advantage. The program had brushed him aside like a fly. Never mind end runs—he'd been buried in his own end zone the whole game! He had no sense whatsoever that his assault had even posed any real challenge to Ultimaya 1.0.

He also wondered what kind of "consequences in the future" the program was talking about. But then he stopped himself. "Heck," he thought. "No point bruising brain cells on that one. No way I'm gonna get close to finding that out till the time comes, the way this thing plays its cards.

"Well, leastways no one's gonna go up in smoke anymore. No one's gonna get hurt. That's good enough for now. I mean, I hope it is. Just have to couch my requests real careful like, to get what I want without collateral damage."

Crawling into bed, Leo mused in an audible whisper, "Whew, I'm ready to sleep like a bird dog in duck season that's been running two full days nonstop. But am I the dog...or am I the bird?"

The last thing he noticed was a feeling that burgeoned into an all-powerful conviction in his heart, before any words came to mind: "Tomorrow, whatever else I do, I have got to see Constance."

THE ONLY MORAL WAY

Early the next day, the morning sun on his face woke Leo from dreamless sleep. From a corpselike position flat on his back—the same way he'd fallen asleep—he jackknifed into a sitting position, instantly remembering his resolve upon falling into bed: "I have to see Constance."

As he sped through his morning ablutions, Leo reflected that this was not going to be easy. What in the world was he going to tell her? How could he prepare her for what he had in mind? Should he even try? And would she even be willing to talk to him? He hadn't exactly parlayed himself into a position of significant ingratiation with her.

Truth be known, Nan Creech was right. He probably did take Constance's attention far too much for granted. Over the last couple of years, she had begun to let him know that maybe, just maybe, she might not be on the receptive side if and when he finally came around with a dozen roses and a little black velveteen box.

Long ago, she'd always laughed pretty heartily when Leo teased her about wanting "one of them high-shine prestige knuckle-sparklers" more than she really wanted him. But lately, whenever he made such jokes, she'd just get real quiet.

How in heck was he going to play this one? What he had in mind was, he knew for certain, to her advantage as well as his. But maybe she wouldn't want to know. Maybe she shouldn't know. Maybe, in fact, she even couldn't know...

"Leopold Stokes, I never seen you fail to eat a short stack of pancakes. No biscuits, no bacon, no eggs over easy—you sure you're all right?"

Nan was sitting across from him at the breakfast table, smiling but with a trace of a concerned frown. Leo looked down at his plate, cup, and glass. He'd chugged his orange juice and black coffee but hadn't taken so much as a single bite of his food.

This surely was unlike him. Leo was a man who appreciated a good breakfast. It was one of the things about living with Nan as his housekeeper that he'd always valued—breakfast was sumptuous, with or without her lectures. But here he was, so absorbed in his plans and schemes he'd forgotten to eat.

"Whew, guess I got some stuff on my mind, Nan. You're right. I better dig in, huh?"

So he made sure to polish off everything she'd given him, and an extra short stack of pancakes besides.

The food calmed him down. He bade Nan good-bye for the day and drove off, feeling rested and free of urgency.

Leo decided he'd just take things as they came today. One way or another, he'd figure out how to work things through with Constance. No need to rush over there to talk with her. Whatever she was feeling, he figured he could get her to cooperate with him on this one. She hadn't given up on him yet. Not that much, anyway.

Driving to the bank, he recollected the many years of his relationship with Constance Cunningham. Three years younger than Leo, she had moved to Ashlin and joined the freshman class just as he and Charley were finishing high school.

Leo had been kind of shy all along. But Constance immediately took to him. All that year and the summer before he went off to college, she threw herself at him—not to get down to anything serious physically, mind you; she wasn't that kind of girl. But she let it be more than plainly known to him, not to mention everybody else, that she wanted to be his girl, and she took every opportunity to try to charm him into taking her out and spending time with her.

Truth be known, Leo was flattered. And Constance, after all, was not plain. She was a little chunky, but voluptuous even as a freshman, and real pretty, with lush dark brown hair and eyes so green they startled you when you looked into them up close. She was always a little embarrassed about her weight and also, especially, her buck teeth.

For that reason, practically from the day she first showed up in school, "Beaver"—with its obvious other anatomical connotations as well—was her nickname among the guys. The more obnoxious of them even called her that to her face, to her mortification and occasional tears. "Yankee Beaver," in fact, since her family had moved down south from Connecticut some years before, even though they were actually returning to the old family home after about a decade in the north.

Then too, back in those days she sounded just a hint like a Yankee trying to talk southern, a strange echo of the north in her Carolina drawl. It took Leo a couple of years to figure out that this was actually her natural way of speaking; she wasn't trying to sound any which way. And she wasn't the kind of girl who would try to make herself sound like someone else. As time wore on, the Yankee inflections fell away from her, so that nowadays she sounded like any other lifelong female resident of Ashlin.

But back then all of that, and also the fact that Constance's folks were in a social class about two echelons below Leo's and Charley's families and the crowd they ran with, had a kind of petrifying effect on Leo. It didn't frighten him. It immobilized him. As often as he tried in those early years to respond to Constance's obvious signals of interest in him, he couldn't get himself to do it. He managed to take her out a few times the summer after his freshman year in college, but Charley and the other guys razzed him mercilessly. "Hey, Leo! Where's your face mask? Don't let her give you a hickey. If she gets all hot and bothered, she might slit your throat!" Their raucous taunts depressed him and made him feel kind of crazy, deflating and flying all over the place emotionally, like a balloon someone had untied and set loose.

He'd start to go nuts in his own head, arguing with himself about whether to pursue Constance. Sometimes he thought he should. Sometimes he thought he shouldn't. When he thought he should go after her, he only wound up stringing her along. When he thought he shouldn't, he tried to give her the cold shoulder but instead still wound up being nice. In any case, he never really went for her.

He wouldn't have had to go too far. Constance meantime had decided that, come hell or high water, she simply must be with Leo. And if she couldn't, well then, she just wasn't going to be with anybody at all.

Leo couldn't imagine why. It wasn't like she wasn't attractive. It wasn't like she couldn't have found a good man. But between his unyielding ambiguity and her unbudging conviction, something got stuck in place between them. And even when Leo returned to work full-time in the bank with graduate degrees in finance and business administration, and all his friends, including Charley, encouraged and more or less expected him to hook up for keeps with Constance, he just could not make the move.

It was weird even to Leo. Maybe the availability to him she was forever broadcasting took away the thrill of the chase. He didn't know why it was that way for him. He just knew it was.

So they dated interminably. At some point, they began sleeping together. He didn't know where she'd learned what she knew; they sure had a good time in bed. But still ...

There was a woman in Ashlin whom Leo found much more attractive: Helen Honeycutt, the one-time Helen Folger, who was also, to spice the stew, Constance's best friend. Helen had been a knockout when their crowd was growing up and she still was today. Of course, she was Paxton Folger's daughter and Ralph Honeycutt's wife, and, it seemed, was determined to stay married, though she was such an uncorked flirt you just never knew.

Leo rarely had any contact with Helen these days, for years in fact, and for all he knew she was unaware of his interest in her. Which interest might as well remain unrequited, he always reminded himself. The last thing Leo wanted was a man the size and temperament of Ralph Honeycutt making physical points to Leo himself, or one with the power and ruthlessness of Paxton Folger making financial points to his bank, about just who were the primary men in Helen Folger's life.

Ralph, Leo could maybe handle over time with a little diplomacy. Ralph was a former football star at State who'd moved to Ashlin from Charlotte after he and Helen married, and a man whose glory days clearly had come to an end way back on the college gridiron. Whatever Ralph's fancy title, the fact was that Helen's daddy maintained Ralph on his payroll as a kind of perpetual wedding gift to her for settling down.

Leo had a hunch that Ralph himself suspected he was a loser and dimly sensed he was kind of dumb. All that pent-up frustration left him trigger-happy; he could easily fly into rage. But even his occasional violent verbal outbursts could be mollified if handled with care.

Paxton Folger, however, was a whole other breed. Now in his late sixties, he was a cotton farmer and mill owner, a man of wealth quite extravagant by local standards. Notorious, feared, old Folger still held the grudging respect of everyone who was anyone in Cotton County—especially for a moonshining operation so vast, sophisticated, and successful that his white lightning was rumored to sell as "Paxton Folger's Best" over the counter in Canada. There—again, as rumor had it—Folger's was supposedly giving Seagram's a run for its money.

Leo avoided tangling with Folger. In fact, he avoided having anything to do with him, and that kept him way outside Helen's orbit too, even though she and Constance were close. There was a kind of unbreakable frost between the old skinflint and Leo. They'd sparred more than once around deals both of them had an interest in; all the business and financial people in Ashlin knew they both made sure to have nothing to do with each other, even at apparent cost.

Once upon a time, Leo had marveled at Charley's boldness around old Folger more than any other show of his pal's teenage bravado. Charley'd been both horny and crazed enough to dare to elope with Helen when he was a junior and she was just a sophomore in high school. For years after the annulment—Paxton Folger had practically signed the notary's form himself—Leo'd half expected to read one day about the discovery of Charley's body out in some field. Maybe near a still.

Well, regardless of the complications she spun into the relations of the men in her life, Helen was a beauty—slender, chestnut hair naturally streaked with blond, movie star looks, and, Leo'd never failed to notice, a gorgeous smile with perfect white teeth. Like a row of Chiclets across her mouth. And she was wild, particularly when they were younger. Like a local Ava Gardner, who, Leo knew, had grown up down in Smithfield, southeast of Raleigh, Helen was that particularly Southern brand of a *femme fatale* who could lay waste to a man's mind and heart with nothing more than a glance. And if she set her mind to do more than that, well, Lord help him.

At the same time, she was also oddly concerned about somehow looking right and being respectable too. In high school, on their crowd's illicit midnight trips to the lake, she'd be the first one in the water skinny-dipping, and the only girl with the spunk to steal her daddy's car to get there. Old man Folger's Lincoln Continental, at that! The girl led a charmed life, and she knew it. Yet it'd also be a matter of utter principle to her that none of the guys would get a clear glimpse of her tits or crotch on those wild nights.

To Charley's knowledge, none of them ever did. Nobody even claimed to. Rumor had it she'd lost her virginity to some Wake Forest basketball player when she was fourteen—if not to Charley during their crazy elopement a year later.

But who knew? Nobody even claimed to.

And, for all that dangerous wildness, Helen had class. No one ever thought she was a tramp, or anything like it. Charley never mentioned a word to any of the guys about whether they did anything together on that fateful one-night marriage, or what that anything might or might not have been. As uninhibited as she could be, Helen still evoked respect. Even from the guys, who all salivated every time they saw her.

The strangest thing was, maybe because her folks were kind of newly minted white trash, and because she always knew everyone else knew her old man was a bootlegger—even though they were members of the Cotton County Country Club and among the richest people in the whole county—Helen also always felt like an outsider. She'd always be bringing her pal Constance to the club events, or just out to the pool there, as her guest. But she often had a nervous glint in her eye, like she was just a guest herself.

Helen's insecurity made for an odd symbiosis between her and Constance, no doubt part of why they became such fast friends. She was at once Constance's ticket into the elite of Ashlin society and her confidant and rebellious comrade in the agonized adolescent world of those who know they really are outsiders no matter what they do, who they do it with, where they live, or how much money their parents have or acquire. Helen was always working overtime for everyone's attention—one day, some wild stunt or a beer party with ten guys and, of course, Constance tagging along—the next day twisting old Folger's arm to buy her way into the Cotton County Cotillion. That was one of the few squeeze jobs the bootlegger ever tried that, to Leo's knowledge, had failed.

Papa Paxton had come down real hard on her about Charley after their fling—so hard, in fact, she did not speak to Charley for a full year. Not long after that, Charley went off to college and things cooled between them. But maybe on a rebound of sorts, and since Leo and Charley were best friends and also among the town's four or five most elite young men socially, Helen, much to Constance's flustered concern, had then started noticing Leo. Helen would, of course, flatly deny any interest in Leo, and he likewise in her. But they both knew it was there. They just never did anything about it.

So now, decades later, Leo lived with his eternal hidden lust for Helen, who he assumed hardly even remembered their teenage sparks, and with his open queasiness about Constance, who had continued to wait for him like a wound requiring salve. After Helen married Ralph, Leo more or less gave up actively dreaming and scheming in secret about her. Everyone went on with their lives.

Helen was a travel agent now, there in town, not so much because she needed the money as because she loved contemplating glamorous, faraway places.

Constance was a nurse supervisor at the county hospital, always seeking to heal and make well.

Leo was at the bank, gumming himself up as large a wad of money and power as he could.

Charley, down in the capital, was presiding over his computer empire, with his own family and his own history—in his own world, really.

And now, here it was near on to thirty years since Leo and Constance had first met, they saw each other regularly—at least up till not long ago—and he still could not get himself to make a marriage commitment to her.

Finally, one recent evening, Constance, in tears, had told him that time was moving on. Either he should take her hand or she felt she just had no choice but to stop seeing him.

In the game of love as in the game of fortune, Leopold Stokes was not one to respond in a meek, submissive way to threats, veiled or not. Constance saying that had really pissed him off. Before that, he'd been dang close to ready to propose. But now, if he did, he'd be capitulating. Consenting to be manipulated. And that was just nowhere to be found in his slightly redneck Stokes bloodstream. After all this time, and knowing him as well as she did, here Constance like a dolt had gone and made it well nigh impossible for him to do the very thing she most wanted him to do, and that he was already right on the verge of doing with no arm twisted.

He could not believe she'd actually said that. Now what was he supposed to do?

So that night, as they talked in the car by her front gate before she went inside, Leo just sat there fuming and smoking like a pile of burning tires. At the time, he didn't say anything to Constance about how he felt. He just silently heard her out.

But he also hadn't said anything about it to her since. Period. Forget spending the night—Leo didn't spend ten minutes at a time with Constance. He stopped going out with her for dinners. On the occasions when he did see her in town, he studiously ignored her or, more often, was courteous but curt, to the point of hardly giving any signs of knowing her at all, much less loving her and wanting her in his life.

That night in the car, and her demand, had been a little over a month ago. She sent a note apologizing, but he had not yet deigned to answer. Truth was, though, Nan was probably right. He was a fool to think Constance would wait for him forever. She was still a very attractive woman, still hot in fact and hot for him.

Well, here he was. Now what? He knew exactly what he wanted in his relationship with Constance. Deep-seated wishes he'd been brewing on for a long, long time, yes indeed. He had a feeling there'd be no problem with Ultimaya 1.0 on the fulfillment of these wishes. But should he tell Constance? Hint at what was happening? Give her any indication at all of what was about to transpire in her life?

Or...just let it rip?

There was no doubt in his mind: Constance would be happier with things the way he was about to set them up. On the other hand, if he tried to explain it all to her, she'd probably flip out.

Charley used to laugh and say Constance made Leo look like a Hell's Angel, she was so squeaky clean and straight, even when she was trying to keep up with Helen's wildness years ago. What in tarnation was she going to make of a machine that could change the physical realities of their entire lives?

Actually, it wasn't even *a machine.* There was no observable mechanism to Ultimaya 1.0. It was just a process of some kind that'd taken up squatter's rights in the dark gray plastic box on Leo's desk, and in his mind, his heart, his whole life. It was a sharecropper that'd appeared out of nowhere and suddenly, in no time flat, was working the whole farm like it owned it!

There was no way Constance was going to be able to accommodate all that. She was probably a good example of why Charley had confirmed Leo's hunch that it was better to tell absolutely no one at all about the program, except Charley himself.

For that reason, the two of them had agreed that, for the time being anyway, Charley wouldn't even attempt to track down where the dang thing had come from, who created it, or how it had come to be and show up, of all places, on Leo's Toshiba.

"Mr. Stokes, this is Ernestine. I hate to bother you again, but these fellas from Strap Rock Baptist Church have been setting out here for quite some time, and I do feel they deserve a little of your time this morning."

His secretary's voice over the intercom snapped Leo out of his reverie. "Whew!" he thought, looking at his watch. He'd been sitting there for more than an hour ruminating. Come to think of it, he'd been so absorbed he didn't even remember parking his car or coming into the bank. "Second time today I've disappeared into my own dang brain! I'm gonna have to learn how to process this stuff better, I'm losing it again."

Aloud, he said, "Certainly, Ernestine; sorry about that, and thank you, ma'am! Send them right on in!"

As Ernestine opened the door and ushered the preacher and several of the church deacons into his office, Leo rose from behind his large burnished walnut desk and went to greet them warmly. "Come on in, fellas, and take a seat. Sorry to keep y'all waiting."

After exchanging handshakes and personal greetings—he knew them all not only by name but also by detailed personal financial history over the last fifteen years—Leo took his seat behind the desk as he began his speech.

"Now, I'm confident, *very* confident, we can find a way to keep that little church of yours in fine financial condition. The reason is, well, I have made what is, for a banker, a very unusual decision, and I think a very spiritual one. Have a seat, and I'll explain."

Because he'd kept the Strap Rock Baptists cooling their heels for a half hour in the bank lobby, the whole rest of his schedule was thrown off. As it turned out, that extra half hour had softened them up even more than they already were, so his refinancing negotiations with them were short and sweet indeed. But Leo remembered his promise when he'd been begging on the kitchen floor for Nan to return to life unharmed. So he made extra sure the final deal was sweeter for the church than it was for the bank. Not without a hint of a sigh—but he did it.

From then on, Leo was at it nonstop with meetings and loan applications all day long, right up till six-thirty that night. By then, when he finally had a minute to sit back and think again, it was pretty obvious. The only smart way, the only humane way, in fact, when you got right down to it, the only moral way to deal with Constance on this one was just to go ahead and fire up the engines.

Time to get on with the launch. She was going to love the changes that were about to happen in her life and her relationship with Leo. But if she had any inkling how they were happening, it'd blow her fuses. It'd be way too much for her to even remotely comprehend. Best to leave her in the dark on this one.

Sometimes Leopold Stokes just knew he was right. This was one of those moments. He felt a sudden surge of power and wisdom. It was a good thing he could discern the right course and act on it without hesitation. Now he was beginning to feel how appropriate it was that he, not Charley Bass or anyone else, had been entrusted with the phenomenal form-building power of Ultimaya 1.0.

It made sense. Charley, for all his skill in business and his knack for computers, would have been both too inquisitive about the program itself and too...well, too dang prissy, when you got right down to it; too afraid to make a decision and act. Not all the time, but sometimes, for sure. Or at least, when it came to something this big, this potent, with this much power to shake the world, Charley might be a tad too thoughtful to be able to seize the day.

But Leopold Stokes was not afraid to seize this day. He had to make real decisions that really affected people's lives and livelihood every hour of every working day. And he had long since stopped fretting about "what" and "whether" and "if only" and "why." Things just have to be decided and done, he allowed, and that's all there is to it. Some folks will like what you decide and others plain-old won't, and there is not a dag-dratted thing you can do about it.

That line of thinking cinched it. Leo gathered a few papers into his briefcase, though he knew he really wouldn't get much done on them tonight, and, locking his office door behind him, departed for home. He wanted to have a good meal. He wanted to relax a little. And then...it was time to get down to some serious wish fulfillment with Ultimaya 1.0.

DOWN TO BUSINESS

Leo and Nan enjoyed another friendly dinner, even convivial, reminiscing about old times in a way they'd neither one of them done in years. By the time she rose to do the dishes it was a quarter to nine. He then puttered around with some of his papers for a while. Finally, once again annoyed at his nervousness and procrastination, he took his seat before his computer. It was already well after nine o'clock.

Enjoying the display of color again, he noticed it'd been different each time, but that each time it had brought about in him this feeling of something dawning, something about to happen that was good and extremely fortuitous. Then he smiled and laughed at himself. "Brilliant, Leo, great deduction! Of course it's gonna make me feel this way. Whoever created this thing needs me to feel this way so I can get altogether into getting my deepest and most precious dreams to come true. *'When you wish upon a star...'"*

Remembering that line from the old Walt Disney Sunday night TV series of the late fifties and early sixties triggered a flood of childhood memories that felt like they were streaming right out of Leo's heart. The feeling was poignant, even painful. To his astonishment and then embarrassment, Leo suddenly began to cry. Not just little snuffles, but deep, drawn-out, aching sobs. Suddenly, he was awash again with the dreams and secret hopes of his childhood and youth, all of which, as a rational and practical man, he had gradually and almost totally stuffed down into his heart and guts, burying them for lo these many years. Till this very night.

Now this strange opportunity to act on everything he most deeply wished for had suddenly been granted to him from—who? what? God? Nature? Some arcane software assembly line in the land of electronic wizardry, California? He could not know, maybe never would. Nor did he care to. Leo found himself just humble and grateful, drying his eyes and trying to calm his breath, as words came onto his computer screen:

"Please state your wishes as previously instructed."

"All right, Mr. Ultimaya. You win! That I will do," Leo muttered, "just 'as previously instructed.'" Hands beginning to type, Leo chuckled under his breath, "Yessirree, 'get with the program' has a whole new meaning here!"

The first thing on his mind was Constance and their relationship. He typed in, "I would like to create a number of changes in Constance Cunningham, and in myself in terms of my relationship with her."

Then he leaned back. This was weird. It'd been one thing, the other night, inscribing his initial, petulant wishes about Nan. He hadn't even really thought anything would happen. But look at everything that in fact did happen! Now he knew very well that if the program accepted or confirmed the reality of his wishes, the changes he wanted were going to come to pass, come hell or high water.

His responsibility here was immense. Another person's life, the whole life of someone who was after all very dear to him, was at stake. So he'd better be for certain sure that what he always thought he wanted was what he really wanted, and that what he really wanted was exactly what he communicated to Ultimaya 1.0.

Leo thought for a long time. The program, as if sensing his seriousness and concentration, did not interject any instructions or questions. He had the feeling it was just patiently waiting to get to work for him. "Funny," he thought, "now that I'm setting here all soft and grateful for its presence in my life, it's ready to serve me faithfully."

Now that he thought about it, that kind of blew Leo's mind. The line came back to him from the previous night: "Ultimaya 1.0 has integrated fully with this User and is consequently bound and determined to fulfill his deepest wishes, when they are truly and fully indicated."

What a promise! What a miraculous opportunity! Was there anyone else on Earth who had been given such a blessing? "And," he thought, "such a responsibility. Well, time to git on down to business."

He continued to type in details of his request for Constance: "Expressing not only my own deepest wishes, but also, I am one hundred percent certain, her own lifelong yearning as well, I would like Constance to undergo certain physical changes instantly. In particular, she should lose about ten pounds of general weight, especially in the upper thighs, waist, and arms; and her calves should be slimmed down too, so they are elegantly slender.

"I very much wish Constance's teeth could simply become completely straight, immediately—like, overnight—so she never again has to suffer feeling bad about herself because she has buck teeth. By the way, she should be able to keep her weight down easily from now on, and not have to worry about what she eats."

He paused, wondering what else to say. The machine murmured quietly.

"Also, I deeply wish that Constance could be"—he struggled for the words—"well, a little more exciting for me to pursue as my bride. Not so exciting that she declines! But I wish that now we can have a hot romance and then, soon, get married and get on with our lives together—both of us completely happy."

With the last word Leo typed, the drive on his computer whirred, and the program interpolated a comment:

"All but one of the elements of this wish-list are acceptable to Ultimaya 1.0. However, the User must understand that this program can take responsibility for phenomenal changes in the content of his experience and his situation only. This is to say, it can provide deeply wished-for transformations only in the realm of causes and effects. It does not operate in the User's qualitative participation in these transformations and transformed conditions."

Leo squinted at the words on the screen, saying aloud, "What? What the—what're you trying to tell me? Dang thing sounds like a White House press secretary!"

He typed, "Are you saying that the 'happily ever after' part is my business, or what?"

The program responded: "The previous statement of the capabilities and responsibilities of Ultimaya 1.0 *vis-à-vis* the User's wishes was complete and clear. No further explanation is forthcoming."

Leo sighed. Whatever Ultimaya 1.0 was, it did not tender any points in negotiations. He scrolled back up the screen to the end of his previous paragraph and eliminated the final phrase, "both of us completely happy." Then he proceeded:

"All right. I furthermore very deeply wish that, effective immediately, my home be transformed so that it is the most expansive and elegant mansion in Cotton County, as befits the chairman, CEO, and principal stockholder in the county's largest bank.

"Now, in the past Nan Creech has always ragged me about how my momma and daddy were frugal folk and would not take kindly to me putting up a movie star home in Cotton County. And she would say, besides, what need did I have of such extravagance when I was just a miserly bachelor with no wife and family? So, of course, Nan should still live with me. But she should have no complaints about my more"—he waited for the right words—"expansive and befitting lifestyle for a man in my position. And she should have nicer rooms, of course, at the opposite end of the house from me, and out of my way. Not exactly servants' quarters, but ..." Leo stopped typing, trying to come up with a description of what he wanted. But then a question came to mind. He typed, "Does Ultimaya 1.0 have knowledge of what I am getting at here? How explicit do I need to be?"

The machine replied, "Ultimaya 1.0 is, again, completely integrated with the User's dynamic wish-field and is fully aware, consequently, of all his deepest wishes. Sufficient direction has been given such that the program can proceed to fulfill all aspects of this particular wish-impulse."

"Hah!" Leo jumped out of his chair, brandishing a fist. "Finally scored one confounded point with this thing! All right!" He sat back down and continued typing.

"Now it is crucial that these changes occur immediately, overnight, and that neither Constance, nor Nan, nor anyone else here in Ashlin, or anywhere in Cotton County for that matter"—he paused for a moment and then completed the sentence in italics—*"even be aware that anything was ever different, or rather they should not be at all aware of how any perceived changes have occurred—except myself, of course.* Myself and Charley Bass, who's down in Wake County anyway, not up here in Cotton County, and is already aware of how the program works. It never occurred to me to wish for this before, but, is it okay, considering that if it was otherwise, things would get very complicated? Does this request work within the parameters of the program?"

There was a soft whirr, almost a mechanical purr, and then a simple confirmation: "Affirmative to both questions."

"Good!" Leo spoke aloud again. He was beginning to feel a little confidence in his interaction with Ultimaya 1.0 now. It was obvious that the program would respond to him—heck, it must've known what his wishes were even before he did, if it was so "fully integrated with his dynamic wish-field." And though he had to be explicit, there were certain things he could rely on it to handle once he'd set the terms and stipulated the conditions he desired.

Likewise, it was now clear that it could and would make adjustments in other people affected by his wishes such that they'd be unaware—blissfully unaware, if he had any say in the matter—of what changes he was creating, for his own good and, yes, for theirs as well.

No doubt about it, Leo was starting to feel the strength of his old powerful self coming into play, in fact, even more than ever before. He knew, of course, that a whole lot of that feeling had to do with Ultimaya 1.0. It was like going from driving a go-cart with a lawnmower engine to racing a Maserati; this program was amazing.

Leo had no doubt that whatever he wished for would come true, provided the program accepted his wish. He also knew that anything it deemed not a true or really deep wish of his, it would explicitly refuse to fulfill. Which was somehow strangely reassuring—"Shoot, it's like it knows me better than I know myself. Which means I can rev this engine way up, 'cause the program's got its own guardrails; it'll protect me from doing damage."

So, buoyed by his increasing success in communicating with Ultimaya 1.0, Leo continued with his requests for the evening.

"It has long been my wish and great intention to make Cotton County Regional Bank into a statewide leader in the regional banking field. And I have been moving in the direction I staked out when I took over for my daddy five years ago when he died in that car wreck. But things have been going too slow. Specifically, there are two things I very much desire.

"First, I wish to have, right away, two successful regional branch offices outside Cotton County—one in, say, Norlands, and the other, well, make it south of here, in Brucks County, in the county seat, Brucksville. Just up and running, no problems, with good, competent, loyal branch managers and staff. Everything I expect in a good branch office. Is this clear?"

The program replied, "Affirmative."

Leo continued. "Good. Second, along with that, naturally I do not want to lose any ground here in my home county. And some of the other statewide banks are trying to move in on what has heretofore been almost exclusively Cotton County Regional Bank business, even right here in Ashlin. I don't mind some of those local upstarts; those boys don't know what they're doing. But Cardinal Bank of Carolina, serious institutions like that, they're real competition. And I don't want them here, now or in the future. I know Bob Jackson, the Cardinal chairman; I like him and respect him and his organization. I just don't want them anywhere around here. Is this understood? And is this wish acceptable to be fulfilled?"

The message came back again: "Affirmative to both questions."

Leo responded on the screen: "Excellent."

His unequivocal success this evening spurred Leo to dare a few more requests. These were a few more things he had in mind that, up till now, he'd been feeling might be too trivial, or self-indulgent, or frivolous, for the program to accept. But at this point, he had succeeded so handsomely during this session he figured he had nothing to lose by trying. He sat thinking for a moment and then started typing again.

"I do have a few more personal and less"—he reached in his mind for a word—"serious requests too, but they are things I have often wished for. First off, I'd like to have"—he grinned and grimaced at the same time, and felt his face flushing red and hot—"an unlimited supply of Lappert's Macadamia Nut and Mango ice creams available to me at all times."

He waited.

There was no response.

At first he felt chagrined, like he'd made an error.

Then it occurred to Leo that maybe since he'd said he would make "a few" such requests, the machine was simply waiting for him to complete his list. Emboldened, he continued: "I also would like"—once again he paused, trying to frame the ask just right—"to in general get a little more respect, like that comic in the movies is always saying. No big deal. Just a little, as befits a man in my position."

He sat back. "These are kinda frivolous," Leo thought, "especially the ice cream." Maybe he should add something with a little more depth or consequence.

He wrote: "Finally, at least for now, I would like to be able to participate in all these changes with"—he hesitated; Ultimaya 1.0 had already made clear what its capacities were with respect to his own qualitative participation—"freedom from this feeling I've had all my life like I'm being constricted or something. I'm not asking to be made 'happy ever after' based on any changes that occur. I understand your stipulations about all that. I'm asking for a very basic and what feels like very physiological distress in my life to be taken away. I mean, this is like Constance's teeth, this is physical. I request that I be set free of that feeling. Except of course, under ordinary circumstances where it's inevitable—"

Suddenly the keys stopped calling forth characters on the screen. Leo watched as a reply from the program appeared: "The User need not elaborate further. All of these most recently expressed wishes will be granted."

Leo typed, "Thank you! Thank you so very much!"

Then he sat back and took a long, deep breath. This was hairy stuff, changing reality at will! He wondered if he was missing anything important. He scrolled up the screen and read back through everything he'd typed in and how the program had responded. It occurred to him that maybe he should get a copy of it all. He wrote, "Is it possible to print out my wishes and Ultimaya 1.0's responses?"

"Affirmative."

Leo spoke out loud, "Very good," and set up the machine to print everything out. While the printer coughed along, he considered whether there was anything else he should request tonight, or if this was enough. He couldn't think of anything. Besides, that was a pretty major menu he'd already ordered there; maybe he ought to digest these changes a bit before ordering any others.

Feeling a need for fresh air, he rose, opened the sliding door that led onto his porch, and stepped out into the night.

It was cool out, but not cold, and the air was invigorating. Every breath he took felt like it reached on down into his legs and feet. Leo stretched his arms high into the air, ran in place for a moment or two, and twisted from side to side, stretching his stiffened back and legs.

Then it occurred to him something was different. And something else was missing.

He looked around him. His porch, which used to be two feet off the ground, was at a level of pine boughs that looked to be two or three stories high. But these were not the familiar, somewhat stumpy trees in his and the Jenkins' yards.

And the familiar lights of downtown Ashlin, which should have been obvious a few blocks away, were nowhere to be seen!

"Oh my God*! Oh my God!"* Leo was stunned. "Where am I? What in God's goldang Creation is going on here?"

He walked over to the railing and looked down. Wherever he was, it was not his little one-story ranch house near downtown Ashlin. He was in fact and indeed standing on what looked to be the third story of a huge mansion!

Leo looked down the length of the porch. He hadn't noticed when he first stepped outside that this was no longer the five-by-eight foot little patch of a porch he'd tacked onto the ranch house back when he moved in. It extended twenty-five feet from him in either direction, with sections disappearing around a great wing of the building. This place was huge!

Then he turned and looked back at the entire edifice. The lights were out, and there was no illumination from any source except a nearly full moon now and again obscured by scudding clouds. From what he could see, however, it looked like his wing was one of three massive sections of what appeared to be a three story, colonial-style plantation home, the far end of which he could not even discern in the night shadows.

"It's already happened!" Leo said aloud. "Holy tarnation, it has already happened! The whole goldang place is different! I don't even know where I am! Must be out in the country somewhere. Look at this place! *Look at it!"*

He felt like exploring the whole house right away. But then, just as suddenly, he thought better of it. Presumably, Nan was sleeping down there at the other end somewhere—seemed in the night like almost a football field's distance. And he wouldn't be able to see much.

Why not save the delight till tomorrow? He knew he'd enjoy discovering his new mansion more in the morning, in the light of day.

Not to mention going to see Constance and finding out how she looked and what she was going to be like now. Yeah, boy—not to mention that!

Grinning, happy, his heart pounding with excitement and gratitude, Leopold Stokes returned to his desk in the—he now noticed—much-expanded alcove of his much-expanded master bedroom. His Toshiba computer was still sitting, faithfully it seemed to him, on a modern, sleek Scandinavian style desk, awaiting his next command.

Well, his next request, anyway.

He typed in that he had no further wishes for the evening, and the machine dutifully went into its Ultimaya 1.0 hibernation.

Leo was once again exhausted. "Working this dang program is a workout itself," he muttered. "Awesome, awesome responsibilities. Mm-mm! Every wish I type in, I feel like I'm moving heaven and earth!"

As he crawled into his very large bed—"This thing," he thought, "must be bigger than a king size, if that's possible"—he noticed a silken, shiny-soft quality to the bed linens. He laughed. "Ha! Right down to the satin sheets! Thank you, Mr. Ultimaya, thank you!"

STOKESLAND!

Even years afterward, and after everything that happened, Leo would always remember the next morning as a kind of ultimate—an Ultimaya!—Christmas day.

Like a kid on Christmas, he awoke long before even the slightest sliver of sunshine crept over the horizon. Unlike a kid on Christmas, though, he disciplined himself to stay in bed and wait till the morning light. He drifted off into sleep again, dipping into pleasant and amusing dreams.

Then, at around seven, he awoke with a start. The sun was up. It was light. And it was time to explore his new world! He leaped out of bed, but what he saw then stopped him in his tracks.

His new bedroom was the size of the entire house he and Nan had lived in until just the night before! The bed itself was huge, a giant four-poster brass antique with an intricate canopy that appeared to be sparkling. Leo crawled up onto the bed and stood to look at the canopy closely. He had the distinct feeling that the sparkling stones studding its entire underside were actual gems, not just rhinestones or glass beads. "Holy goodness Gracious A'mighty," he whistled. "I can't believe it. Either I'm outta my head or this dang thing is strung with semiprecious stones."

But he had no time to answer that question just now, there was too much else to look into! He jumped off the bed with a whoop and ran several yards across the high-pile rug to a closet, sliding open huge, hand-carved wooden doors that extended all the way up to what he reckoned was a fifteen-foot-high ceiling.

Looking inside, he stopped stock still again, his jaw dropping. The closet stretched for at least twenty feet! It had row upon row of suits, ties, shirts, and slacks, what he estimated to be about fifty pairs of shoes, and several adjoining mirrors for dressing, like in a fine men's store.

Leo whistled again. "Heck, Mr. Ultimaya, don't ya think this is a little overdone? I mean, how many suits can a respectable, sober banker get away with in Ashlin, North Carolina?" But he couldn't suppress a grin. "Guess I'll just have to test the tolerances." He handled a few of the jackets' lapels, pulling a couple out to admire them more closely in the bright sun-like lighting from the ceiling fixtures. "Whew, pretty dang fine stuff. Well, 'a man in my position,' I guess."

Just inside the door was a rack of robes, smoking jackets, and other casual wear for lounging and the like. Leo picked out a deep purple terrycloth robe, plush to the touch, and swiftly put it on. He found some warm house slippers that looked to be made of fine leather—he hardly dared even check out the inner linings, but from the feel of them it was obvious that some kind of fine fur now cradled his feet—and then rushed out to see what else had come into his possession through the miracle of Ultimaya 1.0.

His bedroom was a sight to behold. The ceilings rose in the center of the room to about twenty feet high, with skylights on either side of a long beam down the middle of the room. Two walls were full-length sliding glass doors, leading out onto the porch that, if anything, appeared to be longer and wider in the morning sun than it had by moonlight late the previous night.

Yet the room had a cozy feel too, as well as a strong masculine presence. Aside from his work alcove—and Leo smiled at the sight of his computer, monitor aloft as always, now looking small and innocuous at a distance of twenty-five feet from where he stood—there were several distinct seating areas with couches and lounge chairs.

One of them faced a game area that included—what? Leo rushed over, then laughed out loud.

A giant electric train getup sprawled over at least two hundred square feet of the room. Behind it stood a fine billiards table of gleaming hardwoods inlaid with mother of pearl and other colorful, fine materials he couldn't identify. "Shoot! I ain't had a train set since I was a kid! This is too good!" He thought of playing himself a rack of nine-ball, but then thought better of it. Too much to see, too much to find out. Plenty of time later.

Leo ran his hand through his hair, remembering he hadn't peed or washed since arising. Looking around, he realized the huge doors at the far end of the room must lead to his private master bath. He hurried through them, and was once again amazed at what he saw.

The bathroom was a paradise of lovely flowering plants, bursting with greens and pinks and reds and yellows, and gorgeous custom-fired tiling. Leo paused long enough to notice that each gleaming tile contained gradients of teal, maroon, and aquamarine color that faded into and out of one another with more delicacy than he'd seen on many an abstract canvas. Then he looked around at the handsome, dazzling, obviously expensive fittings and features on the finely carved wooden cabinets and on the sink and tub. Under a wide skylight stood a giant Jacuzzi and just beyond it, against the high wall, a shower large enough for two people not only to stand but also to sit in!

There was a bidet as well as a toilet. "Hm," Leo mused, "maybe Ultimaya 1.0 knows something about my romantic future here that I don't?" But then, on further thought, he reckoned he knew quite well what was coming in that part of his life. No need to rush ahead, though. Plenty of time to savor that change when the time was right.

He brushed his teeth, noting that a tube of his favorite brand, Arm and Hammer Baking Soda Toothpaste, was in its appropriate position right next to his hairbrush. Turning on the faucet, he stopped for a moment, leaning down to examine the sink. "Must be marble, all right, but what's this inlay?" he asked out loud. "No, this can't be! Gold on my goldang sink? This is crazy! Somebody got outta hand here...."

Putting down his cup, a stunning crystal tumbler also trimmed with a gold rim, Leo thought, "All right! Enough! Time to get out of the bedroom—though I'm still not done even finding out what's in here—and check out the rest of this place."

First, of course, he had to find the door out of the room. He found ones opening into storage spaces and his home office supplies, and then the one leading to the rest of the house.

Grinning, he walked through the doorway, closing the door behind him, and turned to encounter a hallway as long and richly decorated as one in a huge swank hotel. He glanced at the signature on a colorful, modern still life on the wall, then stepped back with a start. "I can't believe this!" he whispered. "'Matisse '53'—I think this thing is a confounded original! Good God A'mighty." He remembered there were at least four major canvases on the walls of the bedroom that he hadn't taken the time to look at closely. He peered down the hallway. Paintings and statuary framed the full ten yards leading to a stairway down. "This is outrageous! That dang computer program has given me an art museum!"

Leo postponed getting to know his new art collection—at least, the part of it in his private quarters on the third floor—and strolled to the stairway. Upon reaching the second floor landing, he resisted the temptation to explore the rooms waiting down the corridor. He wanted to get to the ground floor and step outside to see what the whole place looked like, to get a feeling for the whole event of this new mansion that he had mysteriously come to own.

But by the time he reached the first floor, he knew he needed someone to celebrate all this with. "Nan!" he called out. "Hey, Nan! Where in tarnation are you, good woman?"

He went running down the parquet floor, sliding along at times in his slippers like a ten-year-old, across the vast expanse of what appeared to be the main living room—more like a main ballroom, with exquisite furnishings every which way he looked—and exploded into what, sure enough, turned out to be the kitchen.

And there the first of the day's more startling vistas erupted before Leo: the sight of Nan, her back to him, addressing a crew of no less than ten crisply attired servants about their day's responsibilities.

"Hey, Nan, wait a minute! Who are these people? Nan, come along with me, will you? I want you to see the rest of my new house with me!"

The shock of running into a whole crowd of unfamiliar servants—"Servants? For me?"—in his home was one thing. What Leo saw when Nan turned to face him was quite another.

She was at least *twenty years younger* than she'd been the night before. And she was stunning.

"Why, Mr. Stokes, I—I'm really quite busy now, as you see, we have such a big day and week of entertaining and all ahead of us. And I had no idea you'd gone and bought yourself another home—"

"Make that thirty years younger," Leo thought. Nan looked exactly like she did when she first came to live with his folks and him in town, when he was a boy. If not exactly, then darn close. And she was, sure enough, extremely pretty.

She demurely cast down her eyes, and Leo realized he'd been staring at her with his mouth wide open. He pulled himself together.

"Not another home, Nan! This home! I want you to come and—" Then he remembered. His jaw dropped again.

"Uh...Nan, come here for a second, hm?" Disregarding the inquisitive glances of the servants, Leo grabbed Nan's elbow and pulled her aside.

"Look, Nan—never mind about the house. I haven't bought any other place. This is it. I...well, I just wanted to tell you, Nan, how happy I am with the job you and the staff are doing, keeping this place so beautiful. Immaculate, I'd say!"

Nan cast her eyes down again, and this time she blushed. "Mr. Stokes, I certainly am grateful and proud to hear you say so. I—" she stammered and then stopped speaking.

Leo was touched. She was so pretty, so unassuming. "Is anything wrong, Nan?"

"Well, Mr. Stokes, it's—it's so unusual for you to address me by my first name, I just wasn't expecting it, that's all."

Leo couldn't suppress a giggle; it came out high-pitched and garbled, like he was choking on it. "Oh, well, you know, just being friendly, that's all. I certainly hope you don't take offense, M—M—Ms. Creech."

He hoped he'd gotten it right. Did she expect "Ms." or would that be too feminist, too Yankee for her, a proper Southern gal through and through? Maybe she was accustomed to being called "Miss."

Or, the thought flashed through his mind, was this somehow thirty years ago, before women even thought about things like that, and feminism hadn't happened yet? For that matter, not just when, but *where* was this even happening?

"No, no, no—it's completely fine by me, Mr. Stokes. You just, ah, took me by surprise this morning, that's all."

Leo laughed again, this time heartily. "Well, Ms. Creech, I probably couldn't explain just how much this morning is taking me by surprise too! Carry on with the staff, and thank you again!"

He wrapped his robe close around him and strode out of the kitchen. "Whew!" he thought. "This is not gonna be a cakewalk by any goldang stretch! I'm gonna to have to stay on my toes here.... And what in the good Lord's whole crazy Creation has happened to Nan? The woman is totally transformed! She not only looks thirty years younger, I got the no-holds-barred certainty cooking in me that she *is* thirty years younger."

Leo was suddenly possessed by a starting question. "Well then, what about me?" He had to find a mirror right away. The bathroom had probably been full of them, but at the time he wasn't noticing himself like he was right now.

He surely felt stronger and, he sensed, both thicker and thinner, more muscular and more trim, at the same time. He sprinted up the two flights of stairs, making a mental note to find the elevator—there must be one in a house like this—and back into his bedroom. Locking the door behind him, he rushed into the palatial bathroom.

First he examined himself fully robed from a distance of about four feet in a full-length mirror. He could not see any significant changes in his face at that distance, but then something struck his eye. He quickly stripped off his robe, silk pajama top, and T-shirt.

"Whoa!" Leo exclaimed so loudly he wondered if anyone downstairs might've heard him. "Whoa in-dang-deed! Move over, Arnold Schwarzenegger! I am coming to town today, *yessir!*"

Leo knew he was exaggerating a little—in fact, a lot. He was, after all, still only about five feet nine inches tall. But in place of his thick, strong but chunky, and usually kind of sickly white-pink torso, was a strongly muscled, tanned, and highly defined upper muscular development.

He flexed a little for himself, laughing and muttering. "How in heck did I get this? Something's gone cuckoo here. All kinds of stuff I never wished for has come to pass around here. Good Lord only knows what else I didn't ask for that's happened overnight!"

Then he remembered he'd gone downstairs intending to go outside to see the whole house in the light of day. He snorted at himself in laughter—"Never even got there, and I call myself a man of intentional action!"—and strode out of his room again, this time determined to get all the way out to the front of the house.

But after five purposeful strides down the hall, in front of the Matisse still life, without even slowing down Leo made an abrupt about-face and marched right back into his room. He walked straight over to the alcove and—the feeling or perception struck him as odd, but there it was, unmistakable—his *expectant* computer.

He sat down, activated the program, and strummed his fingers on the desk, irritated, waiting for all the preliminaries to pass. It was taking forever. He blurted out, "Can we skip the sunrise commercials and get on down to it here?" Then he typed, "What's going on? Why have all these changes happened that I did not request?"

The hard drive whirred, and a message appeared: "All changes have been made in direct response to the User's express wishes."

"No way!" Leo shouted, and then grinned, enjoying the fact that he could now shout at will in his room with no worry he'd be overheard. "No dag-dratted way!"

He typed, "I did not wish to have my body resculpted, though, fine, I don't mind that. But I sure as shooting did not wish, and never would, for Nan Creech to get thirty years younger!"

The machine replied, "The User may be only superficially cognizant of his own deeper wishes. The Ultimaya 1.0 program suggests a careful perusal of our contract."

"Contract! What contract are you talking about? I ain't signed—" Then Leo realized the machine was talking about the printout of his wish list from last night. He leaped up and ripped through the papers on his desk, trying to find it; then, just as abruptly, he went storming out of the room again, talking to himself.

"All right, confound it, I'll read it later. This is Christmas Day at Stokesland—hah, nice name for this place. And I am not gonna get bogged down today in confounded legalities with the goldang program!"

This time Leo held firm to his intention. He strode down the stairs and across the main living room with the bottom of his robe streaming at a forty-five degree angle behind him, like the coattails of a wild-eyed Groucho Marx. He opened the huge, intricately carved front doors, all gleaming with precious oiled woods and silver inlay, and stomped across his spacious, elegant front porch, out to the driveway and beyond, to a grassy meadow in front of the mansion. Forty or so yards from the house, in the chill of the early day, he turned and finally took the look he'd been wanting to see all morning.

"Yes, indeedy! Stokesland!"

The mansion was immense. He reckoned it had to be the largest home in all Cotton County, and maybe in the whole surrounding region. "About goldang time too," he thought. "I've been playing poor boy long enough!"

What he saw now in the bright morning sunshine confirmed his moonlit observations of the night before. He noticed with deep pleasure that what he had here was arguably the largest, finest, and most aesthetically pleasing colonial mansion he'd ever seen—far larger even than Paxton Folger's ostentatious house west of Ashlin.

By contrast to old Folger's almost garish spectacle, this home was altogether balanced in its design. Four pure white columns, a good three feet in diameter at ground level, tapered up to something a tad more slender at the point where they joined the beams supporting the roof. Dark green shutters, crystal clear panes, and white trim on what appeared to be the dozens of windows he could see from this vantage alone complemented the broad white exterior wood paneling of the home's massive front and its visible wings. It was a beautiful residence in the traditional, colonial plantation house style, imposing, yet not overwhelming the landscape of low hills covered in deep green pine forest with a rich blue sky all around—gracious, elegant, like a queen in a court, a jewel in a crown.

Well, maybe he was getting carried away in his own estimations, Leo thought. But this was a fine home, and quite suitable for a man whose name would soon resound across the state, if not through the whole Southeast, as one of the most innovative, successful bankers around.

As he glanced at the two great wings of the home and the larger central main section, Leo wondered first what corresponding rooms and features there must be in the east wing, the one opposite his own. Then a thought struck him that tickled him no end: "I wonder whether, proceeding from the library or somewhere, there is a hidden hallway or secret tunnel." Like the old landowners used to build in the days when men really did have to resort at times to arms and cunning to protect family and property.

Leo laughed out loud. That was the kind of thing he always felt should be somewhere in a house like this. And now he had such a house. "Good! About confounded time!"

He made a mental note to set aside some time to find that tunnel as soon as he could. He knew it would be there somewhere. After all, the place had appeared in response to his deepest wishes, and for no other reason. If there was something he required, well, it was just very well going to be there. And if it wasn't there yet, it would be soon. Leopold Stokes would see to that!

A slender, elderly fellow with a pale but pleasing face stepped out of the main door and came walking toward him. He was wearing a fine English cravat and a greatcoat with tails. "First time I ever saw anything like that in Cotton County," Leo said to himself. He smiled, narrowing his eyes with amusement and curiosity as the man halted at the end of the walkway by the drive, his left arm crooked in front of him with, sure enough, a little white towel folded over his forearm.

"Aha, this gentleman must be my butler," Leo surmised, just as the man said in—sure enough—a clipped British accent, "Mr. Stokes, sir, your brunch is being served in the breakfast room. Won't you come in, sir? Ms. Creech is frightfully concerned that you'll catch a chill out here. It is still winter."

Leo looked down at his bare stocky calves—nicely tanned, he noticed—sticking out from under his robe, his feet all furred up in the plush slippers, and laughed. He began walking at a rapid clip toward the door. "You're quite right, my good man! Freezing my butt off out here! What's for brunch?"

The butler allowed himself the barest of smiles. "The usual, sir. Would you like to dress before taking your meal?"

"No, no, I'm starved. Just make sure the heat's on, hear? Hm, I suppose I don't have to worry about the cost of heating this place, right?"

"Indeed, you don't, Mr. Stokes, assuredly you don't."

Leo, shooting forward, reached the front door before the butler and moved to open it. The man looked at him with an instant's consternation, then recovered his composure. Recognizing he'd broken protocol, Leo chuckled and stepped away from the door. "Sorry about that." He realized he didn't know the old man's name. "Sorry, old fella. Heh, heh."

The butler made no reply but gestured him through the door. Once inside, Leo sensed he should wait, which he did. The older man, visibly relieved, stepped forward and led the way to the breakfast room. Which was a good thing, Leo reasoned, since he himself did not have the slightest idea where it was.

The room turned out to be behind the main dining room, off a sunny courtyard next to the east wing of the house. Leo strode in with as much elegant grace as he could muster—it was going to take some work, stepping up to the role of Lord of the Manor—and allowed himself to be seated. Two serving maids stood by deferentially as the butler spread a fine linen napkin on his lap. Leo suddenly felt a howling hunger.

"Great! Thanks, old boy! Now, what's the spread this morning? Oh right, the usual...well, good, ladies, hm, yes—let's get on with it!"

The serving maids smiled, curtseyed, and bustled off to get his food. Meanwhile, the butler moved to a console and pressed a button. Leo grinned, first with curiosity and then with high amusement, as what turned out to be a giant screen descended from the ceiling on the far wall of the room, straight in front of him.

The butler turned and asked with calm gravity, "Would you like to begin with *Mighty Mouse* or *The Flintstones* this morning, sir? Or considering matters at hand, perhaps you would prefer *Betty Boop*?"

Saturday morning cartoons every day of the week! Leo couldn't restrain a whoop—another wish he'd forgotten to ask for, now fulfilled anyway! Then he glanced at the butler, furrowing his brow. "Hate to have to ask...but what day of the week is this, my good man?"

"Why, Tuesday, of course, Mr. Stokes. Surely you haven't forgotten your most important meeting here today?" The old man had a hint of a twinkle in his eye.

"Oh, no, no indeed. Of course not, just joshing you. And yes, by all means, go for the oldies today: Miss Boop! But not just yet, my good man; let me see what kind of feast I've got coming at me here."

As the maids served him mounds of pancakes and eggs and poured his orange juice and coffee, Leo puzzled over the butler's replies. "Tuesday?" he wondered. "The whole thing with Nan happened on a Wednesday night, right after my golf game got frozen off the course. I spent the next day, Thursday, down talking with Charley. I did business all day Friday and decided not to see Constance that night. And that should've been last night! What happened to the weekend?

"And this is confounded ridiculous—I mean, I don't even know these folks' names!"

Aloud, he said to the butler, "Say, old fella, would you mind asking Ms. Creech to come in here for a moment?"

"Certainly, sir." The man turned crisply and disappeared through the swinging door. Within moments, he returned, with Nan behind him. She came to Leo's side while the butler took up a position of attendance a few respectful feet away.

"Why don't you go ahead and turn on the cartoons? This'll only take a moment." Leo gestured with his chin to the video screen. The butler nodded and went to the console. Leo turned to Nan.

Once again, he was taken aback by her beauty. "Goodness gracious, she really was a looker in her day!" But then he wondered again, "Does this mean I've traveled back in time? Or is she just plain old that much younger right now? Which is when, exactly? Space and place are one thing—I mean, look at this house!—but time's something else again. I lost a whole weekend, but I regained who knows how much youth without getting unnecessarily young. Is this crazy program playing time games on me too?"

"Yes, Mr. Stokes? May I help you?"

Nan was smiling with a radiant innocence that made him forget why he wished to speak with her. Leo cleared his throat.

"Yes, ah, yes, Nan—I mean, Ms. Creech. You certainly can." He beckoned her with a finger to come closer. She leaned over so that her ear was near his face. As he lifted his head and face closer to whisper to her, the fragrance of her perfume billowed over him. Leo felt it was the most heavenly scent he'd ever been exposed to. His nose had no frame of reference for it. He wanted to forget everything and just breathe it all the way down to his toes.

But that would not do. He pulled himself back into the room, tried to ignore her fragrance, and rasped out his question in a whisper. "Ms. Creech, I know this may sound a bit odd, but, well...I seem to have forgotten the servants' names. Heh, heh—mm—I was wondering..."

She whispered back, "Well, Mr. Stokes, that's no surprise, land's sakes; we just hired these folks the last few days. Your butler is Mr. Chatsworth, from one of the finest estates in England, we've been told. This one young lady is Miss Hollowell, and the other is Miss Jackson. I'll be sure to remind you about the others' names when you have occasion to be served by them, so no need to worry, bless your heart, sir."

Leo chuckled to himself. "Sir!" Nan had never called him anything more respectful than "young man" in the past. But "bless your heart," that was pure Nan all right; she'd been saying that to and around him since he was ten...whenever *that* was!

Things were definitely changing for the better around here. "A little respect," indeed!

"Well, good, that'll be fine, Nan—um, Ms. Creech. Thank you very much indeed. I am truly obliged."

Nan smiled and took her leave.

"Ah yes, Mr. Chatsworth!" Leo boomed. He noted that his butler had waited to turn on the cartoons; "nice touch!," he thought. "On with Miss Betty, if you don't mind!"

After finishing his breakfast, and a few charming and sassy, black-and-white Betty Boop cartoons from the thirties—he made a note to get Charley to see one, a Betty Boop takeoff on *Alice in Wonderland;*

psychedelic before its time, he reckoned—Leo suggested to Chatsworth that they take a tour through the house and around the grounds.

Just getting through the rooms alone, moving at a pretty rapid pace, took them more than forty-five minutes. The place was nothing short of vast, and Leo inwardly marveled at the elegance, opulence, and downright class of every room, every furnishing, every piece of art. He was certainly no connoisseur, but it seemed to him that this mansion of his must have been done by some kind of extraordinarily tasteful decorator—and it must have cost a fortune. He couldn't even estimate what the art alone must be worth. Virtually every piece was world class, to his knowledge, the kind of art he'd only ever seen before in museums. And now he owned this stuff!

He tried to ask Chatsworth a few questions without letting on how little he actually knew. The older man indicated that the security guards were on duty at all times. They had three men on three shifts each, so the ones on any shift were always fresh and alert. Chatsworth confirmed that Ms. Creech and the security chief had indeed briefed him on everything he needed to know. Two of the security officers were outside, and one in the house, every moment of every day. In addition, the most sophisticated electronic surveillance system available maintained a continuous, highly sensitive reconnaissance of every square foot of the grounds.

"May I say, Mr. Stokes, this is a home I am truly proud to serve."

"Well, good, Chatsworth. I am mighty pleased to have you with us." He had a sudden stroke of inspiration. "Just out of curiosity, old boy, um, if you were me, say, just how would you prepare for that, what did you call it, 'most important meeting here today'?"

Chatsworth's thin, almost blue lips lifted a degree or two from rigid horizontal, just at the ends. Leo could sense he seemed to take a kind of pleasure in Leo's informality with him and his request for the old man's counsel.

"Really, sir, are you quite certain you want my, after all, relatively uninformed and rather inexperienced opinion on a matter of such great personal consequence?"

Leo grinned. They were now standing at the bottom of the grand stairway, on the ground floor. None of the other staff were in sight.

"Why, yes, Mr. Chatsworth. In fact it is precisely your unique and rather fresh angle on this question that impels me to seek your sage advice. And I do hope you understand that this is, indeed, a matter of 'great personal consequence' for me."

Chatsworth was dead serious. "Oh, I do understand, sir, I most certainly do. Well, eh, indeed." Chatsworth looked off through the huge picture window in the living room, out over the meadows and forest. He was quiet for a moment. Then he turned to Leo with his brow all creased. "Sir, considering the very matter of how important this meeting is, I wonder if I mightn't—eh—think it over for just a few moments privately—not wishing to inconvenience you in the slightest, of course ..."

Leo nodded gravely. "Of course, Chatsworth. Of course."

"... and then I could return and give you my humble estimation of this matter, for whatever it may be worth to you, sir."

Leo nodded. "That will be just fine, Mr. Chatsworth. I'll be in my quarters. Don't knock, feel free to come right on in."

Chatsworth bowed and took his leave, evidently to chew on what was for him clearly a weighty question.

"Dang!" Leo thought, mounting the stairs. "What in tarnation have I got myself into now? A little respect is one thing, but I don't recall a brace of professional servants on my wish list. Suddenly, I'm a man with an extended family of people I never even met! And this poor old bird is so excited, he's practically drooling out his ears just at the thought of giving me a little personal advice. Shoot, all I want to do is find out who I'm having this Lord-A'mighty-important meeting with."

Leo sighed and entered his room. With nothing better to do, he played himself a rack of nine-ball. With each shot he delighted in the feel, balance, and beauty of his cue stick and the fine lines, crisp new green felt, and ornate inlay of the massive table.

Finally, there was a knock.

"Come on in, Chatsworth. I told you, no need to knock."

The butler entered. At a glance, Leo could see he was still flustered.

"Yes, sir, ever so sorry. It's a lifelong habit, sir, rather ingrained, I'm afraid."

"No worry, Chatsworth. Now." Leo took a seat in an old Victorian leather chair, motioning Chatsworth to a nearby couch. "What can you tell me?"

"Well, sir, allowing that this meeting today may truly change your entire destiny for the rest of your life, as you yourself informed me yesterday, and recognizing that Miss Cunningham is, in your own words, if I may be so bold as to quote you, 'no pushover,' I feel you must take advantage of the rest of the morning and early afternoon to plot your strategy quite carefully. Now, quite respectfully, sir, and again, rather timidly I'm afraid, because, as I have indicated, this is admittedly not my area of expertise as a manservant, but, nonetheless, here is a detailed plan for what I think is to be done to secure the most auspicious outcome for your meeting with her."

Chatsworth pulled a yellow sheet of legal paper off his clipboard and spread it before Leo on the low table of polished rosewood between them.

Leo leaned over to look at it, thinking, "Miss Cunningham, huh? Well, yes, that is a big meeting indeed!" Proud of himself for having extracted that information from Chatsworth so innocuously, he perused the numbered, handprinted items on a list that took up nearly the full length of the page.

The more he read, the more he smiled, his eyebrows lifting high on his forehead. After reading only a few of Chatsworth's "considered recommendations," he looked the elderly man in the eye.

"Well, my good man, I have to say, I'd be mighty goldang interested to see what you can come up with in areas that *are* your expertise! You wanna maybe flesh these suggestions out a little bit for me?"

The old man smiled proudly, nodding his white-haired head. "Certainly, Mr. Stokes! My pleasure, sir."

THE RING

Several hours later, as the winter sun sank down toward the rolling hills west of Stokesland, Leo watched from his third floor bedroom porch as his two-tone Bentley limousine, one of four vintage automobiles he'd discovered in his spacious garage, approached along the main drive from the east.

Two thoughts sprang to Leo's mind at once. First, it occurred to him that he still didn't know where in Cotton County, or in relation to Ashlin, his estate was located. He'd been so busy all day with preparations for tonight, he'd forgotten to even sleuth out where he was! And second, he wondered with delight what it would be like to meet Constance in her new incarnation.

He would find out very soon. Joseph, his quite reserved and proper chauffeur, a black man who said he was from "the Deep North," was just now driving her to the front door of the mansion. Though Leo couldn't see inside the car, since all the windows in the limo were tinted dark for privacy, he waved vigorously to Constance, assuming she'd see him. Then he turned and headed out of his room, down the hall, and down the stairs to greet her.

The house had been bustling with preparations all day; everyone was excited. There'd been only one aggravating moment for Leo. Chatsworth, egged on by Nan, had gotten Leo to agree to present a beautiful ring to Constance that night to mark their engagement—assuming of course that Constance would be ready to consent and accept it. And Nan had come to Leo's room in the late afternoon with a ring she and one of the maids had selected on an outing to town with Joseph to pick up flowers and decorations.

When Leo saw the ring, he did a double take. It was unlike any other diamond he'd ever seen. It wasn't just large and elegant, tapered for Constance's slender fingers; it also appeared to shine of its own luster. Even the setting and band were of a gold so luminous anyone viewing the piece would find it hard to see all the fine lines of the diamond itself. Talk about a knuckle-sparkler! It genuinely shone.

Leo was thrilled with it, but Nan—who'd pushed for him to get it—had been subdued about the whole thing. Looking at it side by side with her, he casually said, "Well, this is gonna look mighty fine on Constance's hand tonight, don't you think, Nan?" He grinned and looked at her out of the corner of his eyes, expecting her ready agreement.

But Nan only managed a thin smile and murmured softly, "Yes, I—I hope so, Mr. Stokes. I do feel in my heart, though, that you should be aware—"

Leo chortled. "Come on, Nan! She's gonna love it! Shoot, at this stage of the game, old Con'd be ready to wear a pop-top from an RC Cola can, if I told her it meant we're engaged! Don't you know?"

To which Nan nodded, wanly.

Then the oddest thing occurred. Leo hadn't seen anything like it from Nan since long ago, when he was still a boy and she had just arrived in the Stokes home. Nan stood up from the low table in the breakfast room where they were examining the ring and turned to walk away, but then turned back, facing Leo and nervously smoothing the folds of her dress. At first Leo didn't notice. He was still contemplating the engagement ring and wondering what it was going to be like when Constance opened its sleek black velveteen box and first saw it.

But after a minute, he became aware of Nan standing there and turned to face her from his chair, asking, "Yes, Nan? Is there something else?"

The words were already out of his mouth before he really saw her expression. If he'd caught on sooner, he might've said the same thing but with, maybe, a little more sensitivity.

As soon as Leo saw the cast of Nan's eyes, he could tell something was troubling her, something was on her mind, on her heart. She looked at him for just an instant, then looked down and away. It was as if a cloud had passed over her face, across the windows of her gentle blue eyes. She opened her mouth as though to speak, then closed it in the same instant her eyes fluttered up to meet his again. Then she turned her head away, though her body, youthful and soft, almost girlish, still stood before him.

The silence was agonizing. Finally, Leo felt he had to help her out somehow.

"Nan, are you okay? Is...is something wrong?"

Her face was still turned from him, but he could see her pressing her lips more firmly together, her eyelids fluttering fiercely. She said nothing. The only motion in the room was that of her hands, slowly and steadily stroking the pleats of her skirt. Then she shook her head, vigorously, from side to side.

Leo felt agitated, without knowing why. He could tell she was not going to say what was on her mind, though clearly it was quite disturbing or at least important to her. He coughed and cleared his throat, then tried to make light conversation again.

"Well, Nan—oh, I mean, Ms. Creech—I surely have you to thank for picking out such a fine engagement ring for me to give to Constance. I am deeply in your debt for this, and for ..." Leo halted. Could he say it? Was it even true here in the time-space continuum of Stokesland, which seemed so different from Ashlin? He felt he had no choice. He'd started the sentence, and she was still standing there distraught about something. "I just want to tell you how much I do appreciate how strongly you have—you have for so long—tried to help out, you know, between me and Constance; it—it means a lot to me. You do know how grateful I am for that, don't you, Na—Ms. Creech?"

Still looking down and away, Nan closed her eyes, then nodded. Leo could no longer bear whatever this pain was between them. He turned his face and gazed again at the ring, held it up to his eye just to do *something* in that awkward tension, and then looked at her again and said, "Well, Ms. Creech, please...don't let me keep you. I know you've got plenty to do for tonight. Big event, yes! Again, I'm real grateful for this incredibly beautiful ring you chose, real grateful, yes I am."

Nan nodded again, eyes still closed. She let out a long sigh. "Thank you, Mr. Stokes. I am...truly glad you like the ring. Miss Hollowell and I thought it was perfect for you to give to—to Ms. Cunningham, but we were a little nervous about whether you'd like it too. And yes, I do have quite a bit to do; I'd best be getting on with the other arrangements."

Then, without waiting for another word from Leo, Nan turned and walked briskly from the room.

The interchange left Leo unsettled. The only thing he could think of, and it was almost unthinkable, was that, bottom line, Nan was...yes, no denying it, Nan appeared to be *jealous*. That was weird enough for him to contemplate. What was even stranger was—it was hard for him to acknowledge this even to himself—on this very day of becoming engaged to Constance, there was no denying it: he was feeling more than just a twinge of attraction to Nan.

In his old life, back in Ashlin, the very idea would have been preposterous to him. But with Nan looking to be in her mid-thirties again, mature but still eye-poppingly beautiful..."Well, a man is a man," Leo thought, "and I guess something in me must've wanted this or it wouldn't have happened. But no way I'm gonna try to do anything about it. Not today, for sure, and I can't imagine any time ever."

Besides, he hadn't seen Constance since the move to Stokesland and the momentous effects of Ultimaya 1.0. If Nan Creech had been so delightfully transformed without any conscious desire for it on his part,

Lord only knew what he would be seeing in his lady friend of so many years. Leo was so eager to lay eyes on her that, on his way to greet her, he almost tripped and sprawled down the stairs. To keep from falling, he had to yank his hand out of the pocket of his maroon silk jacket, where he'd been turning the ring box over and over, to grab for the smooth polished wooden banister.

He reached the second floor landing with some semblance of dignity, and was standing still there in full view from the living room and the grand foyer of his house just as Chatsworth opened the massive front door. Constance entered but turned to the side without yet seeing him. While Chatsworth took her coat from her shoulders, Leo descended the stairs one slow step at a time. Constance then turned, saw Leo, and began walking toward him. Their eyes met, she smiled, and so did he, but neither said a word. He reached the bottom of the steps and continued walking toward her, each of them gazing into the other's eyes.

He stopped two feet away from her, and turned his gaze from hers to look her over. "Constance," he said at last. "You look ravishing, darlin'! Absolutely gorgeous!" His lady had her lovely dark hair done like never before in her life, that he knew of anyway—a wild, curly and tangled perm, but swept up to the back and held in place by a beautiful green hairpin. She was wearing an elegant evening gown of resplendent white silk that clung to her from her bust line to her knees. He had never seen her so svelte, so statuesque. Certainly, still voluptuous, but slender, silken—gorgeous!

"I know I do," Constance said, her lips parting for an instant to reveal perfect and perfectly white teeth. "Don't I always, Leo?" She held her arms out and did a model's turn for him, coming to a halt again with her eyes beaming her love deep into his, smiling and waiting for his answer.

Leo was dumbfounded. "The program really did it!" he thought. "This is too good to be true." Aloud, he said, "Yes, oh yes, my dear, you certainly do. Oh my yes, you certainly do!"

He continued to feast his eyes on her, up and down. She didn't seem in the least self-conscious or in any way embarrassed, as she'd been in the past when he openly delighted in her beauty. But after a moment or two, she put her fists on her hips and caught his eye again, a pout on her lips. "Really, Mr. Stokes, I appreciate your admiration, but don't you think it would be proper manners to ask a lady if she'd like to see your home? This is my first time out here, if you recall!"

Leo laughed. "Of course, of course, Con! I was, uh, just a bit taken aback by your beauty, my dear. Come on, I'll give you the grand palatial tour! 'Lifestyles of the Rich and As Yet Unknown'!"

As he turned toward the living room, Leo saw that Chatsworth was still standing in attendance by the door, waiting to be dismissed. He had to have heard their whole conversation. Leo couldn't help but blush. "Oh, yes, Chatsworth, that'll be all for now. If you could just attend to, um, those other matters, we'll be in the dining room shortly."

Arm in arm with Constance, Leo walked with her through the whole mansion. She oohed and aahed and wondered at everything he showed her. For his part, Leo found his appreciation and respect for his English butler increasing by leaps and bounds. If the man did not have behind him a life of deep study and practice (Leo could think of no better word) in relation to women, Leo could only conclude he was a tragic prodigy, discovering the art vicariously at the end of his life.

Chatsworth had earlier said to Leo, "She won't be truly interested in learning all about your home, I daresay, sir, so much as she will be interested in discovering how interested you are in her. I suggest you converse with her a good deal and ask her about herself, and allow her to ask about you and about the house, meanwhile displaying the place and the art and the furnishings, speaking of all this with pride, certainly, but always returning your conversation to her."

He continued, "Ms. Creech and I will have drinks and little nibbles here and there through the home, sir, and fresh flowers all about. Encourage her to experience the place with you. Give her every indication of your ardent feeling for her, but at the same time I would hold yourself in some reserve, sir, that is to say, with a playful mien, gently allowing her to feel altogether comfortable while entirely attended to by you. A woman of her beauty and intelligence needs to find a man deeply set in his own character, not overly swayed by her charms to the degree of losing his balance, yet at the ready with a heart full of passion for her and her alone, if she will but be his."

Such had been the general drift of Chatsworth's recommendations to Leo of that morning. Now, arm in arm with this lovely lady, he found them borne out, step by step. In all their years together before the program (Leo found himself thinking of that previous life as "BTP"), he had never shown much real interest in Constance. So often he had let her generate all their conversation, and she had been so intent upon snaring him that he'd always held back from showing any signs of abiding feeling and deep love. Maybe he had never really felt any such thing.

But now she was a different woman, not only physically, but altogether. Self-confident, poised, vivacious, aware of her uncommon beauty but not self-obsessed with it, sensuous…Leo was thrilled to see and feel the changes in her, inside as well as out.

And for her part, Constance seemed to sense and delight in the changes in him, physically and in his character too. It really was as if they were meeting one another for the first time after many years' distance and no real previous intimacy.

So the evening sped by like a dream, an enchantment. They roamed the house, with stops at the artwork, a curious moment in his alcove ("Con, please don't touch the computer. Yes, I know the switch indicates it's on. No, I'll let you see what kind of programs I have on it some other time, hm, honey?"), the ballroom for some private dancing (Chatsworth had arranged for a pianist from the city and had had the staff partition off a portion of the room and turn it into a virtual replica of an elegant metropolitan club), and the gymnasium, where Constance marveled at the heated pool, sauna, and other amenities. After the grand tour, at around ten o'clock, they finally arrived in the dining room.

There Chatsworth and Nan saw to it that they enjoyed a delicious meal—"California cuisine, sir, chosen tonight for its lightness, given the lateness of the hour, and at the same time, its excellence as nourishment, and with wines corresponding, the best of the Sonoma Valley; will you taste this Chardonnay for the lady now?"—followed by superb Colombian coffee and one of Nan's incomparable blueberry pies topped, Leo did not fail to notice, with abundant helpings of Lappert's Macadamia Nut ice cream.

Throughout the evening, as he had all day, Leo became more accustomed to the curious balance of secret knowledge and extreme vulnerability that was apparently his destiny ATP (After the Program). None of these people, he soon understood, realized what had happened. Only he was conscious of that, as he had expected. At the same time, he didn't and couldn't know what they knew or thought about what was happening until they revealed it to him. More than that, he didn't know what they thought about the past and how their minds and memories had been, it seemed to him, reconfigured to accommodate their transformations by Ultimaya 1.0.

So, as he'd done with both Nan and Chatsworth earlier in the day, he now spent much of the evening delicately fishing for information from Constance about how she understood what had happened and what was now transpiring in their lives. He hadn't planned on having to do this, but there was just no way around it. "Shoot," he reasoned, "that information is vital to me."

And, when the time came for the ultimate matter of conversation between them, something came to pass that Leo would never have guessed possible. Even Chatsworth, given his ignorance of how his new post had actually been made available to him, could not have anticipated this one, despite his almost miraculously acute instincts about how Leo should romance and court Constance on such a—till now—lovely evening.

By this time, they were wrapped in each other's arms on a couch in the main living room, listening to Chopin and Pachelbel on Leo's extraordinary CD and stereo system. Leo waited until the end of Pachelbel's "Canon in D Major" to broach the subject. No way to listen to *those* strings, he felt, and not have a heart full of tender love.

"Constance?"

"Mm-hm?"

"I have something important I want to talk to you about."

"Why, Leo, I was under the distinct impression we've been talking important matters all night long."

"Yeah, Con, that's true, but this is, well, something of another order of importance."

"Am I maybe underdressed for the occasion? Or should I have Joseph take me down the drive and back, so I can make a proper entrance?" She giggled and snuggled up closer to him.

"Naw, Constance, I'm serious about this."

"I know you are, Mr. Stokes, and I'm teasing you because I'm enjoying myself immensely here tonight. I'm enjoying being with you here, just plain old being with you, more than I ever have before, and I just don't know if I want to get all bankerly serious. For all I know, you're going to pull out some spreadsheets or something. Sheets—well, my, my, that would be rather forward of you, since this is in some way like a first date, Mr. Stokes, but spreadsheets?" She crinkled up her nose in mock disdain.

He chuckled, momentarily distracted by both the sweetness of her humor and the openly risqué way she was flirting with him. "Whoa," Leo thought. "This is a whole new Constance, all right. Don't believe I've had the pleasure to make this gal's acquaintance before. Gotta be the program. Mm, mm, mm!" Tempting as all that was, though, right now he had to make her get serious with him.

"Con—"

She placed a fingertip firmly on his lips to silence him, smiling playfully. "Mm-hm, Leo? Cat got your tongue?"

He pulled his left arm from around her shoulders to remove her finger. "Dang it, Constance, I mean it. I want to talk about us. I want to tell you something you've been waiting a long time to hear me say. Now I'm ready to say it and you're playing games with me."

She became very quiet. The violins of another Pachelbel piece filled the room with a depth of feeling, and Leo sensed the time had come. He leaned over and whispered in her ear.

"Constance Cunningham...I want you to be my wife. I want you to marry me, and come live with me here....Will you marry me, Con?"

Constance did not turn toward him but sat intensely still. Leo, suddenly flustered, said, "Oh—heh, heh—I almost forgot." He fished around in his evening jacket for the small black box. "Here it is, hon, that knuckle-sparkler I've been teasing you about practically since we were in high school." He opened the box to reveal the resplendent diamond in its radiant gold setting.

Constance turned to face him now, and when he saw her expression, Leo's heart sank. There were tears in her eyes, but they were not tears of joy and love and gratitude. Love, yes, but—pain.

When she spoke, her voice was no more than a whisper. "Why did you wait so terribly long to ask me, Leo? Didn't you know how much I loved you? Didn't you know how much I despaired that you would ever accept my heart?" She looked away, shaking her head, then turned back with all the pain of the years flooding into him through her eyes. "And what, just what, am I supposed to do now, Leo? What am I supposed to do about Ralph, and what I've started to feel for him while you sat around biding your time? More like, pushing me away. Just what am I supposed to do, Leo?"

Leo felt like someone had spiked him with a harpoon right in the solar plexus. It took him a moment to be able to get out even a single word.

"Ralph?"

Tears were streaming down Constance's face, making a river out of her mascara. "Leopold Stokes, don't you dare play dumb with me! You know very damn well that Ralph Honeycutt and I have been—well, consoling one another. You gall me, you know that, Leo? I've been so happy tonight. This is the first time I have truly enjoyed myself since Helen's accident."

Constance bit her lip as more tears welled up in her eyes. But she didn't want to yield to whatever she was feeling; she wiped her face of a few streams of tears and continued. "Between that and you being so stubborn and cold this last month, I had just begun to give up hope. But Ralph has been there for me, and me for him. You and I haven't said anything about it, but I know you know it. Nan Creech's talked to me about you and me and Ralph a half dozen times and every single time she's told me she was going to get on you about you getting on with it if you want me."

"Ralph Honeycutt? Accident? What're you talking about, Constance?"

Constance stared at him, incredulous. When she spoke, her voice was low and steely. "Leo, don't you play games with me. Helen was my best friend. Just because you didn't care for her—"

"What do you mean 'was,' Constance? What are you talking about?"

Constance pulled away from him in a fury, crossing her arms over her chest. "I just simply cannot believe you, Leo! Are you telling me— and from you I could believe it, I suppose—that you didn't know that Helen Honeycutt died three weeks ago?"

"Died? What? How? Helen is *dead,* Con?"

She still did not move or look at him. Her voice was quiet, exhausted, now even less than a whisper. "You better not be lying to me about not knowing this, Leo."

He was starting to get angry. "Dang it, Constance! Just trust me, will you, please? I did not know about it. I do not know about it. It's been a very strange...month for me. What happened?"

"All right, I'll take your word for it. Okay, I'll tell you." He could feel her sorrow rising again, and he gently placed a napkin from the table in her hand, so she could wipe her tears. She whispered, "Thanks," and continued.

"A few weeks back, I was going out to have lunch with Helen at their farm. No one was in the house. I went out back. Her new horse, a wild stallion she was breaking in, was saddled in the corral, but she was not around. I looked all over, first inside the barn, and then I went out to the corral."

Constance broke down again. It took her a few moments to be able to continue. Her eyes were closed. When she spoke again, it was in a halting whisper. "She was lying there on the ground. Somehow he had thrown her, or else just kicked her—her face. Her teeth. He'd kicked her teeth in and trampled her. I don't know what possessed her to go into the corral with him, but by the time I got there, she was unconscious. I could see she was still breathing.

"No one else was around. I picked her up and carried her to the backseat of my car. I don't know how I found the strength to lift her like that, but you've heard those stories; I guess it just comes to you. Anyway, I sped as fast as I could to the hospital. They did everything they could there, but she was already in a coma."

Constance opened her eyes and looked at Leo with exhaustion and sorrow. "I would have called you, but…things were so wrong between you and me then. I just assumed you found out. I did talk to Nan a few times."

"I wonder why in the world Nan didn't say anything to me."

"What was she going to do, Leo? Tell you to go to the hospital and visit with Helen's daddy and Ralph? Or help you rationalize why you couldn't go to the funeral because of one more business deal you just had to attend to instead?"

Constance looked at him, shaking her head. Then she closed her eyes, took a deep breath and sighed.

"Helen died a week later. Never came out of the coma."

Leo sat with his head in his hands, bent over in pain. She might as well have poured scalding oil into his ears. Constance was leaning back on the couch pillows. He could feel she was very distant, but he couldn't look at her.

"If I had known, I guess I wouldn't have—the ring. You know."

"Damn you, Leo!" Constance said, suddenly sitting up and glaring at him. "Why did you have to wait until all this, Leo? Why? I have not failed to warn you. I have not failed to plead with you to take my love seriously.

115

What did you expect, that I was going to wait forever? I feel guilty enough about it—Helen and all. She was my closest friend. I feel so bad about her, about Ralph, and about you—I don't know what to do anymore, Leo." She sat back again. "What did you expect me to do? You weren't there for me. Ralph was, but he was in shock; still is."

Constance went on to explain that old Mr. Folger had been so devastated, she had to help with everything and handle all the funeral and other arrangements. Helen had been all the close kin he had left.

People had been kind enough, but still—nobody treated the Folgers like family. So Constance had been consumed by both grief and all the practical details, almost like she'd been a sister to Helen, literally.

And now—well, she just didn't know what to say to Leo. "I didn't even think you would have come around anyway. 'Loan' this and 'merger' that! You were always too busy for me. Why should you get less busy for people you hardly even knew or liked?

"I don't know what to say about Ralph. I mean—there really isn't anything between us. But...it's too soon, Leo. It's only been three weeks. I had a wonderful time with you tonight—the first pleasant moments since the accident—but—well, that man's got a heart in his chest, Leo.

"I love you—you know I do—but now I love him too. I don't know what our love means, but I can't become engaged to you with all this going on. He couldn't take it right now. I don't think Helen's father could either. She was all he had left. So I...just can't."

Constance looked down at her hands in her lap and spoke softly. "It's a beautiful ring, Leo. Seems like it almost shines of its own light. It's just lovely. Everything in me wishes I could take it. But I can't. Not now. Maybe later. I don't know. I have to think it over. I have to feel you're serious. I mean, for all I know you just want me in this mansion like some pretty green-eyed statue for your art museum!"

Leo could barely move, but he managed to raise a hand to signal her to stop. "Shh, Con. That's enough. I got it. I hear you." He paused and looked at her face. It was averted and he could see she wasn't going to say more.

"You're not a statue, Constance. I love you. That's why I want you to be with me. I love you and I desire you and I want you to marry me. I'm a dumb redneck cracker with the brain of a mule. You're breaking my heart but I hear what you're saying. I accept that now you've got to think it over. I don't know what to say about Helen. Or Ralph. I'm sorry."

They both fell back into the plush pillows of the couch, their heads turned in opposite directions. Leo was suddenly horribly tired of fishing for information in his new world. He'd just heard more bad news all at once than he ever wanted to hear again in his entire life. "I'm done," he thought. "I'm just done. This ain't working at all."

He thought about the computer and the Ultimaya program. "How in tarnation that dang program worked this outta my simple and harmless wishes I have no idea. I'm gonna throw that goldang thing out the window the moment Constance is out of here. What about all those fancy 'contracts' I thought it signed with me? What about all that?"

He listened to the music from his stereo in the vast silence that had now opened between him and Constance. The distance between them felt like a chasm on a fault line after an earthquake. What he was going to have to do now to win her love he had no idea. Might as well throw that dang ring out the window.

Finally, she turned to him. "Leo, it's late. I have to work tomorrow. I think I better head on home."

"Okay, I'll give you a lift."

She looked aside, obviously uncomfortable.

"All right," he said. "Joseph'll take you."

Chatsworth answered his call and arranged for the car. Leo and Constance walked down the stairs in silence, not touching. He took Constance's coat from the old man and draped it over her shoulders. He walked her out to the drive, his arm tentatively around her waist. She didn't resist it.

They embraced by the open car door. Neither of them spoke. He inhaled the smell of her hair and the light fragrance of her perfume, and also felt her tears on his neck. Chatsworth and Joseph stood by, looking away. Leo thought, "Lordy, I believe I could do without the perk of having hired staff watch my guts spill out onto the dang driveway." Still, he was grateful for their professional respect and discretion.

Leo whispered to Constance, "I'll call you tomorrow, okay?"

She nodded, squeezed him tightly, and then turned and got into the car. She didn't look at him again. For a moment, he stood and watched her being driven away.

It was cold under the wintry Carolina moon. He shivered and turned to reenter the house, where Chatsworth took his evening jacket of blue raw silk and handed him his terry robe. Leo asked his butler to bring a glass and several bottles of wine to his bedside table. He said nothing else and went straight to his room.

SCANDAL

The next morning Leo awoke to see Chatsworth hovering over him. "Sir, so sorry indeed to rouse you, but I have a rather urgent call for you from Mrs. Elkins at the bank. There are some papers for you to sign this morning that simply cannot wait any longer, she informs us. I believe they are associated with a certain Baptist group?"

Leo pulled himself up to a sitting position. The events of the previous evening broke in on him again. He plunged into a foul mood.

"Chatsworth, I don't wanna be bugged by a bunch of loony fundamentalists this morning. Not this particular morning, please!"

The elderly man stepped back a foot or two, though his face and demeanor betrayed no surprise or distress at Leo's crankiness. "Certainly not, sir. I do have a suggestion, however, if you wish to entertain it."

"And what would that be?" Leo was just registering a rotten hangover from the late-night wine. His face was in his hands, his elbows propped on his knees as he sat cross-legged on the bed.

"Ordinarily the fax would suffice, sir, but I am afraid you'll have to sign original documents on this transaction. However, there's no reason we could not ask Joseph to take a run into town and bring them back, and then return in time for Mrs. Elkins' deadline of noon today."

"Thank you, Chatsworth. You are a goldang treasure. 'Preciate it."

"No problem, sir. Also, sir, anticipating that you might need some relaxation and refreshment, I've fired up the Jacuzzi as well as the sauna.

119

You will also find some light breakfast, nothing too demanding, on a tray by the bath. If you'd like, of course."

Leo nodded, smiling grimly. The man was truly a treasure. He hadn't known till yesterday that he deeply desired a personal butler. And it was still a little novel to have somebody else sliding around on the inside of his "dynamic wish-field" anticipating his unexpressed cravings. But hey, why not?

"You're a true treasure, Chatsworth. Thanks so much."

Chatsworth turned smartly and was gone.

Leo continued to sit for a while, head in hands, then groaned and drew himself up. It seemed to him his hangover started in his solar plexus and managed to infect every cell of his body and every convolution of his brain. He groaned again, gingerly got out of bed, and retreated to the bathroom, walking very slowly. He felt like he had about as much energy as a vertical cadaver.

The jets of the Jacuzzi helped, softening his skin and muscles and somehow sucking away some of the harsh dreck of rottenness he was feeling. After about an hour, Chatsworth arrived with a tray of documents, a fountain pen, and several hand towels. Leo dried his arms and hands but hardly read a word of the agreements, just signing them, then groaning and slipping back into the water. Ernestine had mothered hundreds of these puppies over the years. He could give himself a break for once and not chew on every word of the legalese until he could spit them out from memory.

It seemed to him that Ultimaya 1.0 had screwed up everything. Where in tarnation did all this come from? Helen Honeycutt dead, kicked toothless and trampled by a horse? Whoever heard of such a thing? Ralph Honeycutt, her grieving husband, cozying up to Constance?

Of course, he did have to admit, Constance had transformed from an attractive—but in some ways ordinary—gal to an unqualified knockout. And her teeth were perfectly beautiful. It made him wince to think of it, what with Helen and all. Now probably every witless stud in town would be eyeing Constance. Just like they all used to try to make moves on Helen.

So what was he, Leo, going to do about Constance now? How was he going to get her heart turned back to him?

Leo just sat there in the tumult of his bath waters like a rotting log stuck in rapids. He couldn't get up enough energy even to strategize. No ideas. No flashes of inspiration. No way he was going to sit down in front of the computer and try again. *Not now.*

What in God's great Creation was going on with that thing? Why wouldn't it just simply deliver without all the complications and the weirdly explosive kick that seemed to come back at him every time he used it for a perfectly reasonable purpose? He didn't get it. It just did not compute. No pun intended in his own mind.

And what he was going to do next? He had no idea. Leo thought idly about suicide, but then resolved not to spend too much time in that pit—no future in it, and besides, he didn't want the program catching on and then deciding that was what he really most deeply desired.

Finally, after a few gingerly bites of toast, and several sessions alternating among the Jacuzzi, a cold shower, and the spacious sauna in his bathroom, Leo felt sufficiently revived and relieved of his black mood to make a foray into town to his office. On a whim, strange as it might look, he decided to forgo the usual business attire and wear his blue evening jacket with an ascot—and with the jewelry box with Constance's ring right there in the pocket. Leo wasn't exactly sure why, but he knew he wanted to wear that jacket and carry that ring.

Nan and the rest of the staff must have been cautioned by Chatsworth to give him a wide berth. He didn't see a soul except his butler on his way out to the car, and no one there either, except Joseph, who silently drove him away. He started to tell Joseph where he wanted to go, then realized Chatsworth surely already had.

There was a TV in the back of the Bentley, and Leo amused himself for a while watching *I Love Lucy*, an old childhood favorite. Before the show ended, Joseph pulled the Bentley to a halt and came around to open Leo's door.

"Mistuh Stokes, suh, we's heah."

"Thank you, Joseph." Leo stepped out into the bright sunshine. The bank looked the same as it had a couple of days before, the last time he'd been there. Everybody gave him their customary deferential nods and hellos as he walked through the lobby and back to his office. Mrs. Elkins was full of radiant smiles, as always.

"Maybe I'll just settle into an ordinary, routine day of business," Leo thought. "Stop worrying about everything that's been turned upside down. Turn some things right side up, like any other day. Just let the rest ride for a few hours, and then figure out what to do. Always have in the past. Always will in the future. Why should today be any different?"

Buoyed by that line of thought, Leo shuffled a few papers on his desk for a moment or two. Then it occurred to him that he'd been so locked into his interplay with Ultimaya 1.0 for several days—or, who knew, maybe weeks!—he had no idea what was happening in the world. He pressed a button on the intercom.

"Ernestine?"

"Yes, Mr. Stokes?"

"You got today's *News and Observer* out there?"

"Surely do, Mr. Stokes. I'll bring it right on in."

"Thank you kindly, ma'am."

Within seconds, his secretary appeared and brought the still-folded paper to his desk, along with a cup of hot black coffee. Leo thanked her again, took a sip of the coffee, and opened up the paper to the front page.

The first thing that caught his eye was a large headline on a major story, on the top left side of the page: "Cardinal Bank Directors Indicted in Regulatory Fraud—Run on Bank Due to Scandal."

Underneath the headline was a photo of Bob Jackson, whom he liked and knew to be an honest and straight-shooting banker, surrounded by reporters outside a courtroom. The story went on to say that Jackson and the entire board of Cardinal Bank vehemently denied the charges of wrongful acquisition and use of investors' funds, claiming that whatever an investigation might reveal in terms of any accounting errors, there had been absolutely no intentional wrongdoing. Their claims, however, had not deterred a run on the bank all over the state. Already branches in many counties were closing their doors, including, that day, the new Ashlin branch that had just opened two months ago.

Leo slumped back in his chair. "I can't believe this!" he said aloud. "Why does this stuff just keep on happening? Nan and Helen and now this. All I asked was for Cardinal to stay out of Cotton County. I did not want Bob Jackson to be ruined. Or for his bank to go down. This is insane. Why does every positive little change I ask for make a goldang earthquake happen on the other side of it?"

He was whispering most of this. What little energy he'd mustered since bathing and driving in to the office for the day had now evaporated. He felt beaten and weary, up against some kind of force or opponent that seemed far wilier than he, and more ruthless than any human antagonist he'd ever faced.

Leo thought it through a bit further. Yes, he had not specifically asked for changes to happen, or not to happen, to Bob Jackson himself. He had not specified that no grave harm should come to the Cardinal Bank and its executives and board. Bob Jackson was not someone "close" to Leo. But why did such shocking and terrible side effects have to ensue from what he was asking for himself and for people he loved?

True, he couldn't prove a connection. He couldn't be sure that having his wishes fulfilled produced massive deficits in other people's life accounts—even deadly ones, like for Helen. But then he remembered her once-perfect teeth. Kicked in. By a horse! And Constance now with her own perfect teeth.

"Lord only knows," he thought. "Lord only knows what else is going down here that I'm not even aware of. I got that big mansion—someone probably went broke and died. All those servants, cars, art—somebody or some whole bunch of folks are probably on the streets right now. Destitute, and they don't even know why. This is mad. It ain't just crazy-making. It's crazy."

At that moment, it became obvious to him: he'd better go see Charley again. Things were not working out at all as he had hoped. He needed some help. And he had absolutely no one else to turn to.

CALIBRATED KARMA AND
HALFWAY WORLDS

This time Leo didn't even call ahead. He didn't clean up his desk. He didn't notify Ernestine Elkins. He didn't close his briefcase, didn't even bring it along. The moment Leo realized he had to see Charley right now, he just stood up and walked out the door of his office, down through the lobby and out the front door, to the parking lot, where Joseph was waiting by the car. Joseph had the back door open for him by the time he got there, so he didn't even pause. He just climbed right in and settled down for the drive.

His mind was churning so much it only dawned on him a few minutes later that he hadn't even told Joseph where to take him. He looked out the window. They were on the road to Raleigh, all right.

"Joseph?"

"Yes, suh, Mistuh Stokes."

"Where're you taking me?"

"Down to see Mistuh Bass, jes' like you tol' me, Mistuh Stokes."

"I did?"

"Yessuh, Mistuh Stokes, right when I was cranking up the car."

"Oh. Thank you, Joseph."

"No problem, Mistuh Stokes."

"Whew!" Leo whistled to himself, then muttered under his breath,

"Dang, I'm losing it again!" He had no recollection of having said a word to Joseph.

As they drove along, he wondered. Could Joseph have known psychically what Leo wanted? Or had he, Leo, in fact spoken to him, and was he so brain-crazed now by Ultimaya 1.0 that he was forgetting things that had happened just minutes before?

He decided to try his utmost to keep his attention on the road. He wanted to make sure they stayed in the same world in which he'd just read about Bob Jackson's tragedy at Cardinal Bank. Maybe there was some sign he would see that would tip him off, if they were, in fact, leaving the world of Stokesland and Ultimaya 1.0 to reach Charley's office in the real world of Raleigh.

One thing for sure: Charley, whenever and wherever Leo might see him, was reliably living in the real world. And he'd give Leo some straight talk about what was really happening.

Of course, now that he thought about it, Charley Bass the Flower Power Acidhead of the old days was never famous for being grounded in reality. And then, how did Leo know the world of Ultimaya 1.0 and Stokesland was actually the same as the place he'd just been when he saw the newspaper at the bank? He hadn't watched to see if there was any dividing line on the way in to the bank. Like a fool, he'd been watching *I Love Lucy*!

In that moment, it hit him that he'd again been lost in reverie for—who could tell how long? He looked outside. They were already in northern Wake County, only about three-quarters of an hour from Charley's office.

"No way!" he thought. "There is absolutely no way I could've been drifting around in my own brain all that time. So either Joseph flew down here, or somebody's continuing to play with time as well as space on me, or I am really losing it. Extra real bad."

At that point, he gave up trying to keep track of anything going on either inside or outside his brain. After a few moments, Joseph stopped the car and opened the door for him. Feeling like a zombie, Leo stepped out, walked into Charley's main store and up the stairs, not saying a word to the couple of salespeople who greeted him, and then on into Charley's office.

He knew Charley would be there, and sure enough he was, sitting behind his desk in a cloud of Winston smoke. He looked up, a bit startled to see someone barging into his office, then grinned.

"Hey, Stokes, what brings you here? Come down to celebrate the fall of Cardinal Bank? Big story today, huh?"

Leo's smile was thin and pallid. "Naw, that's not why I'm here, Charley."

"Well, what's up, then?"

Charley's immediate mention of the disaster for Bob Jackson's bank had caught Leo off guard. He tried to pull himself together and proceed with his plan. Sitting down, he described, with as much enthusiasm and detail as he could muster, the astonishing results of his wishes for a new place to live—the manifestation of Stokesland.

Charley didn't bat an eyelash the whole time.

Finally, Leo asked, "Charley, you believe what I'm telling you?"

"Yeah, I believe it. I can even see part of it right off. You're looking a little muscular for the first time since we worked in the lumberyard summers during high school—though you definitely got that Freon anti-glow again, despite your tan. So I believe it. What of it?"

Leo could hear an edge in Charley's voice and see a wariness or something, he wasn't sure what, in his eyes. But he went on with the plan.

"Tell you what. Why don't you just take a look out your window at that parking lot you got for a view here?"

Charley stood up and went to the window. "All right. Now what?"

"See that black chauffeur standing next to the big white Bentley?"

"Yeah. Nice car. What about it?"

"That's my car, Charley!"

127

"Okay. So?"

"It came from Stokesland down to Raleigh, Charley! We drove it down from a whole other world that didn't even exist a few days ago!"

"All right—but 'exist' is a pretty big word, Stokes. The world was already a lot wilder and weirder than you thought before Ultimaya 1.0 interrupted your dreams of interest rates and foreclosures. What else?"

"That guy, Joseph. My chauffeur. Says he's from 'the Deep North.' Wherever that is—he sounds like a chitlins and southern fried chicken black man if I ever heard one, but that's where he says he comes from.

"I mean, there's a whole bunch of folks up at that mansion I've never seen or heard about before. I don't know where they came from at all. But, lookit, that guy appeared in Stokesland and now he's here in your parking lot. You could go up and talk to him!"

Charley was unmoved. "So what, Leo? I got better things to do than interviewing chauffeurs from other worlds—if that really is who he is and what he does. So what? You gotta understand something here—I already accept that the world's got more sides than it's got corners, and more corners than it's got sides; it's full of weirdo surprises. I already know that. I told you that the first time you came down here and told me how you incinerated Nan in your kitchen and then pulled that southern-fried-spinster, Lazarus-outta-the-linoleum stunt. What else?"

Leo pulled the small black velveteen jewelry box out of his pocket. "Take a look at this, Charley. This oughta convince you that Stokesland is a reality and that dreams really can come true. 'Cause I don't think you quite get it yet. You say so, but take a look."

He opened the box with his right hand and displayed the ring to Charley with his left.

"Hm." Charley picked it out of the box. "Intense rock, all right." He turned it over, looking at the underside of the band, and then examined the stone more fully. "Not like any ordinary diamond I ever saw, that I'll grant you. Where'd you get it? And how?"

"Nan brought it to me yesterday. She and Joseph and one of the maids picked it up while they were out shopping. Said she got it in town."

"You didn't happen to ask what town?"

"I assumed she meant Ashlin."

"Well, old bud, in your new line of work, or life, I wouldn't bank on assumptions."

Charley eyed Leo coolly.

"Did you bring this ring down here just to impress me—like the car and the driver?"

Leo thought about it. "Well, yeah, partly. But I guess for some reason I just like to carry the ring around."

"To keep your eye on the prize, trying to get Constance back?"

"Well, yeah, that's a lot of it. But...I don't know. What can I tell you: the ring just gives me some kind of special strength I feel I need right now."

Charley suppressed a grin. "I see. Say, Leo, you didn't by any chance happen to read *Lord of the Rings* back in the old days, did you?"

"What?"

Charley sighed. "Never mind, skip it." He lit a cigarette and sat down behind the desk again. Neither of them spoke as he took a couple of slow draws and exhaled fat, tumbling smoke rings. Then he eyed Leo again. "Listen, Stokes. It's obvious to me that the program is still in charge. It's obvious that you're still in a sinkhole of obsession with what you think it's gonna give you. And it's obvious that you're hurting pretty bad, coming down here and trying to impress me, of all people, with hoodoo-voodoo amulets and 'the Brother from Beyond.' All that level of it, to me, is a grade C sci-fi flick. What's up, Leo? What do you want?"

Leo sighed. He sat quiet for a few minutes, wringing his hands in his lap, unable to say anything cogent. Finally, he replied. "Yeah, you're right. I'm happy about all the good stuff, the house—and you should see Constance, I mean, she's so gorgeous she'd blow your mind. But there's this nasty underside I can't seem to get out of the program's system. Or out of me. I don't know why it has to be that way. And I don't know what to make of things anymore. I don't know where the real world stops and the world of Stokesland, the world of Ultimaya, begins. Everything's gotten pretty crazy."

"Well," Charley said, "that I can work with. How about just telling me what's happened since you were down here last. And don't leave out the underside and the craziness, hear?"

So Leo recounted the whole story, bringing Charley up to current, including the real reason, the way he saw it, for the headlines in that morning's paper.

When he finished, Charley leaned back in his chair and lit another Winston. "Hm. Pretty weird, all right. I mean, that is the way they say karma works. You set certain consequences or results in motion through your intention, your desiring, your actions. They keep on going, until and unless another motion deflects them. Repeating themselves, with equal and opposite reactions getting set up besides. Mind makes events, eventually. Or so they say in the books. But who knows what causes how much of what? The world's like a wavy-mirrored funhouse. There's so many different factors influencing any given moment that usually we can't see it all. And it's all kinda slow, kinda vague, how things turn out and why. It takes a lotta time or smarts to pick up on the fact that you're setting yourself—or even somebody else—up for the equal and opposite reaction to whatever you're doing, thinking, or feeling, and for a whole lotta repetition too. Somewhere, somehow, you're not only gonna get something like what you want, but sooner or later, maybe even beforehand, you've set yourself up for the backlash as well."

Charley leaned forward again, eyeballing Leo square on. "So, Leo, I'd say that little devil of a program is delivering exactly what it promised. No breach of contract whatsoever."

Leo sat quietly. He couldn't exactly make out what Charley meant but there was no point interrupting. Another C.B. III sermonette.

Charley gazed out over the cars in the lot and continued. "Now, what you got going on here is kind of like what we'd call in the old days 'instant karma.' Maybe it's a function of the machined quality of this program. Maya in the form of a computer program, producing karmic results that are electronically calibrated or something—we're talking machine-tooled, precision karma here."

He looked hard at Leo again. "I mean, that thing with Constance's teeth and what happened to Helen. And Cardinal Bank. Pretty amazing stuff, Leo." Then he frowned, shaking his head. "And pretty rotten too. I am sorry to hear about Helen—I once loved that girl, you know—and the whole thing with Constance and Ralph. I didn't know how you felt about Bob Jackson—all that's a real drag. A lot of it downright tragic, Greek chorus stuff, I'd say. And hey, I'm not about to skip the 'I told you so' factor. I did warn you about this little devil, didn't I?"

Leo thrummed his fingertips on the desk, agitated. He could tell Charley was on another roll and he might as well just let him yap on for a while until he could get him down to the business at hand.

Sure enough, after tamping out his most recent cigarette, Charley folded his arms on the desk and resumed. "Leo, all this about the real world and where it stops and starts reminds me of this guy I knew back in the late sixties. He was a shrink, young guy, working at the Duke University Hospital. We took a few trips together—classic ones, did the whole Alpert-Leary Millbrook 'set 'n setting' bit. Had some wild experiences. And I remember one night we were reading *The Tibetan Book of the Dead* where they describe the 'bardos'—the transitional realms of desire, craving, and fulfillment that you apparently rattle through like a runaway train after you leave the body, when you die.

"Well, that Tibetan description ain't fun by a long shot, and me and this guy got into some strange spaces there. But eventually things cooled out, we were able to help each other through the bizarre hallucinations.

"Finally, as we're coming down, the guy starts laughing like crazy. He tells me, half-joking but the other half serious, that it just hit him:

131

the bardos are halfway worlds. Like halfway houses for nut cases, see? He says to me that when you're a loon in a halfway house, you know you don't really belong there—I mean, these joints are nothing like 'home'—but, still, you gotta earn the right just to hang in there in one of them every day of your life. And you always got the very distinct knowledge and explicit threat from the Big Nurses and all the orderlies and doctors that you could get shipped off to some place much, much worse. A real-life version of *One Flew Over the Cuckoo's Nest*.

"Well. Even when things are going good in one of those places, you never quite get all the way there. You never fully arrive in a halfway house. You're always at a distance from the real world and always in transit, at least a little. You're only half, or less, only some itty-bitty fraction of where you really are or could be, or of what you really are or could be. And what would the world be like if you were whole and really real?"

Leo was looking out the window.

"Anyway, sounds to me like you tied your butt into one helluva halfway world, Leo. You don't know what's right side up or upside down anymore. 'Course, the whole point of the ultimate wisdom is that *this* is a halfway world too. Ain't nothing but halfway worlds until you get enlightened. And even then, it isn't the worlds that are whole. It's how you meet them, one instant after the next.

"Which gets me to my main point, thank you for listening, O Great Master of Stokesland Manor. I tell you what: you don't need a computer technician to help you out at this juncture. I think you need a shaman. You need a guru. You need somebody who's got a whole other kind of grip on the weirdness of the world than someone like me. You don't need a computer consultant. You need a Zen master, someone who can put you in touch with the actually real reality—and I don't mean some slick-talking TV preacher. I mean someone who can work deep in the spiritual and psychic substrata of the world, someone who can set you up with serious divine protection—'cause, buddy roe, you sure as hellfire do need it!

"'Course, you'd have to give up your whole thing in return; I mean, you can't have this kinda cake and eat it too. You need to go on a psychic diet real fast, Leo, and drop some serious karmic weight."

Charley eyed Leo. Leo's eyes were rolling skyward.

"I mean it, Stokes. If what you think is happening to you actually is happening, then karmically you're not that far off from one of the old heroes of Tibet, Milarepa. Long story short, his momma went on a vengeance rampage against an evil uncle. She insisted Milarepa learn the black arts; he was still a young guy and didn't feel he could refuse. Turned out he had quite a talent for it. But after causing hailstorms and other heavy stuff, his coup de grâce was magically bringing down a stone house on the uncle's entire family on the occasion of the daughter's wedding party. Killed thirty-five people.

"That's when it dawned on Milarepa that he was seriously up the karmic creek, no paddle, not even a boat. He found a super-powerful spiritual adept to straighten him out, guy named Marpa. And old Marpa had to have him half-build and then tear down about a dozen giant stone houses all over the countryside, by hand and by himself—no magic!—to release those karmas. Sarcastically called Milarepa 'Great Sorcerer' and kicked his butt endlessly. Marpa only let up when Milarepa, with his back breaking and hands bleeding from hauling all those boulders around the county, was about to kill himself in despair. When he did let up, Marpa said it was too bad, the purification wasn't quite over; if only Milarepa could've suffered through one more house going up and coming down by his own backbreaking labors...

"Well, Stokes-ey, old bud, I don't think you're a Milarepa but I am definitely no Marpa. So I'd say you need some big-time spiritual help in your life right about now—and on a whole other level than proper old Wellington at your Episcopal Church in town or even those faith-healing, Bible-thumping Strap Rock boys can give. You need someone who can plug you into the presence of the actual God. Who or Which by the way is not reducible to the pictures those folks broadcast in their churches and what the really Big Dog Believers televangelize."

Leo was steaming. What any of this had to do with him, he had no idea. "Mountain Man, could you can the goldang sermon and philosophizing? What in the world does some dude in Tibet a zillion years ago have to do with you and me, here and now? Get outta your head, Bass, and help me out right here. Earth to C.B. III! I got a ring in my pocket and now, after twenty years of her dying to get hold of me, I can't get the dang thing on Constance's finger. What's a shaman gonna do about that? Shoot, I don't even know what a shaman is. What kinda nonsense are you talking to me?

"I got Nan thirty years younger than she really is, twenty times sweeter than she really is, and all of a sudden *she* starts looking real good to me. Nan! Jesus, it feels like incest or something; this is weird stuff, Charley! What's a Zen master gonna tell me about that?

"I got a mansion full of priceless art and high-priced servants and I don't have a hen's brain of an idea where it all came from. And I got some poor innocent woman kicked toothless and trampled to death by her own horse and her husband now cozying up to my lady, 'consoling' each other!

"'Scuse my cracker ignorance, but I don't think this kind of stuff is on the contract when people go find medicine men and gurus to bliss out in the ozone somewhere, Charley. You tell me all this craziness I got going on is right on target for what I asked the dang program to give me, which makes no sense to me, but now I have no idea how to ask for anything else and I'm shaking in my boots at the thought of asking for anything at all.

"We can cogitate on metaphysics later. I don't need God. I don't need a guru. I need a strategy, Charley! I need a plan.

"What's all this let's-go-whine-at-the-feet-of-some-wizard and humbly hope for help stuff? Where's your good old American cojones? We can figure this dang thing out. You built an empire without even trying! I haven't done too poorly myself. And now we're settin' here tapped into a raw source of world-moving power like nothing we ever even imagined before. And it's real, Charley! Think of where we can take it. You're an entrepreneur, man. Look at the possibilities!"

Charley leaned forward over his desk. "You number crunchers and money monkeys are all alike, Stokes. Got about as much interest in the subtleties of what's going on around here as a fat redneck attacking a platter of barbecue."

Leo also leaned forward, glaring at Charley, eye to eye. "If you're so hot for spiritual truth, how come you ain't gone to a shaman yourself? What in tarnation are you doing hanging out in computer heaven? You spending your life monkeying with a bunch of circuit boards and raking in cash and me spending my life monkeying with farm and construction loans and raking in cash sounds like the same platter of fatback to me! 'Scuse me, Mountain Man, but if you were so dang hot on getting in touch with the subtler dimensions of things, you wouldn't be sitting here burying your brains in computers and performing the remarkable charitable act of donating your lungs *before you die* to the goldang R.J. Reynolds Tobacco Company!"

Charley twisted his mouth for a moment, maybe trying to suppress a grin. He looked at the end of his cigarette, then tamped it out. "All right, Stokes. It's real simple. You wanna know what to do? You wanna know what to ask for? Ask Ultimaya 1.0 to allow me to help you compose your requests and sit in on the next conversation with it."

Leo gazed out the window. When he spoke again, his voice barely rose above a whisper. He didn't look back at his friend. "Charley, I told you I can't do that. It ain't gonna happen, understand me? Bringing you in there…I don't know. It'd just pop the whole bubble somehow. I know it would."

Charley lit up again and smoked a while, then turned back toward Leo again. Leo continued to avert his gaze while Charley began talking, also softly.

"Y'know, Stokes, I am definitely beginning, after all these years, to get a take on why your momma made such a fuss of naming you after that big-time symphony orchestra conductor—what's his name, Stokowski. The Grand Maestro, Leopold Stokes! You're just into orchestrating everything and everyone. Problem is, you're not willing to be a conductor of real human life with other human beings. You wanna control it all, have it just your way, have everyone and everything conform to your specifications. You think the whole world owes you big, Leo. You think God owes you big, like God was just another dirt-poor Strap Rock Baptist deacon or something. But it doesn't work that way in real life, Leo, and I guarantee you you're gonna crash and burn this rig you're flying. I keep telling you. You keep not wanting to hear it.

"I don't know what to say anymore. And I'm no great mystic, no shaman, no yogi. I don't know what's going on with you, really. I tell you for a fact that you sure as hellfire need someone like that real bad. You're out there in some very strange territory. People have been known to die out in the kind of skyscape you're flying around in. They've been known to go irretrievably insane. What's to stop you? Who? You won't even listen to my at least moderately sane counsel, never mind someone who could set you really straight and help you make your way out of this madness."

Leo sat with his lips firmly pressed together, gripping the arms of his chair so hard his knuckles were turning white. He wished Charley would just shut his trap, if all he was gonna do was preach. He didn't come for a sermon, dang it. He came for a plan and a real partner.

Charley lit up another of his infernal Winstons. Leo thought about how much he hated all the confounded cigarette smoke in the office. It made the whole place stink and look and feel even drabber than it already was. He pulled out a handkerchief and blew his nose with a trumpet honk. It had no effect. Charley just continued eyeing Leo as he smoked. Then he started talking again.

"Leo, you've always been a pretty private kinda guy—building the bank, doing your own thing. But now you're just all wrapped up around this program. I do believe this thing may be the ultimate in Maya. It's sure got you hornswoggled.

"Hell, I've seen lots of software programs. They come and go. I've also seen lots more guys get eaten alive by computers than you can count. Disappear inside the operating system, so you can't even find the guy anymore. No heart. No soul left. Some kind of 'techno-cide,' suicide by hi-tech.

"Looks to me like that's where you're heading, old bud. Now you told me the program said nobody else could fiddle with it, only the certified 'User,' which is you. And, according to you, this is somehow connected with federal regulations regarding the use of the program. Come on, Leo. People like me look at warnings like that and laugh. We know exactly what that's all about. It's just software companies trying like crazy to hold on to some kind of copyright clout, which is a total pipedream anyway. They figure they can scare the dumb little naïve users. They don't even bother trying to stop players like me.

"So I don't give a hoot what the fool federal regulations on that idiot program are. Leo—heads up—nobody ever heard of a program named 'Ultimaya 1.0.' It's not registered—anywhere! I've been checking it out all over the country, even in Japan. From any point of view except yours, Leo, the Ultimaya software doesn't even exist.

"That's why I want you to show me the damned thing. I'm getting worried about you. I don't want that program for myself, Leo. I know for sure I don't *need* to get any more selfish than I already am, for Christ's sake. I'm just a dumb lazy old fart. I got Maya up one side and down the other, inside and out. I put in twenty years of serious study and reflection on what's going down in this whirlpool of a world. And it's plain as cow pie in the barnyard that nobody's desires ever get and stay fulfilled.

"So no thanks! You can keep your little gem of a wish-fulfiller. I think it's to your advantage, even so, for me to get a sense of what's going down in your little room in Stokesland, specifically when you plug into this sucker. But you won't even show me. You want to keep it entirely to yourself. You believe letting me in on it will knock you out of it. Okay, fine, go ahead. If you have to play it that close to your chest, you're on your own. But I'm here when and if you really need me. If it's not too late. Meantime, you're not just acting like a jerk; you're acting like a fool, and an asshole, to boot."

Leo glared into Charley's eyes. He could not believe he'd wasted all this time to come down here and get a snotty lecture. There was nothing left to say. Charley looked back at him, expressionless.

Leo stood. "Okay, Charley. Guess you've drawn the line. I said it before, and I'll say it again: you ain't got no gumption. Not on this one you don't. See you later."

"See you, Leo. Good luck, my friend."

Leo was already walking out of the office. He didn't acknowledge Charley's last words. He did slam the door on the way out.

A goldang waste of time, that's all there was to it!

No Way Out but Down and Out

L eo's mind fumed and churned all the way home. He didn't think
once of trying to notice a dividing line between the ordinary world
and Stokesland. He'd had enough. It was time to take charge. He
was not going to play around any longer.

He didn't say a word to Joseph on the drive, didn't thank him for
opening the car door for him in front of the mansion, didn't acknowledge
Chatsworth's deference and solicitude at the door, and was so deep in
scowls that when Nan saw him, the smile fled from her lips and she
about-faced and headed back into the kitchen without saying a word of
greeting. Leo meanwhile threw his overcoat to the floor and, still wearing
his blue silk evening jacket, stormed up to his room, shouting,
"Chatsworth! More wine! The best!"

In his room, he paced and stormed some more. When his butler brought
the libation, Leo bypassed the glass and took it straight from the bottle. He
drank sixteen hundred and ninety dollars worth of wine—a full bottle of a
rare, prize-winning Chateau Lafite—in just under ten seconds. Con-
gratulating himself on the longevity of his chugging technique, he caromed
around his spacious room a while longer, waiting till he was roaring drunk.

That condition achieved, he sat down in front of the computer. This
time he meant business. Finally, the screen finished its obligatory "mood

music" of prelude colors, which were really starting to bore him now, and awaited his instructions.

Leo wasted no time. He had no patience for any more preliminary handshakes. There was no referee here, after all, and basically he had taken a continual pounding below the belt ever since the first bell of this match. He typed into the computer his final, summary demand:

"I WANT IT ALL!! I WANT IT BAD!! AND I WANT IT NOW!! I want the ultimate in pleasures and the ultimate fulfillments, and I do not want no danged backtalk from YOU, Mr. Ultimaya 1.0! I want no more black widow backlash poisoning everybody around me and in the world just so I get what I asked for! I want immediate fulfillment of everything in my entire goldanged dynamic wish-field, period! This is final! These requests are nonnegotiable! JUST DO IT!!!"

The hard disk whirred briefly. Then a new legend came on the screen: "Program malfunction. Abort or Retry?"

Leo spluttered in drunken rage, shouting, "Don't you give me that crap! Don't you pull this stuff! Don't you evade my demands!" He typed, "Malfunctions will not be allowed," but then noticed that nothing was appearing on the screen.

The screen blinked, sort of, and then the same words reappeared: "Program malfunction. Abort or Retry?"

Leo pounded the *r* for "retry" at least twenty times in rapid succession, like a man firing an automatic weapon. It did no good. Nothing changed.

He snarled, "Goldang you! You are a snake! You are nothing but evasion, deceit, and garbage!" He hurled himself and his chair away from the desk and leaped up to stomp around the room, yelling in fury.

Then, sloshing drunk as he was, Leo caught himself and reasoned aloud: "It's no dang use. It's got me again. If I want to play, it calls the shots and sets the rules. It is, I do believe, infinitely flexible in its ability to control and manipulate me according to its whims and my need for its powers. The only way I get to play is on its court, with its ball, and it gets to change the rules or even throw them out any old time it wants. *A-goldang-mazing!* But...it's true."

Now becalmed, at least a little, Leo strode—more like wobbled—to his chair and approached the computer again. He pushed *a* for "abort" and watched the program close down into hibernation. Then he started it up again, endured the daybreak color histrionics, and, when it was finally ready, took a new tack.

He typed, "I wish to realize all the primal fulfillments of my dynamic wish-field as quickly as possible. Whatever that means. And I don't care about the consequences, for me or for anyone else."

He was in a mean and sullen mood, and he didn't care about that either.

This time the program quickly replied:

"The User's previous imperatives, as well as this more reasoned communication, have been registered. If the User wishes to realize all the primal fulfillments of his existence in the manner specified, he must be prepared to endure an extraordinary acceleration of the process whereby what is wished for becomes manifest."

Leo typed angrily, "NO PROBLEM. Now get on with it!"

The program continued. "Moreover, the User must understand that in order to be capable of experiencing such rapid and total fulfillment, he must proceed immediately to the border between the worlds."

Leo punched in, "NO PROBLEM. And just where is that?"

The program replied, "Finding the border between the worlds is a necessary part of the User's preparation for what he will experience there."

Leo shouted out loud, "Goldang it! I've had enough of this mumbo-jumbo compu-speak runaround!" Then he typed in, pounding each key: "TELL ME WHERE I'M SUPPOSED TO GO, GOLDANG IT!!!"

The program went into balk mode again: "Abort or Retry."

Leo screamed, "Aaaagggghhhh! Confound you, you idiot box! Tell me where I'm supposed to go!"

But try as he might, Leo could not get the program to proceed.

Finally, with an angry sigh, he punched the *a* again and the program went into hibernation.

For the first time since Ultimaya 1.0 had introduced itself to him, Leo closed the computer, slamming down the monitor so hard, in fact, that he worried for a moment he might have cracked the casing. He stood and looked at the machine with raw contempt, reeling slightly from his drunkenness, which was suddenly coming on very strong.

"Awwright!" he slurred aloud. "You wan' me to go find the border between the worlds. Fine. I think I'll do jush that. I don't need your dang help. But when I get there, you better deliver. That's all I got to say, Mr. Ultimaya! Or Miss Ultimaya! Or Mrs. or Ms. or Madame—*Mad-am*, accent on 'Mad,' is more like it! And you know *exactly* what I'm talking about!"

Fuming, sputtering, and sopping drunk, Leo spun out of the alcove. After two steps, he lost his balance and stumbled against the bookcase lining the wall, knocking several books off a shelf. Muttering angrily, he stooped to pick up the books and was about to smash them back onto the shelf.

But there on the wall behind where they had stood, he noticed something strange: *A red button.*

"What in tarnation is that?" he asked aloud.

Curious, suddenly sober, Leo lifted his arm and advanced his right index finger to the button. A fraction of an inch away from it, he paused. He couldn't push it. Didn't dare. God only knew what it was!

But he couldn't not push it, either. He had to push it and find out—whatever it was for.

Maybe it was a secret summons for Chatsworth—but he had an intercom for that.

Maybe it was a hidden way to reach the security guards.

Maybe...but then, in a burst of frustration and damn-the-torpedoes daring, Leo just stopped thinking and wondering. He jammed his finger straight into the button.

As he looked on open-mouthed—"Oh my God!" he thought, "just like in the goldang movies!"—half of the bookshelf and the portion of the wall directly behind it disengaged slowly from the rest of the wall and rotated outward. Leo had to step aside to make room for it. The other half of the wall and bookshelf rotated inward, into the internal framework of the mansion.

He peered into a dark, gloomy, very narrow space. "Holy good God A'mighty!" he said out loud. "This is it! The secret tunnel! I knew it was here. I found it!"

Leo stood before the looming emptiness. The whole world was silent. Suddenly he didn't feel the least bit inebriated. He thought, *"Whoa. Just had that fancy bubbly shocked right outta me."*

Under his breath, he whispered to himself, "It ain't just a secret tunnel. This has gotta be the hidden passageway to 'the border between the worlds.' But how can the border between the worlds be right here in my house?"

He was silent again. The darkness was so intense, Leo felt he was being magnetized into it, like a planet being pulled into a black hole.

"Well," he said, "Nothing to it now but to get on with it." He wondered how he would find his way in the dark and flirted with the idea of calling Chatsworth for a flashlight.

"No, no way," he thought. "This thing's like to close right up on me. And what if I can't get it open again when I come back? Nope. Gotta jump on in, even if it means groping in the dark."

Just then a small, pulsating red light flashed near his right thigh on the inner wall of the tunnel. Leo peered down. The light was actually in the shape of an arrow, pointing downward. And there, on the concrete floor of the tunnel right at the entry, were a tall candle and a box of wooden matches.

Leo chuckled. "Little low-tech, don't ya think?" he asked, a little louder than actually felt comfortable. "If you could provide a candle, why not a flashlight?"

No sooner were the words out of his mouth than a shudder went down his spine. It dawned on him that he was addressing some kind of living presence. His questions presumed a listener, but when he'd begun asking them he was just talking out loud. Now he felt certain that some *one* or some *thing* was actually listening. More than that, he knew somehow that by entering this tunnel, he was going right into that living presence and subjecting his body, mind, and soul to its whims.

"All right," he said boldly, but with secret annoyance since he couldn't keep his voice from quavering. "I'm gonna trust you. Despite my better judgment, I am going to trust you. Here I come!"

He lit a match and used it to light the candle. Holding the candle before him, and shielding his eyes with his other hand so he could see what it illuminated without being blinded by its light, he scanned the area where he stood to see if any other aids to his adventure might be awaiting discovery. He looked again at the pulsating red light, which was set in a metal box the surface of which was flush with the wall. There appeared to be some kind of written legend on it, in tiny lettering. Leo squinted and moved the candle as close as possible. Then he leaped back with a start.

The legend consisted of a single word and a number: "ULTIMAYA 1.0."

"Jesus!" Leo whispered. His whole body shook again with an involuntary shudder. "This is plain, plumb weird!"

He blew out a long breath, trying to gain composure. The silent darkness yawned before him. It occurred to him that old Jonah in the Bible might have felt something like this, staring into the gullet of the great whale, and that thought prompted another shudder.

Jonah had no choice. He was busy being swallowed, whether he chose it or not.

He, Leo, did have a choice. But this was no time to turn back.

He stepped into the tunnel.

As soon as he did, the wall and bookcase wheeled and creaked shut behind him, making his heart skip a beat.

He pretended to be unflustered. "What is this?" he asked aloud.

"*Raiders of the Lost Ark* or something? Come on. Don't you think this is all just a touch too tacky?"

The secret passageway seemed to arc or gravitate to the right and spiral steeply down. Leo noticed nothing on its walls except a sheen of dank slime. He held up the candle as high as he could, to see if he could make out a ceiling; he couldn't.

That disturbed him a bit. It confirmed his edgy feeling that the ceiling was either way high up or else—he didn't how to make sense of this, architecturally, but there it was, a stubborn sense he had of the space—maybe there was no ceiling at all.

He tried not to think about that. He was glad he'd found the candle and not just gone off into the tunnel groping by hand. For one thing, it was draped with thick cobwebs. He could smell them burning away as the candle flame seared them one after the other.

For another thing, after what he assumed was only a few moments of walking down, Leo realized he had no idea how far he had come. And when he turned to look back in the other direction, he saw only the wall sheering to the left above him, and the floor rising sharply behind him. He didn't think it would even be possible to be able to go back up, with those fancy leather slippers on his feet. Clearly, he wasn't dressed for spelunking.

"Dang," Leo thought. "No way back. No way up these slick and slimy walls. So no way out except straight ahead. And straight ahead seems to mean way down. No way out but down and out. If I'm lucky."

On and on he descended, placing each slipper with care for fear of slipping and tumbling down. If he could've, Leo would have grasped the stone floor with his toes through the shoes.

A strange thing began to happen. At first it was just a reverie. He recalled again how beautiful and young Nan was now—or whenever in time he'd seen her last in Stokesland—and how different she was from the way she'd been for so many years in Ashlin. That led him to thinking about his parents, and the accident.

145

He thought of his mother, lying in that final hospital bed. Of how he'd wanted to see her, and yet not wanted to. How much he'd resented Nan's monopolizing her attention, and yet how relieved he felt by her doing just that. In his mind's eye, he could see his mother again, bandaged from head to toe. Her right leg had been in traction with massive fractures in four places, her chest and ribcage crushed by the impact of the crash, her face bruised, swollen, and sliced from the shattering of the windshield. He had found it almost impossible either to look at or speak to her. So, truth be known, he'd welcomed Nan's mother-henning of his mother, even though it made him feel guilty about his own avoidance.

All this was running through his mind when he turned a slight corner in the passageway down—and looked up to see his mother lying in her hospital bed right there in the tunnel!

"Momma?" Leo stood motionless, barely able to whisper the word. The hospital bed was canopied with jumbles of cobwebs that glistened in the flickering light of his candle. The old woman turned her head with a grimace—might have been from pain, but it hit Leo as terror—and opened her mouth as though to speak.

Then in an instant both she and the bed disappeared!

Leo stood trembling in the musky tunnel. "What in God's holy Creation is going on here?" he thought. He took a long, deep breath and exhaled. Then he whispered, "Oh, boy, I'm starting to hallucinate. I better keep my attention on what's in front of me—getting down this tunnel and out of here. This place is …" He didn't want to say out loud what he was thinking, but a numbing terror had gripped him. And he knew it was not going to let go.

He began gingerly walking down once more. Soon his attention drifted away again to other times and places. For some reason, the image of his grandfather, Abner Stokes Sr., kept coming up to his mind's eye. It was the picture in the photograph Leo had recently retired from the mantel in his former living room. In that stern visage, the angles of the old man's jaw and brow were hardened and chiseled by what Charley Bass laughingly used to call "the Ancient Stokes Code of Clench." Seeing his forebear's face, Leo had always sensed that his grandfather had held his life to rigid order, at peril to all emotion, spontaneity, and pleasure.

Abner Sr. had worn one of those archaic, moustacheless beards that made him look even more Victorian than he already was, so that his ever-compressed lips stood out as the primary feature of his face. Leo had met him only a few times, when he was a little boy. The experience had always terrified him, especially when the severe old man opened his mouth and spoke to him.

"LE...O...POLD...STOKES!"

The garbled tones reverberated through the tunnel—it was a man's deep voice. Leo didn't want to allow himself to acknowledge it was his grandfather. It had been so long ago ...

Within seconds, he came to a place where part of the tunnel seemed to recess off to his left, while the main passage continued to wind around and down to his right. As he peered anxiously into the darkness—he couldn't fathom how deep the recess might be, this could be a subterranean chamber, a cavern within his own home—the voice echoed again, from the depths of the darkness he was staring into:

"LE...O...POLD...STOKES!"

No doubt about it. It was Abner, Sr. Or, at least, it was the old man's voice.

Leo thought, "The last thing I need right now is a lecture from my goldang, long-dead granddaddy. If he wants me, he can come get me!"

He kept walking straight ahead and down. Full of dread, he stopped now and again to listen, but there was no sound of anyone following him. He shook his head, trying to rid himself of the cloying terror that these visitations were at least as real as anything else he was experiencing right now.

But the visitations did not stop. As he came around one sharp turn in the tunnel, he saw Constance and Helen standing before him.

Constance was weeping, shaking with silent sobs, her eyes cast down. Helen was looking at him mournfully, dressed in an informal skirt and sweater, almost like school clothes—except for one thing that stopped him in his tracks: her entire body, head to foot, was covered in translucent sheets of what appeared to be ice. Ice that her body was not melting. The sight of these two women he knew well and that stark, strange iciness on Helen made Leo gasp aloud—and in that instant they vanished, as if his involuntary croak had dematerialized them.

He made up his mind to continue down, down, down as far as the tunnel was going to take him. There must be a way out somewhere. More images kept flying from his mind into the caverns, and then back, it seemed: strange and murky specters, vast spaces, enticing women he didn't know, dreams and traumatic moments that had been buried since his childhood, bizarre displays of imagery combined with frenetic scheming about the bank, his accumulation of great wealth, more memories of his parents and the images he'd conjured long ago of their violent death in the accident, horrid shapes and visions as though whirling out of nightmares; on and on and on.

When he could even think deliberately at all, it seemed to Leo that he was somehow walking through his own mind—but then another spectacle of his memory or his fantasies would arrest his attention, standing before him as concrete as the glistening walls of the tunnel.

Leo noticed the candle was burning close to the holder now. He only had a few minutes, maybe ten, before the flame would go out. The thought of being stranded in this bizarre place with no light whatsoever petrified him. "Confound it," he thought. "Why in the world is this happening to me? What is the point? When am I going to get out of here? And what can all of this possibly have to do with finding that place the program told me about, 'the border between the worlds'?"

"Leee...ooo! Leee...ooo!" The lilting, teasing tones of the voices of several women sang to him from the gloom in front of him. He could just make out their shapes in the darkness.

Something about their energy puzzled him. Then it hit him: it was like he was on a trip down Movies from World Literature Lane. "First my own 'ghosts of Christmas past,' now a bunch of tacky sirens! Now Ultimaya's going Greek on me!"

Out loud, trying to sound brave and commanding, he shouted, "Enough! I know you're not real. You're just...you're just tacky bad dreams. Hallucinations! Leave me alone. Or better yet, get me outta here!"

The women came closer. He could see there were three of them. He had never met or, best he could recall, seen any of them before. He could also see they were all wearing erotic lingerie. Close as he was to freaking out, that did get his attention.

One, a striking brunette, stepped forward. Her hands were behind her back. She was grinning slyly.

"Just hallucinations, Leo?"

"That's right, ma'am," he said. He was tired, and exhaustion had cut into his fear. It also made him pretty testy. "Nothing but a goldang mind-form. To what end, I do not know. And I don't even care."

"Well, in that case," she said with a giggle, "I guess you won't be wanting or needing this!" She pulled a hand from behind her back, revealing—of all things—an ice cream cone!

She held it a few inches from his face, so that he recognized the flavor by smell, just as she said, "Mango, Leo—but I guess you're not interested in hallucinated ice cream, right?" And before he could say a word, she grabbed his right hand—he could feel her nails digging into his wrist—and, laughing, smashed the ice cream cone down on the candle, snuffing the flame!

The other two joined her in teasing laughter and ran away down the tunnel. Leo was shocked and outraged at the same time. He shouted, "Hey! Goldang it, you come back here! Who are you? What are you? Where are you going? Come back here, dang it! *Come back here!*"

It hit him that the candle was useless now; it was under a whole scoop of ice cream, and in the confusion he'd dropped the box of matches.

That did it. Stark terror overwhelmed him. Frantic, he began running after the sounds of the women's laughter, which seemed to be receding swiftly far beneath him and around many more curves in the tunnel.

Leo abandoned himself to his terror and anger and went running, sliding, shouting through the pitch black tunnel, his right hand on the slimy wall to guide him, and his left hand, still smeared with ice cream, held out in front of him in the darkness. He could still hear the women's giggles and peals of laughter, but they seemed to be coming from so far, far below him that he thought the tunnel must never end.

Suddenly, he crashed full speed, with a great clang and clatter, into what must have been a metal wall right in front of him. His outstretched left hand and arm served no protective purpose at all. Leo went full force into the wall so fast that, for several moments afterward, he lay senseless on the dank tunnel floor.

Eventually, he tried to pick himself up in the darkness. His cheeks, nose, chest, knees, hands, arms, and elbows felt bruised and battered from the impact and fall. He groaned aloud, then stopped and didn't move.

There wasn't a sound. Anywhere.

He put a tentative hand out to touch the wall he had collided with. It was very cold. He began to trace all along its surface to see if maybe it might lead him to another opening. The blackness of the tunnel was now absolute. Except it wasn't exactly a tunnel anymore. Whatever tunnel there was, was behind and stretching above him now. But who knew? Maybe that was all walled in also. Where in God's good Creation did those women go? What had just happened?

His brain racing, Leo again and again felt along the surface of the wall that had stopped him, as well as the slimy walls beside him. What was in his mind anymore, and what was outside it—if anything? Maybe the tunnel was his own brain and nervous system somehow. Maybe the house was his own total mind somehow. Maybe the border between the worlds was really just code for the boundary between sanity and madness.

Maybe it was madness itself.

Maybe the presence he'd encountered when the tunnel first opened up to him, and which he had felt pressing in on him more and more, almost suffocating him as he descended—maybe that was his own unconscious mind, but conscious in its own way, and fully in charge of his fate and his choices.

This last wondering stopped Leo cold. His terror, already at high volume, ratcheted way on up to extreme paranoia. It was like he was confronting a dimension of himself that was entirely "other" than his usual sense of who he was. Not just other, but coldly antagonistic to him and about to destroy him, like a black widow or praying mantis about to devour a no longer needed mate. Another shudder passed up and down his spine, the hair on the back of his neck stood on end, and goose bumps rose all over his body.

Standing there in the tomblike silence, trapped in fright and despair, helplessly freaking out, Leo one more time tried moving his right hand to the right and down on the wall in front of him. Suddenly—in a place on the wall he knew he had already felt his way over several times without feeling anything there—his hand grasped a shape. It was a handle one might use to open a door. Suppressing another shudder, not daring to admit to himself how petrified he was, Leo pressed down and heard the click of a mechanism inside the wall.

Once again, as when he first entered the tunnel, he hesitated. "God only knows what's beyond this door—if that's what it really is," he thought. "But no way I can stay where I am right now. No way out but out."

Out loud he said, "No way out but down and out!" Taking a deep breath, he pressed down firmly on the handle and pushed on the metal in front of him.

It opened! It was a door after all!

A burst of icy air blasted his face and the front of his body, pushing him back. He managed, however, to keep the door open, and stepped through it into a chamber of a size he couldn't determine in the dark.

He let go of the door, and it clanged shut behind him, its echo reverberating in the chamber. Now he had to grope again. He stuck the candle in his left jacket pocket. He cursed the remnants of the ice cream dripping from it and, while he was at it, also cursed his own failure to find the box of matches again after he'd dropped it.

He felt all along another wall, shrinking back from it whenever he came across more cobwebs. "Shoot," he wondered, "what if there are black widows in here? I gotta watch out."

The chamber was so silent, even thoughts seemed explosive, like pistol shots in his brain. He groped along with both hands and feet and tried not to think.

What if there was a sudden drop in the floor?

What if he just fell right off a precipice into nothingness?

Just when Leo was feeling he could jump out of his skin from paranoia, his hand struck—another door handle!

With no hesitation, Leo turned the handle and pushed to open the door with his shoulder. The latch clicked and the door gave way, so that he stumbled forward and was suddenly blinded by blazing light and hit by another cold wind.

For a moment he stood blinking, trying to get accustomed to the brightness.

"Good morning, sir. I do hope you had a restful night."

Leo's vision came into focus quickly, and he looked around to get his bearings. He was standing outside the house at Stokesland, on what appeared to be a lower back stairwell.

And Chatsworth was right in front of him, with a napkin over his arm and a small tray with a glass of orange juice!

"Chatsworth, what the—whaddya mean 'good morning'? Have I been in there all night?"

"Why yes, sir. It is not possible to leave the tunnel until you have begun a new day."

Suddenly, Leo understood something about Chatsworth—well, it was just a hunch.

"Chatsworth, I don't suppose it would be a, shall we say, *profitable* use of my time to try to get you to tell me what's really going on here, would it?"

The elderly fellow frowned. "Why, sir, forgive me, but I do not comprehend your question. I do hope there is nothing amiss in my service or that of any of the rest of the staff. Surely, sir, no one has been failing to evince the proper respect for the master of the house."

Leo shook his head in resignation. If he pushed the issue, he was all but certain Chatsworth would have no memory of what he had said just seconds ago about the tunnel. Not that the old man would be pretending to have no memory. Leo was pretty sure he plain old actually wouldn't have any.

"No, no, Chatsworth. Everything's fine. Just a strange notion there for a moment—please, take no heed. And thank you for the juice."

He drank down the orange juice, which obviously had just been squeezed from fresh fruit. It was so delicious he closed his eyes to savor the taste; so delicious he didn't even mind that it chilled him again. When he opened his eyes to hand the glass to Chatsworth, the old man had a touch of a smile on his lips and a twinkle in his eye.

"Mr. Stokes, sir, if you wish to pursue larger questions than those I am qualified to respond to, perhaps you would like a private moment with...?" He gestured deferentially to a small table and folding chair behind him.

Upon the table, on a crisp white tablecloth, sat a sleek black laptop computer.

Leo looked suspiciously at the old man. Just how, he wondered, did this computer he'd never seen get out here? "Chatsworth—"

Chatsworth's expression assumed a characteristically innocent, if uncharacteristically befuddled, mien again. "Yes, Mr. Stokes?"

Leo had that all but certain feeling once more. He wanted to ask but thought better of it.

Chatsworth didn't meet his gaze, but said, "Sir, I will be happy to stand by if you need to use the machine for a moment—"

"Thank you, old boy. Don't mind if I do—but hey, wait just a second here."

Leo turned to look at the door out of which he had moments before emerged into daylight. It looked like an ordinary wooden door with glass windowpanes and, apparently, blinds on the inside fully closed. It did not look like that last big metal door he'd cranked open had felt to his touch.

"What in tarnation?" Leo shivered, the hair rising on his back and neck again. Timidly, he reached out, turned the doorknob, opened the door slowly, and looked in.

Inside he saw a stairwell, a few knobs on the wall for coats and a low rack for shoes. Just the sort of things one might expect to find inside a small back door on the bottom floor of a country mansion.

Nothing like a tomblike tunnel.

Leo muttered, "Whew!"

He closed the door and turned back around. Chatsworth was now standing a couple of paces behind the little table, napkin on his arm, waiting for Leo to take a seat. Leo did so and pressed a button on the side of the computer. The screen leaped to life.

Now there were no preliminaries. The cursor was pulsing on the screen in front of him. Leo typed in a request: "I assume this is Ultimaya 1.0 and you're plugged into me perfectly. I have one question: where was I just now?"

There was a swift whir, then a legend appeared on the screen: "The User was inside his own house."

Leo sighed and typed, "That is a pretty smart-ass, obvious answer."

The machine replied, "To an unnecessary, obvious question. The Ultimaya 1.0 program, furthermore, can no longer accommodate such questions, due to the extreme acceleration of wish-fulfillment processes the User has irrevocably set in motion. It is strongly recommended that the User waste no further time and proceed directly to the border between the worlds."

Leo sighed again, then looked at his butler. "Chatsworth, what's it talking about, 'irrevocably set in motion'?"

The old man blushed and stammered. "Sir, I do feel this is outside my province, but—well...you may recall you closed the other machine rather forcibly in your quarters last evening. And that your communications to it just previously were, shall we say, somewhat peremptory?"

Leo nodded with a rueful smile. "I see." He typed in a final question: "Is there anything else I need to know?"

The computer replied, "You will find your answer in the red heart of the wood." Then the machine abruptly turned itself off.

Leo ran his hands through his hair, blowing out a long breath. "Wouldn't you know it?" he muttered. "As if it weren't all enough, now riddles too." He shook his head in silence. He was so tired, it was like the marrow of his bones wanted him to get and stay horizontal in a seriously comfy bed for a week.

"Will that be all, sir?"

"Yes, Chatsworth. That'll be all for now."

Chatsworth wheeled and walked away into the sunlight and up what looked to be stairs to an upper deck just on another side of the building.

Leo stepped out of the shadows to look back at the house. "Now this is weird," he said out loud. "I walked all over this place and all around the grounds the other day, but I never saw this part of it at all. I don't think it was even here."

The main building lifted high above and behind him, vaguely looking like the mansion as he knew it, but vaster, with more stories, wings, and sections. In the other direction from the house, a steep hill stretched below him that he had not noticed before, and, in the distance, wintry cornfields he hadn't seen. "They weren't there," he muttered under his breath. "The whole place is different. 'The User's own house.'" He chuckled. "Ultimaya's changed everything again."

"You be wantin' t' head to th' border, Mistuh Stokes?"

TO THE BORDER

Leo turned sharply to his right. There was Joseph, standing by an odd-looking car—maybe it was a truck. Its right front door was open, apparently ready to speed him away.

Leo eyed the man. Joseph had a look of complete sincerity, trust, and even respect on his face. There was no knowing smirk or ironic glint of superiority in his eyes. His question was honest and open.

So Leo responded in kind. "Yes. Thank you very much, Joseph."

He didn't even bother to ask how Joseph knew where Leo was supposed to go. He just got into the car. "Where's the front of the house, Joseph? Where's the main drive?"

"Oh, round back t'other way, Mistuh Stokes. Bit of a drive. You wantin' t' go that way, suh?"

"No, no. We have our business. Let's drive on." He no longer had a clear map in his mind of how Stokesland was all laid out—but then, maybe what he'd had in mind wasn't really accurate even before his journey through the tunnel. Leo knew he was somewhere in Stokesland. And he knew, and he knew Joseph knew, and that Joseph knew he knew, that his business was to find the border between the rest of the world and the place from where Ultimaya 1.0 was supposedly fulfilling his deepest wishes.

He noticed Joseph was driving him out over the meadows behind the mansion in an all-white, four-wheel-drive Rolls Royce custom designed to serve as a two-seater, mini pickup truck—like one of those old Ford Fairlanes with the back seat and trunk scooped out flat, pickup style.

For a while Leo looked around inside the vehicle, marveling that this could somehow be a fulfillment of his own deep desiring. He'd never even imagined such a car, truck, whatever it was, could be possible. But here it was, in his world. It could only be here because he had somehow, somewhere deep inside, wanted to have it.

Right?

Or what?

How, where, and why Ultimaya 1.0 had supposedly tapped into him to produce this bizarre, super-posh yet working-class roadster, he couldn't imagine.

Leo was starting to get another picture in his mind's eye, though. It was of a dark space, somehow pregnant with possibility, which was a part of him he didn't and maybe couldn't know. Wherever his "deepest wishes" or "dynamic wish-fields" were constellated, they were beyond, or before, or elsewhere and greater than, and somehow or sometimes contradictory to, the imagination he could tap into and consciously activate in his mind.

That was what made dealing with Ultimaya so risky. And that was why he felt he had to find out what it could show him at his destination—the border between the worlds.

They tumbled across the hillsides for a mile or two, Leo gazing upon the rotting old gray stalks of last summer's corn and, beyond them, out into distant chalk-gray skies. If he had thought about it, he would have wished this kind of wintry day not possible in Stokesland. But then maybe that kind of wish would be superficial, not really deep or "deepest," and unacceptable or unworkable for Ultimaya 1.0.

Even so, he didn't like these chalky, chill days in Cotton County. Somehow they put a mute on his soul, so he felt cold and lifeless from the inside out. Then again, the events of the last twenty-four hours and more were enough to put a cold pall on anyone, regardless of weather or the season.

A sensation of the vehicle slowing pulled Leo out of his glum reverie. He saw they had pulled up to the edge of a forest that stretched along a line in either direction as far as eyes could see. By his feet, under the dashboard, Chatsworth had provided a pair of boots for Leo, which he pulled on. He climbed out of the car and, looking back and forth along the tree line, stretched and took a deep breath. The cool air felt good inside him, gave him a little life again. He turned to his chauffeur.

"Joseph, is all this my property? I mean, what is, and what ain't, that we can see from here?"

Joseph nodded gravely. "Mistuh Stokes, as a matter o' fact, suh, evuhthing you can see heah is your'n. Not only that, but your property line, it's way on back in these heah woods, Mistuh Stokes. Way on in thar, ah reckon."

"Well, good." Leo looked at the edge of the woods. It seemed to stretch along the fallow wintry fields for miles in either direction. Leo knew the distances must be deceiving, but still, it did appear to be miles. "Come on, Joseph, let's lock up the truck here and head on in there."

Joseph looked down at the ground, then spoke in little more than a whisper. "No, suh. Ah think ah'd best stay heah by the truck, suh."

Leo was surprised. "Why not, Joseph? Is something wrong? I mean, ain't nobody really gonna mess with the truck, out here in the middle of nowhere on my own land."

Joseph didn't look up, but his voice had a charge to it. "Well, suh, ah just cain't do thet. Ah jes' cain't go where you want t' take me, suh. Mattuh o' fact, ain't no way ah'm goin' into them woods, Mistuh Stokes. That walk ain't for me. It's fo' you, Mistuh Stokes. Ah'll be waitin' heah by the truck when you get back. But ah cain't go where you want t' take me, and that's a fact."

Leo stared at the man, whose gaze was still riveted to the ground. He sighed. "All right," he said. "So be it. Alone. I guess it makes sense. If I'm trying to find the border between Stokesland and the rest of the world, I don't reckon anybody but a Stokes is gonna be able to do it. And

I sure hope what I learn there puts me in a position to know what you and Chatsworth and apparently every other body on the property except me already seems to know about me, and what I own, and where I'm supposed to go, and what I'm supposed to do!"

Joseph let that last outburst pass, then looked up at Leo. Their eyes met. Joseph was calm. He said, quietly, "Good luck, Mistuh Stokes. You gon' need it."

"Thank you, Joseph. I know." Leo felt a bit unnerved by the steadiness and—he wasn't sure what exactly, a kind of depth maybe—he detected in Joseph's gaze.

But larger matters confronted him now. Leo turned and walked into the woods.

There was no path and, for what seemed like a long time, he fought his way through tangles of underbrush, thorns, and thickets of small trees. He had no idea which way to head, except what appeared to be deeper in.

Soon he was in dense forest. When he'd emerged from the tunnel, he hadn't noticed exactly what time of day it was. It had seemed to him that he'd come out into a noonday sun, even though Chatsworth had given him orange juice and wished him a good morning.

Now he felt the forest around him entering into the quiet of dusk. The birds were calming. Already there was the occasional hoot of an owl. Once again he felt a darkness coming to enwrap him and his world. "I don't get it," he thought. "Time's gone haywire. Or else I'm on somebody else's time scale here."

That thought made him tense and jumpy. He stopped and became very still.

There it was again: the unmistakable sense of a living presence or personality, other than his own and yet tied into him somehow. Maybe it was the spirit of the forest. Or maybe, Ultimaya.

A shiver went down his spine as he realized that once again, with no defenses available to him, he was plunging somehow into uncharted regions of his own wishes and dreams, the chaos of what he desired even before his thinking mind came up with any of its schemes.

The forest had a grandeur and a somnolent silence all its own. For a while, pushing through the woods, Leo thought of whistling a tune or singing a song aloud. But he couldn't get himself to do it. As darkness drew down around him, in fact, he became increasingly quiet in his progress. He didn't know where he was going, and there was still no path.

Yet the farther Leo went, the more he had an unaccountable certainty that he would find the right path sooner or later. He knew he had to stay attentive, alert. And he felt he had to remain subdued, as if the solemnity of the woods required a certain respect, even when he had to muscle and thrash his way through brambles and thickets.

Soon it was so dark Leo couldn't see more than a foot in front of him. He groped along, sometimes moving only a few yards in what felt like a quarter of an hour. His mind was spinning. "Shoot, what's it gonna take to find this border?" Ultimaya had talked about "the red heart of the wood." Joseph had said it was deep in there somewhere. What and where could it possibly be? How would he notice it?

Finally, after what seemed like hours—his face and hands all scratched, his muscles rigid from the evening cold, his clothes ripped and snagged by thorns and boots caked with mud and undergrowth— Leo emerged from thick forest into what looked in the darkness to be a wide clearing. From its center, he could see stars and a full moon high above.

His eyes suddenly felt like the moon had magnetized them to it; he couldn't look away from it. He watched for a long time as it climbed to the zenith of the night sky, directly over his head.

The moment it reached that highest point, a shimmering, laser-intensity ray of its reflected light shone down on a large boxlike shape standing at the other side of the clearing. A rectangle of red light pulsed from the center of the curious structure.

Leo groaned, grinning and shaking his head. "Tacky, tacky, tacky," he said. "I mean, really, 'the red heart of the wood.' So now what? This must be where I'm supposed to find 'whatever else I need to know.' Whatever that could possibly be!"

He walked across the clearing to the structure. Its red light kept pulsing. As he got closer, he saw that the thing resembled a phone booth, or an ATM, situated right there in the middle of the forest! He couldn't stop chuckling.

The booth was framed of metal, with three clear plastic sides. The side facing him was open. Leo stepped inside, noticing there was no floor; the booth was sitting on the grass of the clearing. Three-quarters of the far wall was a console, much like that of an ATM but with a large computer screen built into it.

Leo laughed aloud and muttered, "This is too dang droll!" Now he saw the red light had appeared to be rectangular because the entire screen of the computer was flashing, periodically, with a bright, uniformly red color.

As he stood there, puzzled, the screen prompted him: "Use the pen and write directly on the screen. Because this computer is on the Ultimaya network, it will recognize the designated User's characteristic script."

Then he noticed a special pen, hanging on a holder by the screen. Leo grinned, whispering, "My own personalized, customized, computerized wish-fulfillment network! Kinda thing a man in my position oughta have."

Curious, he did what he'd been told. He wrote on the glass screen, "What do I need to know?"

The computer screen flashed back at him, "Is this all the User wishes to ask at this time?"

Leo wrote yes.

The machine replied, "Very well. The User should readily know what to do in the following situations."

Leo scrunched up his face, confused. He said aloud, "What following situa—"

He didn't complete the sentence, because the earth beneath him gave way!

It must have been only sod covering a trapdoor through which Leo, squawking, now tumbled. He fell through what seemed to be a pitch-dark chute wide enough so that he didn't touch and couldn't feel any sides, but somehow sensed they were there.

"All Bad Now"

Leo froze in fear, expecting to smash any instant into dirt or rock at the bottom of the chute, but he kept falling. And falling. He continued to fall freely for so long that he began to relax a little. Leo knew he'd hit some kind of bottom somehow, but he reasoned that the program didn't simply want him to die. Somehow, he assumed, his fall would be broken.

It also occurred to him, in free fall, that if he was a real-world Alice who just fell down the rabbit hole, well, he'd already met the Red Queen in his maybe not so real world. And her name was Ultimaya 1.0. Which got his attention. "Maybe," he thought, "me calling the program 'Mr. Ultimaya' misses a whole big piece of this puzzle. Maybe it ain't 'Mr. Nobody.' Could be a big 'She' like Bass keeps saying."

By ordinary non-subterranean standards, after a time Leo felt he must've covered, falling, the height of a good-sized skyscraper. He seemed to be traveling faster and faster, at incredible speed. But neither time nor distance had any reliable referents.

Just as he reached this conclusion, he popped down out of the chute into the sky above a bright landscape. He was tumbling right toward the open top of a booth that appeared to duplicate the one he'd dropped out of somewhere way above.

Leo shouted, "Hey! *Whoa!* What? No! *No!*"

He tried to draw himself into a tight ball, hoping he wouldn't smack into the sides of the booth from above and get cut in half.

But then something became evident that released Leo's fear. The sky of this place, the air, was so redolent and hazy it seemed to cushion his fall. By the time he fell into the booth, Leo had slowed down so much he was hardly more than floating. It was easy to aim himself into the open center of the booth. He plopped onto the earth with a thud, not hurting himself at all. He stood up and, brushing dust off his clothes, looked at the computer console standing beside him.

He laughed again. On the screen were two large words: "The Bottom."

With the pen attached to the console, he printed on the screen, "OK, I've hit bottom. Now what?"

New words appeared: "Prepare for acceleration."

"Acceleration?" Leo questioned out loud. "Wonder what that's supposed to be all about."

The computer responded: "Immediate situations will give the User a taste of the 'All' and 'Now' fulfillments of his wishes. Other fulfillments will appear shortly."

Leo could make no sense of any of that. He shrugged and looked around at the landscape surrounding the booth.

During his fall, he'd noticed a large number of tables spread out across a nearby meadow. It seemed to be spring here, wherever he was. The close-cropped grass of the meadow was a radiant new green, clusters of jasmine, honeysuckle, and flowering trees were in fragrant bloom, and bees and butterflies were flitting from one bright flower to the next. It was a delightfully warm day, not too hot, quite comfortable.

Leo took off the blue silk evening jacket he was still wearing and noticed that the small ring box was still in the right side pocket. He slung the jacket over his shoulder and turned to walk out of the computer booth. He shuddered with the oddly pleasant feeling of having just descended in a psychic elevator from one realm of reality to another.

Then another strong sensation, and an equally strong perception, distracted him.

The sensation: of his own ravenous, deep-gutted hunger.

The perception: every one of the countless picnic tables dotting the meadow was laid out with a magnificent spread of the best food and drink imaginable!

He saw every kind of meat and fish he'd ever eaten before, and many he couldn't identify; eggs prepared in at least twenty different ways; vegetables in steaming platters of all sizes, Greek and Italian salads, casseroles, gumbos—an amazing feast. Even what looked like fine Carolina barbecue!

Yet there was no one else in sight.

"Hm!" Leo grunted. "Guess all this is for me! Maybe Ultimaya 1.0 is gonna deliver, after all."

He roamed around among the tables, gorging himself to his heart's content for what seemed like hours. At last, he was so full he couldn't take even one more step. A vast weariness overtook him. With immense effort, he yanked one of the red-checked tablecloths—"Another nice touch, Ultimaya," he thought, "tacky as usual, but nice"—and, with the cloth, all the trays and platters of food went tumbling off the table, spilling onto the grass. He could have cared less. He rolled onto the tabletop, covered himself with the cloth, stretched out, and instantly passed into sleep.

The moment Leo fell asleep on the picnic table, he woke up on a beautiful white leather couch in an immense office. At least, it felt like that very same moment. Yet somehow time must also have passed because Leo saw he was now dressed in an exquisite, charcoal-gray, pinstriped suit. In fact, he realized on closer inspection, it was—or was just like—one of the custom tailored suits he'd seen in his closet in Stokesland. Leo felt energetic and lively, as if he'd slept long and deeply, yet the suit was as fresh as if it had just come out of dry cleaning. A pair of what looked like expensive Italian shoes embraced his feet.

For a moment, Leo was bewildered. He wasn't dreaming, he knew that. But how had he gotten from the meadow into this office building? How had he changed clothes? And when?

Just as those questions were flashing through his mind, Leo spied a thin, elegant gray computer—he guessed it was the kind called a "notebook," it was so thin—sitting on a table by his side. He tried to find a catch to open it. There wasn't one. Puzzled, he said, "Wonder how this dang thing opens?"

The instant he spoke, the machine opened itself.

"Oh, I get it," Leo said. "Voice sensitive. Charley told me there'd be stuff like this around. All right, then, assuming you're listening, Mr. Ultimaya 1.0—or excuse me, I guess that'd be Ms. Ultimaya 1.0—how did I get here? How did I get dressed like this? Not that I'm complaining, mind you, but what am I doing here? What's going on?"

The computer flashed a message on the screen: "The answer to these questions should be obvious to the User from our most recent interchanges. The User is advised to eliminate speculative wonderings and to savor the particular quality of the fulfillment of his wishes that is available to him at this immediate time."

Leo snorted. "Well, thank you, your usual goldang much! That's a pretty snooty message, don't you think?"

The next lines came up on the screen: "The Ultimaya 1.0 program does not make value judgment determinations about its own processes. It does, however, offer the User the following salutation—"

Leo waited to see what was coming onto the screen next.

Nothing did.

Then, as he watched befuddled, the monitor portion of the machine lowered, clicked closed, and the hard drive stopped whirring. The computer had turned itself off.

Leo snorted again. "Definitely your basic Ultimaya," he thought. "Real forthcoming." But what 'recent interchanges' was it talking about?

Immediately, the last words he'd seen on the screen in the meadow booth jumped into his mind's eye. "Oh," he mumbled, "acceleration." So this must be the acceleration, but what was the salutation?

Bright yellow light streamed out from above the main doorway leading into the room. An electronic screen was built into the wall there. On it, Leo saw words form one at a time.

"Welcome...to...Stokes...BankGlobal!"

"Stokes BankGlobal!" Leo snorted, taken aback. "Hm! Some salutation, all right. Well, I'm ready! Bring it on!"

He looked out across the vast expanse of the office, which featured an ornate conference table larger than any he had ever even heard of before, and out its dozens of huge plate-glass windows. It suddenly struck him that he was seeing nothing but sky outside. He strolled over to a window—and then jumped back away from it.

This was no ordinary skyscraper! He felt he must be hundreds of stories up in the air. If he was seeing clearly, the floor he was on had to be at least a half-mile up in the sky!

A huge city sprawled all around down below. Yet there was no other skyscraper anywhere—for he could see 360 degrees—that even remotely approached this height.

A voice buzzed through an intercom. "Mr. Stokes?"

It was Ernestine Elkins!

"Yes, Mrs. Elkins?"

"Everyone is here, sir. And they are all ready for the final signing of the documents."

"I see." Leo knew he was going to have to be fast on his feet again. "What dang documents?" he thought. "Here we go. Guess I'm about to find out about Stokes BankGlobal." To the intercom, he said, "By all means, send them on in, Ernestine."

Leo took what he presumed was his seat at the head of the giant oval conference table that must have had a hundred plushly upholstered and carved mahogany chairs stretching around it. The table was decked out in a festive manner, apparently readied for a celebratory business meeting, with multiple bouquets of flowers and dozens of champagne glasses.

No sooner had he taken his seat—more like a throne, he thought—than doors opened around the room and people came streaming in, all anxious to catch his eye and full of words of praise.

"What a marvelous event this must be for you, Mr. Stokes!"

"Truly an historic event—the acquisition of the four largest banks in the world all at once by what was once little Cotton County Regional, now the mighty Stokes BankGlobal! You must be so very proud, Mr. Stokes!"

"What a coup, Leo! No other regional banker in history has accomplished so much so quickly. Look at this place—Stokes Tower! Incredible! How does it feel to own the tallest and most beautiful building on Earth?"

Leo greeted everyone with pride and a regal bearing fitting the occasion. Ernestine Elkins arrived at his side, looking her matronly best. "Actually, way hotter than that," Leo mused inwardly. "I always did think she was a kinda homegrown, down-home Sophia Loren or something, that Ernestine. Now she looks even better than ever! Thank you, Ultimaya 1.0!"

Ernestine motioned for everyone to sit down. As soon as they were quiet, she opened the meeting.

"Now, y'all, as Mr. Stokes's vice president in charge of acquisitions, it is my honor to officiate at this supremely historic occasion. I wish to thank the heads of all the participating institutions for your generous cooperation in our various negotiations, whereby we have now created the single greatest bank on Earth, and this one is truly everywhere—*Stokes BankGlobal!*"

Everyone applauded and cheered. Ernestine impatiently hushed them with her gestures.

"Plenty of time later for applause and celebration. In keeping with the genius of Mr. Leopold Stokes, who engineered all the various transactions to make this event the swiftest and I am so proud to say, most painless, single—actually, multiple—sequence of mergers and acquisitions in history, we have all worked together today to make it possible for him to conclude this marvelous event, a first in modern financial history, with a single signature on a one-page document. I want to bring to your attention that, with this signature, Mr. Leopold Stokes"—once again applause interrupted her, and once again Ernestine swiftly quelled it, with a flashing smile and then a fake frown. "As I was saying, with this very signature, Mr. Leopold Stokes is creating the single largest bank in the world, with more assets than any other financial or corporate or even governmental institution on Earth. And, as our new chairman and president, he is becoming the single most financially powerful man on Earth, controlling an empire of financial service institutions so vast we have not yet been able to count up what it's worth. And, last but certainly not least—thereby, he is becoming the single wealthiest man on the planet.

"Leo, will you do us the honor of taking this pen and this document and doing the deed? And after he does, we're all gonna celebrate with the finest champagne, and with a round of Leo's favorite, Lappert's Macadamia Nut ice cream, all on the house of Stokes BankGlobal!"

Everyone laughed in delight. Leo was amused to realize that this whole crowd must all be aware of his penchant for Lappert's. He was less amused as it dawned on him that these men and women, of all colors, shapes, and sizes, dressed in all kinds of ethnic finery as well as classic Western business suits, must be some of the most powerful financial people on Earth, and now he was their boss and they were all looking to him for leadership.

And he didn't even know who they were. He could recognize a few from furtive glances but with lots and lots of them, he was clueless as to their names, what they stood for, what his past connections with them might have been, and what they all thought he had in mind for them going forward. He broke out in a sweat and hoped nobody could see it on his face.

They sure were looking, every one of them. There was a hush as Ernestine Elkins leaned over to him with the single page document and a Mont Blanc fountain pen. A murmur stole through the room as Leo took the paper and pen from her hands. He quickly perused the document. He didn't recognize the names of most of the financial institutions over which he was now gaining control. But then a sweet thought struck him: "Shoot, I don't need to know. I'm in charge. We'll work it out. Like we have with that crew of folks I never met before who take care of things for me back home at Stokesland."

Leo took the cap off the pen, set it aside, and with a proud smile, signed his name at the bottom of the page. A roar of applause and cheers rang through the room as he sat back, grinning broadly.

As everyone offered him toasts and cheers, he leaned over to Ernestine Elkins and whispered, "Ernestine, you piqued my curiosity there. How much am I worth?"

She smiled and whispered back into his ear, "Near's we can tell, Mr. Stokes, about five hundred billion dollars. It's accruing so fast we can't keep track."

Leo smiled and turned back to acknowledge the standing ovation the others in the room were giving him. A waiter poured him a glass of champagne. He noticed that other waiters were already placing huge bowls of Lappert's in front of the celebrants, while yet other servers were walking around the table dispensing ice cream toppings of every kind.

Someone tapped his left elbow. He turned to see Ernestine Elkins raising her champagne flute to him and smiling sweetly. Leo smiled back and lifted his to her in return. As they clinked the glasses together, he realized that she reminded him of an older, more mature but equally beautiful Helen Honeycutt—something about the shape of her eyes and nose. For just an instant, he had a troubled feeling about Helen, though he couldn't remember why.

But this was his dear helpful Ernestine now raising her glass to him. He quickly thought of a toast to offer her—and was opening his mouth to do so—when a ray of light striking the side of her glass arrested his attention. Leo looked into it deeply.

In the next instant, he was all alone in an ornate room, dimly lit, all full of red and purple couches, cushions, rugs, and heavy velvet draperies. He was downing the glass of champagne that was still in his hand. Startled—could this be the same glass?—he kept on drinking anyway. As he placed the empty glass on a table near the chair on which he sat, Leo noticed that now he was once again wearing his blue silk evening jacket. He fished around in his right pocket—the box was there too!

He was about to pull it out to make sure the ring was inside when a beautiful young woman approached him. She was wearing only a wisp of a gown and erotic lingerie underneath. Something about her looked familiar, but he could not remember why. Smiling, not saying a word, she took him by the hand. Leo was amazed and confused, but he allowed himself to be led down a hallway, up a flight of stairs, and to the end of another hall.

The place was quite opulent, done up in expensive Victorian and Edwardian antiques. Leo sensed there was nothing in the whole house that was not very fine and very old. But why was it all so red and purple? Who would decorate in such a fashion?

Then a door opened, and two other young women, similarly attired and also breathtakingly beautiful, welcomed him and his companion into a lavish suite.

Leo closed his eyes, shaking his head. "I get it," he muttered, not so loud they would hear him. "I'm in a cathouse."

The three young ladies giggled and squealed with laughter. As if on cue, all three said at once, teasing, in a stage whisper: "Lee...ooo!"

His mouth dropped open. He narrowed his eyes to look more closely at them.

"Oh, no!" he mumbled. "You're not...?"

All three grinned and nodded.

"But...I don't..." Leo looked from one to another, stammering.

Then he stopped and got hold of himself.

"All right. So you're the gals I met in the tunnel in Stokesland. Are you gonna disappear on me again, or what?"

Still grinning, all three shook their heads no.

The Asian one, a little sylph of a thing, stepped forward. "My name is Chana, and I am Malaysian."

The tall, slender blonde stepped forward. "I am Karina, and I am from Norway."

And then the third, a buxom brunette said, "Ah'm Mary Jo, and ah'm from Memphis."

Then all three said at once, again as if on cue, "You don't need to introduce yourself, Mr. Stokes. We know all about you. Now you just relax and let us get you ready."

"Get me ready for *what?*" Leo mumbled, but Karina silenced him with a firm and luscious kiss right on the lips and the other two turned him, pushed him backward, and then tripped him, so that he fell on the bed with all three of them.

The girls chortled and giggled and started taking off his clothes. Leo struggled out from under Karina's kiss.

"But wait! What're you doing? I mean—what about, um, safe sex? You know, AIDS 'n all? What're you doing?"

Chana seemed to be the spokeswoman. "Oh, no worry about safe and unsafe here, Mr. Stokes. This not the world you came from!"

"Then what world is it? Confound it, where in God's good goldang Creation am I?"

The three vixens looked at each other, mugging, and shrugged with vaudevillian panache. Then they squealed with laughter again and returned to their task. Leo gave up struggling, though he was more than a little nervous. He cleared his throat.

"All right, ladies. I give up. Have to be a durn fool not to. But, um, I think any one of you gals, I might could handle—maybe two—but all *three*...well, that might be a bit—"

Mary Jo put a finger to his lips and shushed him. She smiled, and her eyes danced as she shook her head. "Not us, Mr. Stokes. Not any one of us. But y'all're just gonna have to relax, now, you're making our work a little extra hard."

Leo looked at her, then sighed deeply. And then he gave up and tried his best to relax.

The women soon had all his clothes off. They began to massage him all over his body. They were in no rush, and their every touch was deep and sensual. The room was quite warm, suffused with a pleasing fragrance, maybe some kind of incense, Leo thought. Soft classical music was playing, it might've been a string quartet, but Leo couldn't identify it.

Now and again one of the ladies propped him up for a moment to ply him with a beverage he'd never tasted before, but which was so delicious—not too sweet, but somehow heavenly to taste—Leo didn't even want to ask what was in it. Or what effect it would have on him.

Leo could feel he was beginning to unwind like he hadn't in years—maybe ever. Their expert hands were loosening what felt like the tensions of a lifetime in the muscles all over his arms and legs and torso, his face, head, feet, and buttocks. Leo just let go into the pleasure of it...

Then he awoke with a slight start. The women were nowhere in sight. "Is anyone here?" he asked aloud.

Another woman's reply came from behind a beautiful Oriental screen in the middle of the room—a screen Leo was sure hadn't been there before. "Mm-hm."

The tone of her voice was vaguely familiar. Leo felt he was with someone he already knew, though just who would not come to mind. Whoever she was, he was real happy to hear her purring at him from behind the screen. He stretched, not wanting to rise or even hardly move, still so unraveled from the massage he felt like he was just a lake of bliss on the bed. He spoke again, the words taking their time getting out.

"And with whom...may I ask...do I have...the distinct...pleasure of conversing?"

The woman stepped out from behind the screen. She also was clad only in a silken nightgown and lingerie. She looked like someone he'd known all his life, but for the life of him he could not bring her name to mind. A coy smile played on her lips.

"Need an introduction, Mr. Stokes?"

The voice—now he knew! Leo was dumbstruck.

"Helen! Is that you? I thought—I thought you were...Helen, I heard you were dead!"

It was Helen Honeycutt. *She was alive!*

Helen sauntered in her four-inch heels over to the side of the bed and leaned over Leo's upper torso, her hands on her hips.

"Do I look dead, Leo, honey?"

Without waiting for him to answer, she gracefully stretched herself out on top of him. She pulled her head up so her eyes were within inches of his. Her silken chestnut hair, its blond highlights shining in the room's low lighting, fell on his cheeks, ears, neck, and shoulders.

"Do I *feel* dead?"

Again without waiting for him to reply, she kissed him, swiftly inserting her tongue deep into his mouth.

They kissed for a long time. Finally, they stopped. Their faces and lips were still close. Helen looked into Leo's eyes. She giggled and whispered in his ear.

"What do you think, Leo? Do I *taste* dead?"

Leo whispered back, "Helen...I still can't believe it's you. And that— and that we're..."

He didn't know how to finish the sentence. But he didn't need to say more. She just nodded, then lay her head down beside his. They clasped one another tightly.

Leo was overcome with love, and joy, and sorrow, all at once.

"Where are we, Helen? Is this Stokesland?"

She responded, her face still turned away so he could barely hear her. "Well...not exactly. At least, I don't think so."

Leo asked, "Then is it real life?"

Helen whispered again, "No, not exactly that, either. I mean, I'm not sure. Something's happened to me...I've—I definitely crossed over into something, or somewhere, that's for sure, but what, or where..."

Leo chuckled. "For a travel agent, ma'am, you're pretty vague on this trip."

She turned toward him and pushed herself up on her elbows. "Yes, that's something I used to be, but I don't know what I am now. Wherever it happens to be, Mr. Leopold Stokes, here we are. Just you and me. Right here. Now...after all these years...what're we gonna do about this...just you and me...hm?"

She smiled and pushed the tip of her tongue between her lips.

Leo didn't fail to get the picture. He grinned but said, "Y'know, Helen, I really want to be with you now—nothing I'd like better in some ways." He looked her over and sighed, smiling. "But, well, for the future...I mean, I've got a ring over there in that jacket that's specially for Constance. And if I ever get to be in the same place where she is again, I am going to give it to her—"

Helen looked deep into him, eyes and heart and soul. When she spoke, her tone was still lighthearted. But there was a depth, a sobriety about her he'd never felt before. "Leo, I don't think I can adequately communicate to you just how little I am now able to count on anything or anyone in the future. Far as I'm concerned, we've got this time together to make the most of. Who knows whether we'll even see each other again? Or where? In what circumstances? All I know is, I've always had a thing for you. Sometimes a big thing, sometimes just a little teeny one. But I always did have one. And I always felt you kinda did for me too. I'm right, aren't I?"

Leo had to nod his head. He didn't mind hearing all this. Shoot, he'd wondered and hoped for it practically his entire life.

"So now that I've got you in this bed—somebody's bed—I ain't gonna let you up till I'm done with you, Mr. Leopold Stokes!"

Surrendering, Leo laughed and pulled her down roughly to kiss her. Then they made love—slow, delicious, with passion and gentleness, abandon and sweetness—for what felt like hours and hours. The last thing Leo remembered before passing into a long, dreamless sleep was the musky fragrance of Helen's hair on his shoulder.

Sometime later Leo awoke. He was in a bed, but she was nowhere to be seen.

"Helen? Helen?"

No answer. Leo looked around. He was not in the room they'd been in. It wasn't the same bed either. In fact, he wasn't in a place he could identify at all.

Then an extraordinary sequence of things began happening—way more amazing than anything else yet.

The first thought that came to his mind was an image of a pancake breakfast—and then he was eating one, on a sunny veranda somewhere on a warm early morning. Along with the breakfast, there was a suspicious looking bowl of—he took a spoonful—yep, Lappert's Macadamia. He chuckled and then set in on the meal.

While Leo was chewing on a link of spicy sausage, as he put the knife and fork to a short stack of blueberry pancakes to cut himself a bite, it occurred to him, "Hm, think I'd like to play golf today." Suddenly, he was lining up a putt on a gorgeous, huge green—while still chewing the sausage!

As he stroked the putt and watched the ball head toward the hole, out of the corner of his eye he saw a red Ferrari pass by on a distant street—and in a twinkling he was inside, driving it, thrilling to its elegance and power, and knowing it was *his*.

With a sudden burst of longing, he wished Constance could be with him—and then, there she was!

"Constance!" he exclaimed. "Is that you? Is it really *you?"*

She was as lovely as she'd been in Stokesland, though he had no idea where they were now. Constance was wearing shorts and a bikini top and looked ravishing. She turned to him, a sparkle of delight in her eye, smiled and said, sweet and coy at the same time, "Of course, Leo, my love."

Leo felt a deep peace settle in his heart. He wondered for a moment if he should tell her about Helen, but decided against it at least for now.

For now, at last, again, after all this, he was with Constance Cunningham, the love of his life, and she loved him after all!

Leo looked back at the road before them. A billboard promoting some lawyer's campaign for state attorney general caught his eye. Driving that fine car, with his gorgeous lady beside him, Leo thought about how he'd always fancied someday he might run for public office—and in the very next instant, he was walking into a government office building in what, best he could tell, was Washington, DC.

As he walked, several people approached him, treating him with deference, calling him "Senator Stokes." He smiled. He was beginning to get the picture. No forewarning, no briefing in advance. "Okay, so now I'm a U.S. Senator!" First chance he got, he ducked into an interior room.

Constance was nowhere in sight. "Why," Leo thought, "does that not surprise me?"

It was at this point, letting out a long and troubled sigh, that Leopold Stokes began to get nervous. Things were happening way too fast now. He lifted his hand to loosen his bold, colorful silk tie—and found himself on a magnificent beach, with fine white sand, a deep blue sky, applying sunscreen to his neck and face.

"Whew! Maybe a little break here," he said out loud. "I wonder if there's some way I can suspend the, uh, superflash want-it-you-got-it mechanism for just a few moments?" He had the odd feeling he was sort of praying to something or someone; he wasn't just talking to himself.

Leo stopped moving for a moment. Nothing else happened.

"Okay," he said aloud again. "Um, whoever or whatever you are, thank you."

He lay down on the towel stretched out beside him. It was a magnificent beach, fine white sand, deep blue sky, and clear aquamarine water in what looked to be an island lagoon. He noticed a Styrofoam cooler next to the towel and opened it to look inside. There was a bowl of—he began laughing—"Gotta be Lappert's, right?" He took a spoonful and tasted it. "Yep. Mango."

Leo laughed again and lay down. It was so calm and peaceful there on that sunlit beach that he soon fell asleep.

Then he began dreaming.

He was driving a strange contraption, something like a cross between a big Caterpillar dirt mover and a Rube Goldberg machine. He was trying to escape from some dark, ominous place just behind him. But the contraption got stuck in what appeared to be an abandoned mine shaft that tunneled up into a hill at a forty-five-degree angle. He couldn't get it to go forward.

Desperate, even though it meant going backward toward whatever he was fleeing, Leo tried every gear to find reverse. Finally, by incredible effort and maybe good luck, he found the gear and was able to back the machine out. But when he got back outside, the landscape was now dark.

Then he saw, coming straight at him, a dark little man whose presence, from a distance of fifty yards or more, immediately caused the hair all over his body to rise. Leo knew, without any doubt, that this was a dreadful, evil creature.

He turned and began to run for his life, yet the ground seemed to be slipping back beneath him, like a treadmill going too fast and dragging him back toward that evil being.

Leo tried to scream for help, but no sound came from his lips.

Frantic, he tried imagining anything and everything he could wish for just to get away from that place. He wished to see Constance. He wished to be back on the beach. He wished to be on the golf course, in the office, in Stokesland, in the Ferrari. He shrieked inwardly, "Give me the tunnel! *Give me anything anywhere but this!*"

None of it worked. Nothing changed. He was still running at top speed away from that horrid, malevolent creature who was gaining on him even though, as Leo could see looking back, the man was walking without effort, almost strolling along.

Then he was back at the contraption he'd just jumped out of. "Oh my God," Leo muttered, "I've been running in a goldang circle!" He quickly leaped into the driver's seat and tried to start the colossal machine. The engine wouldn't turn over.

"What in tarnation is wrong with this dang thing?" he shouted. He pulled a switch that lit the dashboard. In the rearview mirror he saw the evil man, no more than twenty yards away now and grinning hideously. Shaking with fear, Leo turned back to the dashboard, to find that it was—what?

A computer screen!

"No!" he screamed. "No, goldang it. This is no time for your little commercials, Ultimaya!"

On the screen flashed red words on black: "THIS IS NOT A COMMERCIAL. THIS IS LIVE ACTION. THIS IS REAL."

Leo shouted, "Get me out of here! Right now! Why aren't my wishes working?"

The screen replied, "The User suspended what he referred to as the 'superflash-want-it-you-got-it mechanism.' Does he wish to terminate this suspension?"

Leo screamed at the top of his lungs, "YEESSSS!"

In that instant, he felt a slimy, at once almost metallic and yet fleshy hand grip his neck and yank him from the elevated seat of the machine down to the ground. The impact knocked the breath out of him and dulled his vision. But when his eyes came into focus, he saw the evil being's face, disfigured with open gashes and leprous malformations, gleaming in the dim light above him. The man's hands rushed forward and clinked into place around Leo's throat.

Leo grasped those horrible robotic hands and screamed in so much terror that he passed out.

The next thing he knew, he was walking through the doors into his bank in Ashlin.

Leo stopped in the entryway, hardly daring to breathe. His right hand still cradled his throat. He was dressed in a business suit once again and in his left hand carried his briefcase.

The old security man, Jim Barnes, looked up. "Howdy, Mr. Stokes. Fine day, ain't it?"

Leo looked at him and exhaled very slowly. "Yes, Jim. It certainly does seem to be a...fine day." His voice was croaking, but he didn't care. He walked through the bank, smiling at the tellers and waving to the loan officers, hoping the trembling he could not stop was not something they could see.

Once inside his office, with the door closed behind him, Leo glanced at himself in a mirror. He was still affecting the same smile he had flashed to his subordinates, and he noticed with no reaction that it was about as animated and convincing as that of an embalmed corpse. He had to remind himself to keep breathing.

Leo was now desperate not to want or wish for so much as a single thing. For a second, he wondered what had happened to the Stokes BankGlobal office, but he determinedly put his attention on the practical matters before him.

He set the briefcase down on the rug and took his seat. On his desk, Ernestine had placed a loan application from Dwayne Jedediah Tompkins, a farmer from the poorest part of the county. "Ah yes, poor old Dwayne," Leo murmured aloud, relaxing a bit—and then there was Dwayne beside him.

Leo, now in boots and jeans, was sitting with Dwayne on the front porch of his farmhouse, talking about whether he'd have to foreclose on

Dwayne's land. "Now, Jed, I'm gonna do my very best to work out another loan for you. But in large part, it depends on what kinda guarantees I can secure for fellas like yourself down in the State House next week—"

And then he was in the State House, talking with Morton Rydell, the Speaker of the Assembly and chairman of the Farm Board. Rydell suggested they go have a few drinks—which in a flash they were imbibing in a low-rent dive of the type Rydell was notorious for frequenting. Leo was looking at the go-go dancers with fascination and lust, and at the clientele, including Rydell, with revulsion, when suddenly there was a crash at the backdoor.

Everyone started shouting and screaming as axes broke through the doors. A crowd of uniformed police and undercover agents came running in, shouting, "Don't anybody move! This is a raid! You're all under arrest!"

In that moment, something in Leo began to die.

He didn't feel any fear. He didn't even feel any particular concern about his future and his reputation.

He felt numb.

Stokes BankGlobal, Cotton County Regional—whatever he was in charge of—was going to ruin now, just like Bob Jackson's bank had only days, or whatever period of time had passed, before. His demise, however, would be far slimier. He could already see the headlines in his mind's eye.

Leo let out a long, deep sigh. While the place all around him exploded in pandemonium, he could feel that, underneath everything that was happening, he was incredibly uptight. For a moment he wondered why Ultimaya hadn't yet taken this uptightness away from him; he'd certainly asked for that from the beginning. But then he questioned whether that request was really one of his "deepest wishes." He'd been so busy wishing for everything else; maybe he hadn't asked hard enough for relief from being so wound up.

Leo could also feel that, in fact, he'd always been this uptight. That terrible sense of constriction, that squeeze of the life in him…as a young police officer almost apologetically clamped handcuffs on his wrists, Leo closed his eyes and wondered if he would ever get at the root of that terrible clamp on his own life.

Then the cold metal was gone from his wrists, and his hands swung free. A rush of intensely humid air surrounded and smothered him, as if he'd walked into a steam bath. Leo opened his eyes.

He was standing in old clothes and boots in what appeared to be a tropical jungle. He looked up. The jungle canopy was so thick and stretched so high he couldn't see sky anywhere, though he could tell from the shafts of light penetrating to the jungle floor that the sun must be shining above the trees.

"What now?" he asked aloud. "Where on Earth, or wherever, could I possibly be now?"

His question reminded him of his and Charley's little chant so many years ago—"Where in God could hell possibly be?" Silence descended on the forest. He hadn't noticed the cacophony of bird and animal calls, the buzzing of insects, until now. The silence was so sudden and so complete it was as if all sound, even all possibility of sound, had been vacuumed from the environment.

A rush of terror overwhelmed Leo—and then he was lifted by a tremendous force and hurled to the ground, except he never reached the forest floor. He was rolling and roiling and turning in some gigantic coiling thing that was wrapping itself around him with monstrous power and crashing through the undergrowth along the jungle floor so swiftly that the trees, bushes, and vines all seemed to blur right past him.

Then everything once again was deathly still. Leo took a breath, as much of one as he could. He tried to look down, to take stock of his situation. He couldn't move his head or most of his body. His left hand and arm, however, were free.

Gingerly, not wanting to provoke it, he touched the thing that had encoiled him. It had gigantic...scales.

Whatever it was, the thing was breathing. He could feel its coils tighten and loosen slightly with each breath. But with each breath, it also tightened far more than it loosened on the breath before.

The moment that fateful fact became clear to him, from behind his head there was a horrible, deafening hiss, and a blast of putrid air.

"Oh, my God," Leo mumbled. "It is a goldang anaconda or something... this is not happening. This is not happening. THIS IS NOT HAPPENING!"

A familiar voice addressed him. "Yes, indeed, Mr. Stokes, dear me, you really do seem to have stumbled into quite a frightful predicament."

Leo struggled to get his head free enough to see where the voice was coming from.

There, to his amazement, not three feet away, stood Chatsworth.

Even more amazing, in the midst of this stinking, steaming jungle, the old man had a pure white linen napkin draped over his left forearm, an elegant small white tray with a white cup balanced on his upturned left palm, and not so much as a drop of sweat on his face. His brow, however, was furrowed with concern as he looked at Leo in the giant serpent's coils.

Leo tried to shout, but it came out more like a hoarse whisper: "Chatsworth! You've got to help me!"

The old man nodded gravely. "Sir, this really is a most terrifying situation you're in. I thought perhaps you'd like a spot of tea?"

Leo exploded, gasping for breath. "Chatsworth! Goldang it! I'm getting crushed to death by a forty-foot anaconda and you offer me a confounded cup of tea?"

The butler became a bit flustered. "Oh, dear, dear me, Mr. Stokes, quite right. Yes...just...well. Would you prefer something else, sir? Perhaps some...Lappert's ice cream?"

From a small table behind him he brought forth a bowl and held it up to Leo's face.

"I thought, sir, that, under these circumstances, the most appropriate flavor would be Mango. I do hope this conforms to your wishes, Mr. Stokes!"

Chatsworth was all but grinning in his pleasure at being able to serve, which, under the circumstances, struck Leo as wildly out of touch with reality. He felt the snake tighten its grip still more on him, and then grimaced as he heard and smelled another horrific hiss.

The appearance of his butler from Stokesland and their insanely insipid conversation so far stunned Leo's brain to a standstill. He closed his eyes and muttered aloud, "This cannot be happening. This cannot be happening. I just don't believe this is happening to me!"

Chatsworth whispered, "Mr. Stokes, at the risk of overstepping my prerogatives as your butler...if I may be so presumptuous as to offer a word of advice—may I suggest, sir...this may not be the ideal moment for propositions about reality and declaration of one's belief."

Leo opened his eyes. The man's face was only inches from his own. He was about to groan and berate the old fool for being such a dolt at a time like this when he noticed a curious gleam, a knowingness, an intelligence in the old man's eyes that he hadn't seen before.

Chatsworth raised one eyebrow, tilted his head, and darted a knowing glance toward the head of the snake.

Leo now realized he could move his own head slightly. He looked in the direction Chatsworth was pointing. The head of the serpent was also very close, maybe two feet away from his own.

He let out a gasp—the thing was huge!

Its head was at least two, perhaps three feet across. Its dull black eyes were empty of all life, certainly any animal warmth. Only its giant flickering tongue betrayed its awareness of him.

Then it moved closer and began to open its mouth.

Leo shrieked and closed his eyes. It was going to swallow him alive!

Chatsworth again whispered urgently, "Mr. Stokes!"

Leo felt the motion of the snake's head halt only inches away from him. He opened his eyes.

There was Chatsworth again. This time his expression was intense, fierce. He once more nodded toward the head and open mouth of the snake.

Leo looked up at it. The snake's mouth was wide open, but it did not have teeth. It didn't really have a mouth, in fact. Its tongue continued to flicker from underneath what Leo dimly perceived in the dark and dappled jungle light to be—at first he couldn't accept it, but there it was: the keyboard and monitor of a computer!

"No," Leo groaned. "Oh, no, this is not happening."

On the screen, a question flashed: "Does the User have any further wishes or questions?"

Leo mumbled. "Why is this happening to me? What is going on? Where is it leading? Am I going to die?"

A reply appeared on the screen. "The User will recall having locked the Ultimaya program into a procedure of absolute acceleration of wish-fulfillment: 'I want it,' with the following further descriptive stipulations, 'ALL,' 'BAD,' and 'NOW.' This process of acceleration, with minor permissible modifications by the User, has been in force ever since. It will necessarily proceed to termination at this time unless the User wishes to enter into a completely different context and structure of the wish-fulfillment process."

Leo felt numb. Whether from terror, exhaustion, or both, he didn't know. Or really care. He couldn't think anymore, couldn't make out what the mechanized monster meant by all that. He looked at his butler.

"Chatsworth..." he whispered, then moaned. "No idea what it means. What's it saying?"

"It is asking, Mr. Stokes, if you are ready for something, and somewhere, quite different. Remarkably different and yet, ultimately, you may find, quite the same."

"What are you saying now, Chatsworth?"

The old man lowered his gaze, flushing in the heat. "Really, Mr. Stokes, my position in service to you does not permit—"

Leo sighed loudly. "Dang it, Chatsworth, all right already. I give. Never mind explanations. Just tell me what I have to do now!"

Chatsworth smiled. Taking the crisp white hand towel from his arm, he daubed the sweat from Leo's face. He looked at him with a gaze of loving kindness.

"You have already set up the next sequence of fulfillments quite thoroughly, and you have repeatedly reinforced that request—if, indeed, one can call it such—in your own way. Given the circumstances, my dear Mr. Stokes, may I suggest...you might as well just completely relax and let go."

With sudden clarity, it dawned on Leo. His enslavement to his own endless wanting was just going to go on like this for him forever unless he did something like what Chatsworth was suggesting. He was still in the dark about plenty. He had no clue what Chatsworth meant about his having "set up the next sequence of fulfillments" and then "repeatedly reinforced" it. But he was too tired and terrified to care.

What Leo did know—well, he had a pretty strong hunch by now— was that from now on his every impulse, fascination, even every perception or act of attention—who knew, maybe even every slightest wavering of awareness—was going to spit out an instantaneous or at least extremely fast fulfillment and then be followed by a whole train of inexplicable events. And he knew, or at least now surmised, that not even a shred of it was going to satisfy him permanently, because, in the world of Ultimaya anyway, nothing ever lasted.

Leo found it all revolting even to think about. Every next fulfillment of his wishes was immediately all over him like a very heavy and horny woman. It was like he was fighting his way through the billowing flesh of his own random desires, wishes, perceptions, and noticings. All of it was now coming to some weird fruition just about instantly and then dissolving just that fast, yielding to the next random impulse and then the whole rest of the cycle, all over again.

Now here he was in this unlocatable jungle—he would've lost big bets if it were ever proved to be anywhere on physical Earth— crystallizing dreams like a queen termite on opium popping out one little baby mite after another. The whole cycle was getting sickening to him.

The snake now seemed to embody all his desires and whatever in Creation prompted them—all of the roiling, monstrous machinery of his "wishes" had him endlessly trapped, imprisoned, constricted, and encoiled. And then the fulfillments—so fast, so intense, he barely enjoyed them for an instant before they were gone and the dreadful, stinking cousins of their consequences were all over him.

If there was anything Leo wanted right in that moment, it was summarized in one word: *out!*

But since there looked like absolutely nothing he could do to extricate himself from this maze, he figured he might as well listen to somebody else. For a change.

Leo sighed again, so deep his chest almost rumbled with it. "All right, old friend. Whatever you say."

He closed his eyes. Within seconds, everything fell away. The feeling of the giant snake's coils. The jungle. All awareness of Chatsworth, of his own body, his mind, his fear, his bone-grinding tiredness. He was falling into a depth of something beyond sleep, beyond unconsciousness, beyond anything he'd ever known or imagined before.

Except soon he wasn't even there to notice anything about it.

He was gone.

"Go with the Program!"

Leo came to consciousness lying on a bare hillside in broad daylight. He wasn't sure where this place was—but then, he hadn't been too godalmighty sure where he was, or when he was, through so many sequences of time and place, that there was no longer any way he could get his bearings.

The ground on the hillside felt like soil. The grass smelled like grass. Blue sky, one sun, clear light, a cold breeze—he seemed to be somewhere on Earth. But he had seemed to be somewhere on Earth everywhere and "everywhen" else he'd been too. He couldn't trust any appearances any more.

For some reason, Leo was struggling to catch his breath, and he felt his hands and feet becoming unbearably cold. He wanted to rub his palms together to generate some warmth, but discovered he couldn't move his arms. Then he tried moving his legs. Nothing happened. Then his head, then his lips—then he realized he couldn't even close his eyes. They weren't blinking naturally either. They began to ache.

His stare was fixed on a granitic hillside off to the right where his head was turned. He lay under an icy sun, the cold now starting to stream up his arms and legs. "Good God A'mighty! I must be dying!" His mind raced, trying to come up with some way he might survive.

Then something appeared in his field of vision that diverted his attention. A vague spot of light appeared to be forming before him, scintillating as though with many-colored electronic pulses of energy. Suddenly, with a whistle and a pop, a man was standing before him, looking into his eyes.

The man's gaze was so arresting that Leo couldn't break away from it to look at his other features or his body. (Then he recalled that he couldn't move his eyeballs in any case.) In his peripheral vision, though, he could see that the fellow appeared to be an Indian or some other kind of Asian, with long, brown-black hair pulled back in a ponytail, what appeared to be stripes of ash smeared across his forehead, and a full navy blue, pin-striped Western business suit, complete with a white shirt and a bright red tie.

"A yogi in a power suit. Gotta be kidding me," Leo thought.

There was a glint to the man's gaze that reminded Leo of something or someone; he didn't know what or who.

"You seem to be dying."

The yogi's voice boomed all around Leo, though he didn't notice the man so much as open his mouth. The voice was also familiar, but how or why, Leo couldn't fathom. It didn't seem to be particularly Indian or Asian.

In any case, the yogi's matter of fact comment annoyed him. "Brilliant deduction, Sherlock," Leo thought.

"I don't think you can afford such foolish, snide communication at this stage of your quest," the voice boomed again. The yogi smiled and raised an eyebrow, his eyes twinkling.

Leo was angry. He surely didn't want to die, and he felt he'd been totally ripped off by Ultimaya 1.0. In the silence of his own brain, he shouted, "Then get your goldang ears outta my brain matter, butthead, and you won't get no communication whatsoever!"

He was in no mood for conversation. The cold had now numbed both arms and legs and he felt it rising up through his stomach and vital organs toward his heart.

The yogi lowered his eyebrow and the sparkle went out of his eyes. He folded his arms across his chest. Leo noticed that the yogi's cuff links had the same luster as the engagement ring for Constance; the two studs gleamed.

Leo suddenly remembered he was still, or once again, wearing the blue silk evening jacket he had on when he first entered the tunnel in Stokesland. And, though he couldn't move to touch it, he could feel the jewelry box in a pocket underneath his body. The front of his jacket must have gotten partially twisted under him, so he was lying on the pocket with the box and ring in it.

The man's voice boomed forth again, this time seemingly from a sensitive point right smack in the middle of Leo's brain.

"Stop being an idiot. You are dying. Do you want to die?"

"'Scuse me, Sirrrrr"—Leo kept that word going in his head for several seconds, drawing it out in defiant mock deference—"but I ain't noticed I got any say in the matter."

The yogi looked to one side, his eyes flashing. "White boys," his voice rang out in Leo's brain. "Insolent fools. Stupid, arrogant fools. Know what I mean, Mistuh Stokes, suh?"

He turned his gaze back to Leo, his glance again riveting Leo's motionless eyes to his own.

It was then that Leo recognized him. "Wait a minute!" he yelled inwardly. "Are you—you're Joseph, aren't you?"

"'At yo' suhvice, Mistuh Stokes, suh.'" Each mocking word cut into Leo like the blade of a saw.

Even so, knowing it was actually his trusty chauffeur from Stokesland standing here before him in this godforsaken, freezing place gave him a surge of hope.

"Joseph, what in God's name is happening? Where am I? Is this the border between the worlds? It's so unbelievably cold! It must be way on up north somewhere. But what's going on? Please, Joseph, I beg you, man, you've got to help me!"

The glint in the Indian Joseph's eye did not soften, nor did he uncross his arms. His voice was acid. "I am under the clear impression that you have already received all necessary answers to most of these questions. As for helping you, that is precisely what I am employed to do. In fact, as it happens, at present I have no existence except in service to you. To me, however"—there was a pause, during which Leo realized that Joseph's voice piercing his brain was giving him a searing headache—"this service is merely and only a job. This is just a job for me, 'Mistuh Stokes, suh!'

"You could say this is north—but in relation to where? Could it be 'the border between the worlds'? That depends on you, 'suh.' Maybe you're north of that border, and maybe you're not. Or maybe this border has no sides, no spatial configurations, no vector or direction. You did wonder what I meant when I said I am from 'the Deep North.' Maybe now even that wish has been fulfilled—you've found out. Then again, maybe not…

"In any case this is not Stokesland and I am not 'Joseph Fetchit,' Mistuh Stokes, suh. I am still doing the driving, but now it appears I am the one who determines our destinations. If, indeed, you are going to proceed any further at all."

All through this speech Joseph had continued to fix Leo's gaze with his own. Leo felt the man's eyes were drilling into the core of his soul. Now he looked away again, his crossed arms confirming to Leo, along with his tone of voice and his business suit, just how much the power dynamics between the two of them had changed.

"Curious turn of events, wouldn't you say, Leopold? Of course, you don't mind, surely, if I address you by your first name, do you, Leopold? I am not your nigger anymore, not your servant. I am not anything you can even imagine. But I am here to serve you…if you will simply *cooperate.*"

Leo was still raging inside. But he knew he needed help and that he had not the slightest leverage for negotiating. He thought, "Okay, then, dang it. What do I have to do to proceed further?"

Joseph's voice softened. "From the moment Ultimaya 1.0 began to communicate with you, you have frequently muttered invocations to 'God,' 'Jesus,' or 'Lord,' usually preceded or followed by colloquial honorifics, such as 'Good,' 'A'mighty,' 'Dear.' In your speech patterns, these are hardly more than exclamations of surprise. You bring no heart to them, no ardor, no sacred intent, no true need for grace.

"Nonetheless, they are prayers of a sort. And you have, in general inadvertently, offered them frequently, as a kind of communication in code to a greater reality.

"If you are to proceed in this life beyond this crisis, you must become serious. You must learn sacred intention. You must give your life to that greater reality, to that God—however, and by whatever name, you sincerely want to address, approach, and know Him, or Her, or It."

Leo despaired. Images and words from his apparently religious exclamations, particularly right after Nan's spontaneous combustion, flashed through his mind. He almost wanted to cry.

"Joseph," he thought, feeling like he was about to break open with sadness, "you know me. You know I am not a religious man. You know my churchgoing is basically a business investment. Shoot, I even write off the time I spend there—at an inflated hourly rate! You gotta be kidding me. I can't do what you're saying. It's just not in me."

Joseph's voice in his mind felt like it sliced through his whole body. "Listen to me, you ass. I am not talking about churchgoing. Where we are heading, should you choose to come with me, there are no churches remotely like anything you have known. I am not talking about childish games of superficial belief and imaginary salvation played by fools who know neither themselves nor their so-called 'Lord'! The real God knows real believers in their hearts and souls—even in churches of the kind you desecrated with your crass, hypocritical presence. You've been nothing but a moneychanger, Leopold Stokes. Now look at what has happened to your table in the temple."

Leo listened, dimly remembering stories from the New Testament. But he was in agony. The cold was becoming so painful, it felt white-hot. And now it was spreading all over his body. Even his lips seemed frozen shut, and his tongue felt like a log of immovable ice in his mouth. The only parts of him that still held any warmth were his heart and lungs.

Joseph continued speaking in Leo's brain, his own lips compressed, a fury coming through his words. "You are dying. I ask you again. Do you want to die?"

Everything below Leo's chest felt as frozen as his head and face. The cold began to penetrate his lungs. He could still hear distinctly, but his vision started to fade in and out. He felt like a human iceberg.

Then he began to sense a building motion, somewhere in him; maybe it was in his soul. It was like a wave starting to form and crest rapidly toward some unknown shoreline, as if his spirit were about to crash and burst out the top of his head.

Leo knew if he allowed himself to go with that wave, he would certainly die.

He heard again from the yogi. "So?"

Leo felt something give way in his heart. If his tear ducts could respond to his feelings, he would have wept. Words formed clearly and with great emotion in his mind. "No, I don't want to die. I really don't want to die. But I don't know what to do. Am I supposed to ask this 'God' I don't even believe in for help? Tell me what to do, Joseph. I'll try my best. I promise."

Now he could no longer see anything at all, but the yogi's voice was louder and more clear. It had a metallic or electronic ring to it, and was still broadcasting to him from a point somehow more intimate to his sense of being than the place where he was hearing it. This too made a kind of innate, nonsensical sense to Leo; it seemed absurdly appropriate even as he lay there knowing he was dying. But that whole reflection slipped by as he contemplated the yogi's offer.

"You do not have to die if you do not want to. Not now. Your acknowledgment of your need and your weakness before God is itself the simplest prayer for divine help. You will learn more later. You will also be tested. To continue, however, there will be a price."

193

Leo sighed. "I'll pay it. What is it? What do I have to do? I can't do anything anymore with my body. What do you want? What do you mean?"

"You have to be willing," Joseph's voice intoned, "to give up everything. And you have to come with me into my world, which has a different time scale from yours. You have to spend one night and one day with me there."

"No problem!" Leo practically screamed inside. "No dang problem! What world? Where? But no, that's okay, I'll go anywhere with you. Just don't let me die. Please, thaw me out. I feel like I'm about to go—please, I'll do whatever you want."

There was a turbulent silence in the center of Leo's brain and all around. Then another voice broke through into his mind.

"Not so fast, old bud! I don't know about this sucker."

It was Charley!

"Charley! Where are you, Mountain Man? God, I can't believe you're here, but where are you? What's happening, Charley?"

Again, the weird turbulence without a sound. No sight. No feeling, no sensation. The wave in him pressing fiercely upward to break, Leo struggling, with no energy left in him to hold it back, like a dog barking at a tidal wave, somehow miraculously holding it at bay for one more instant at a time, then another, then the next …

And then he felt the tension and pressure ease, ease, ease on down.

There was a tingle of warmth on his face.

His vision started coming into focus.

The arctic grip of cold all over his body retreated like a tide, in waves, and he began to breathe again.

As the cold dispersed into his further extremities, he realized he could move his head—just as two forms came into visual focus.

One was the yogi, Joseph.

And the other was Charley!

Leo was so overjoyed he began to weep. He opened his mouth to call out to his friend. But then he saw, felt, or understood—it was another of those now commonplace, absurdly normal, bizarre things about what was happening here; but however he knew it, it was obvious to him—Charley and Joseph were locked in some kind of fierce argument or invisible combat.

Neither of them moved. Neither of them spoke. Yet it was like they were hurling javelins of fire at each other.

If Leo had enough strength he would have tried to crawl away—the fury between the two men felt like it was escalating into an almost nuclear confrontation.

Then, just as suddenly, it died away.

Charley looked at Leo with a frown. He opened his mouth—Leo was relieved to see a man start to speak out loud for a change—and said, "Well, Stokes, you've gone and done it this time. Deal's a deal. But you can trust him. He's a good man."

Leo nodded weakly. But a terrible foreboding stole into his heart and the pit of his stomach. He too now could speak aloud. "Do I have to, Charley?"

"Yep. This is it. The border between the worlds. You got no choice. You already signed up."

"But what's gonna happen to me, Charley?"

Leo's friend looked at him in angry disbelief. "How am *I* supposed to know, Stokes? I already told you, I'm outta my league in this mess of yours. I did the best I could for you. That's all. From here on—who knows, buddy roe?"

Leo panicked. "Charley! Come on, man! You gotta help me. I don't want to go! Help me out here, Charley!"

Charley yelled at the top of his lungs, "Leo, it's too late! Shut up! Just go with the program!"

Then Charley turned back to Joseph, and their silent, motionless, somehow visibly ferocious interchange resumed. Leo had no idea what was happening. A sense of dread enveloped him like a demonic wraith. He felt immobilized, rooted to the spot.

With mute agony, he watched Joseph lift his arm with seeming nonchalance, point at Charley, and flick his index finger. A bolt of energy sizzled at light speed into Charley's solar plexus. Then, while Leo looked on in disbelieving horror, Charley started to curl and burn from his feet up, like a six-foot-six sheet of tinder-dry parchment. In an instant the flames consumed him. Leo saw a last grimace of inconceivable pain on his dear friend's face.

Then even his drifting ashes disappeared from sight.

Joseph then turned to Leo, who stiffened with fright—until the man smiled at him. His smile, in fact, was so plainly sweet that Leo was disarmed. Despite his fear, he couldn't help but grin back. Once again, Joseph's voice—there sure wasn't anyone else around to talk, though Joseph's mouth was not opening—boomed at Leo from every direction: "He could not have come where you have asked me to take you. Don't be perturbed. He lives on elsewhere, in another form. He's okay."

Leo was still troubled. "But you killed him!"

Joseph's raised a warning eyebrow at Leo. His voice boomed again, in measured, somehow quiet tones: "The time has come."

At first Joseph's calm friendliness, along with Charley's assurance to him before burning up and dematerializing, soothed Leo a little. But then Joseph's meaning sunk in.

Leo felt another wave of fright. "Is this really necessary?"

The man's eyes flashed. "No further negotiation is possible. Any further attempts will not stand you in good stead."

"But I don't want to go."

"Nonsense! You insisted on it."

"When? What do you mean? *I did not!*"

Joseph glared at him. Without will or effort, Leo shut his eyes. Instantly, as if in an open space in the middle of his brain, he saw what appeared to be a computer screen. A blast of colors played on it, and then words appeared one letter at a time:

"I beg…to differ…'Mistuh Stokes…suh.'"

Leo's heart felt like it was being squeezed in a vise. "Oh no," he murmured inwardly. Sure enough, as he continued to view the vision in his brain, the letters in the sentence on the screen began clicking off audibly one at a time, leaving only, first, the "s" in "suh," and then…the "b" in "beg." Then all the other letters disappeared in a flash.

Leo read aloud in his mind what he saw on the screen. "B-S," he gasped in silence. "I don't believe it. This can't be happening to me *again*." He felt so much rage and helplessness at the same time that his body shook and shuddered. "I don't understand," he beamed angrily in his mind.

"Then it's a good thing you don't need to understand," Joseph's voice replied. "The time has come."

"All right," Leo muttered inside. Charley, after all, had told him to "go with the program." Strange—plain old weird, in fact—that Charley Bass would ever say such a thing about any commands from Ultimaya's direction. But he had said it, so Leo supposed Charley's encouragement made it okay. He felt a pang of excruciating pain in his solar plexus. "Oh my God," he thought. "I've just been the cause of yet another horrible death of someone I love who loves me. Why is this happening to me? What in God's good Creation have I done that I keep causing pain and death to people I love, and who knows who else? And keep getting out-negotiated by a goldang computer!"

Then, in a moment even more stark, so focused with simultaneous insights and understandings that Leo felt like he was being lifted into an eternal vortex of meaning in his own mind, Leo caught on. At least, so he thought.

"Wait a minute," he shouted inside to Joseph. "Wait just a goldang minute! You *are* Ultimaya, aren't you?"

Joseph betrayed no sign of acknowledgment. "That is an extremely simplistic way of understanding your situation. Stop thinking and come with me."

But Leo was consumed by everything he was beginning to comprehend. "No way! Wait a minute! *You are Ultimaya 1.0 in person,* and you are responsible for all this. For everything that's happened. Not only that, you reneged on our agreement! You *promised* no one close to me would be hurt!"

"Correct. And?"

"You lied! Look at what you just did to Charley Bass!"

Now Joseph scowled. "You, Leopold Stokes, are a fool who sees very little and understands even less. Nonetheless, in time everything will be made plain, even to you. It might take an eternity, though. You're a touch on the—how'd your Shakespeare put it?—'beef-witted' side."

Joseph flashed Leo a friendly grin.

Molten Fog and
Significant Differences

The question, "*My* Shakespeare?" flashed through Leo's mind—but he quickly forgot it. Suddenly he was rising and moving again, though just how was kind of strange. It seemed like he just flowed up to a vertical position and then kept on flowing toward Joseph, without moving any muscles and without even the slightest sense of wanting or trying to on any level. Joseph then began flowing with him toward the hill a few yards away. Just as they reached the rock escarpment at its base, two images hit Leo at once with equal force, so he couldn't make out whether they were things he was seeing or things he was imagining.

One was the visual image in his mind that however he was locomoting himself, he appeared to have the consistency and mobility of heavy fog moving over a hillside. He knew somehow that he still looked like himself, but now he was like the fogs he'd once seen when traveling with his parents, decades ago, along the California coastline.

The second thing he saw, or maybe imagined, was behind him. Leo wasn't looking backward, but now he seemed (and what was weird was how normal it felt to him) to have natural 360-degree vision anyway. And that second thing he saw or imagined at precisely

199

the same moment was his own physical body lying behind him, looking distinctly—no, unmistakably—dead.

Whether he saw or imagined it, Leo had no time to react to that image, because in the next instant he felt himself and Joseph passing into the hill through a wall of what appeared to be solid granite. For the barest moment, it was as if they were being strained through a giant, dark sieve. Then suddenly they oozed out into a vast and glorious landscape. Leo felt himself continuing to move like fog, though now he had the sense that he was almost a molten form.

"Molten fog!" he thought. "Who ever heard of such a thing?"

A sudden breeze twisted his garment along the side of his thigh. He looked down to see that from the waist down he was garbed in a flowing garment so white it shone of its own luster. In fact, it was a robe covering his whole body. "Here we go, getting tacky spiritual again," he thought, but then he felt distinctly that thinking such things was way out of place here. What Leo was wearing came with the place he was in and the way he was moving through it.

What made all this all the more ludicrous, yet also quite sensible to him—Leo was starting to notice that things were making complete sense to him that in his ordinary world would have been altogether bizarre— was something else he noticed he was wearing. Over the shining robe on his upper body was the jacket of blue silk that had become, for him, the uniform of his adventure.

He oozed his hand into the right pocket of the jacket—now that was a strange and perfectly normal sensation, both at once—and sure enough, the box was still there. He pried it open with his fingers. The ring was still there too. Feeling it snugly in his pocket made him more comfortable, though he hadn't exactly felt uncomfortable before, about vibrating through space and hillsides like molten fog—until he turned to speak to Joseph moving beside him.

Then he saw that Joseph was gone. Or else he'd been transformed beyond recognition.

Moving along beside Leo now was a woman of unimaginable beauty, clad in a shining garment like his own—but she appeared to be about forty times the size of a normal human being!

Leo let out a squawk of fear. In his mind—he was now accustomed to telepathic talking—he shouted, "What happened to Joseph? Who are you? Are you Joseph? Where are we going? Why is this happening?"

The giant woman turned her face toward him. She opened her mouth, so that he expected her to speak, but then the mouth just kept on opening.

In seconds, her mouth became a huge chasm that soon surrounded him and even contained all space, so that now Leo was hovering there in what seemed to be an endless void.

Leo was petrified: open-mouthed himself, and bug-eyed with shock and dread.

In the depths of the darkness before him, he saw a bright, rectangular object coming toward him. He squinted to make out what it was. Then he sighed, with something like the rattle of a dying man's last breath.

It was a computer screen.

On it he could now see two questions flashing, the second just below the first, mimicking his own.

"What happened to Charley?"

"Are you Nan?"

Without waiting for Leo even to try to formulate a response in his mind, the screen emptied and then a new question appeared: "Is the User certain he wishes to proceed along such lines of questioning?"

Leo got the hint—or so he felt. He screamed inwardly, "No! No way! No, I don't want to ask those questions at all. Furthest things from my mind. Uh-uh! No way!"

Instantly the vision of nothingness dissolved, and he was in the air flowing alongside the glorious giant woman again. He breathed a raspy sigh of relief. Then he looked at her again. Her face and form were beautiful, though not in any way that might arouse a sexual response in him. Besides, she was way too big.

Leo asked, in a soft voice and with genuine humility, "Are you a god? Should I worship you?"

The woman turned her head slightly toward him and her voice resounded around him, as Joseph's had before: "No. I am a goddess. *You* are a god. There are a number of important differences." She smiled and a twinkle shot from her huge eyes into his, seeming to melt his heart. "And I will tell you what you should do."

It was a bizarre, weird, and wonderful thing, but Leo actually tasted her voice in his brain. It had the flavor of an unimaginably delicious ambrosia. Still, what she actually said bewildered him. "What?" Leo thought. "I'm a god? No offense meant, but that's the craziest thing I've ever heard."

"Perhaps, but it is true nonetheless. At least, potentially, while you are in my world, it is true."

The goddess smiled at him. He had the palpable sensation of her radiance bleaching his mind with some kind of nearly liquid joy.

She continued. "Then again, if you attain a realization of this truth, you won't be able to find much difference between my world and yours.

"Of course, you will have to pass your tests. Which, given your history..." She shrugged, raising her eyebrows. Then she smiled again, her giant eyes like beacons.

Leo sighed. So much was happening so fast, he could make little sense of any of it.

He and the goddess continued to waft and vibrate across the landscape until they reached a high plateau. There they both spontaneously stopped.

The goddess turned to him once more and spoke again in his mind. "Ordinarily, beings must become great saints or mystics to enter this realm, at least in the manner we have. In your case, certain allowances were made—though not on account of any virtue of your own." She beamed with brilliant sweetness.

"Your willingness to open to whatever God can be for you certainly had a part in the postponement of your death and your entry here. What you do while you are here will determine your further progress. What you aspire to will determine what you do. And what you are, the nature and quality of your being, will determine your level of aspiration. Unless, of course, you allow a different principle, which humans sometimes call grace, to change what you are in the deepest, core dimension of your nature."

Then there was silence. Yet curiously, Leo knew that this remarkable being's communication was continuing.

He silently heard or felt her confirm to him that he was still in process with the accelerating fulfillment of his deepest wishes. He was still engaged in active interplay with Ultimaya 1.0 (for which, or for whom, he felt increasingly awed respect). And, he would do well not to assume that the goddess now before him was herself Ultimaya, any more than Joseph had allowed him such simplistic ideas.

Yet it was confirmed that, in communicating with her, he was also communicating directly with, or to, Ultimaya 1.0. He would do well, he felt her implying, to maintain focus on what would be presented to him and not waste time speculating about the nature or significance of other beings and events he encountered.

Leo was listening with his whole soul and every fiber of his body. He felt like his brain was about to melt or, recalling his visions of Nan not so long ago, spontaneously combust. He had a fleeting remembrance of himself when he first took an advanced accounting class for which he turned out to have been quite ill prepared. He'd managed to muddle through, but not without feeling like a dunce most of the time.

The goddess's voice interrupted his recollection. Now she was speaking aloud, through her mouth. "There," she pointed.

Off in the distance was what appeared to be a city.

"What do you see?"

Gazing at the faraway place, Leo discovered he was seeing, or feeling, every single one of its inhabitants—human and animal. In fact, he was even aware of all the mineral and vegetal life forms, and also what he gathered were spirits without visible forms or bodies, a whole teeming mass of all kinds of beings. What was more, he was somehow conscious of the thoughts, feelings, histories, and even destinies of each and every one, all at once!

He could not speak. The vision was at once sublime and harsh, stark, both blissful and painful to an extreme.

He felt the goddess's pleasure and sensed she knew what he was experiencing.

"You see?" she asked, once again from the core of his brain—maybe from the center of his heart and soul, the words were so intimate to his feeling of being himself. "I told you, in this world, you are a god. At least, for now. Potentially."

Leo nodded and turned again to gaze into the heart of life in the distant city. He could not tell where it was, but he had the feeling it must be a real place, a place in his real world, somewhere on Earth.

A sense of dignity and peace came over him, and a serene curiosity. He became aware that, while conscious of all the beings and things there, all at once, he could also focus his attention on one person or a few or even gatherings of people. And that, still maintaining a thread of diffuse or all-embracing attention, he could in many ways help individuals and influence them to do things that were best for themselves and also for others, for everyone, for life.

He saw that this world was at least not unlike that of the Earth, if it was not actually on his home planet. People here looked and acted like Earth-bound human beings. They had the same problems, the same fascinations, the same illnesses, elations, pleasures, pains, desires, reactions, and setbacks.

His attention drifted into what appeared to be a hospital. An old man was gasping for breath on an operating table. Leo sensed the doctors and nurses were so distracted by the complexity of the surgery they were performing that they weren't noticing their patient's labored breathing. By simple will, he influenced one of the nurses to look up and see the patient's endangered condition. She quickly administered oxygen—or whatever kind of air these people breathed—and the old man's breath and heart rate steadied again.

A shiver of compassion mingled with pride ran through Leo. He felt he could do more, so much more. It was strange. He had never before just done things for others, without thought of himself.

With his clairvoyant vision, he scanned the streets of the city. A crying child caught his attention. A lovely little girl, about eight or nine years old, she was sitting in a bedroom, weeping bitterly. In another room in the apartment, her parents were having a vicious argument. The man was slapping the woman, hard, and she was vainly trying to protect herself and fight back. They were both shouting curses at each other.

"The pain and blame game," Leo thought, sadly. "Same horrors everywhere."

He became aware of invisible mechanisms above the man's and the woman's heads, which he could see were actually extending up from their hearts. He saw that they might, just might, be receptive to a silent communication of love, empathy, remorse, forgiveness, and peace.

From his heart—he had never done anything like this before, but the ability was suddenly obvious to him—Leo radiated tenderness and tranquility to the two adults.

For a moment they seemed oblivious, continuing their verbal and physical strife. Their tempest of hatred seemed to rage even more. Leo didn't know what else to do, so he just persisted in sending them blessings.

Then, maybe under the influence of his benediction, they began to calm down. The man stopped slapping the woman. She stopped screaming curses.

Leo kept blessing them silently. The thought flashed through his mind that he didn't even care whether his intention was actually causing them to be more peaceful. He was just grateful they weren't fighting any more.

The two adults became quiet, and then aware of their daughter, weeping in the nearby room. They looked at each other with tears in their eyes, wounded and abashed, even ashamed. No words said, they tentatively reached out to touch each other, then fell into one another's arms. Leo could hear their whispers of apology and forgiveness.

Then they rushed to their daughter. The mother swept the child up in her arms, and the father encircled both of them with his. The parents told her they were sorry and promised never to do that again—to each other, or to her.

Leo was moved by what he saw happening, yet also by what he could see would likely happen in their future. He could feel the very impulses that had produced their battle would likely produce another, soon enough. But maybe they had learned a little something. Maybe next time they'd be able to catch themselves earlier, and to prevent an argument or disagreement or hurt from becoming a violent emotional, verbal, and physical conflict.

Once again, as he drew his attention out to the larger field of the whole city and all its inhabitants, a surge of potency shot through Leo's heart. What blessings he could bring to all these people! How much he could help them in the midst of all their struggles and travail!

Scanning far and wide again, he became sensitive to a crack forming in the dam of a reservoir high above the city. He perceived that if unattended, this hairline crack would soon enough lead to a major collapse of the dam, flooding the entire area and killing perhaps tens of thousands of people, not to mention who knows how many other living creatures.

Leo activated his newfound clairvoyant vision and psychic sensitivity again, though not without a moment of slight embarrassment at himself. "Shoot," he thought, "I must think I'm Superman or something. But what am I gonna do? Someone's got to handle this. If I don't, who will?"

With his visual power—"I guess it is something like X-ray vision!"— he penetrated the control center of the dam. There he quickly located the bank of machinery the technicians used to monitor all of the dam's technological functions. Leo saw a row of television screens hooked up to other dials and monitors. He sensed these devices were used to gauge the strength and integrity of the huge dam's hundreds of thousands or maybe even millions of cubic feet of concrete wall. One of the screens was out of order, flashing distorted images.

Through sheer mental and heartfelt intention, Leo generated a terrific force of light and electronic energy that reactivated the internal circuitry of the screen. Within seconds, it began to function again. In less than another minute, two of the technicians noticed it—and saw what it was now clearly revealing: the section of the dam it was monitoring had a crack widening and lengthening so fast they could see it happening right in front of them.

Shouting to their team, the technicians also alerted their supervisors, who put the entire staff on red alert. Within minutes, work was under way to repair the crack before it could lead to catastrophe.

Still focused with his clairvoyant vision there in the command control room, Leo was happy and proud, but then he noticed that the same screen appeared to go dead. No one at the site saw it. He looked closely, and the screen blazed back into colorful activity. Then it went white. On it, these words appeared in stark black print: "Welcome to Stokes LightGlobal."

Leo wasn't sure he understood what was happening, except he had a feeling something was not quite right. Some kind of point was being made to him once again, that he felt for sure. He deactivated his all-seeing vision and soon found himself again on the plateau, with just his ordinary senses and the sense of his body and mind intact for the moment.

He was standing next to the giant goddess. She towered above him, so that he had to lean way back just to look up at her face.

She was regarding him with a gaze that combined compassion and exasperation. "You have not yet noticed, have you, Mr. Stokes?"

She was speaking to him telepathically again. He replied in the same way.

"Noticed what? What do you mean? I was doing those people some good, wasn't I?"

The goddess-woman sighed, and the rush of her breath down at him nearly knocked Leo to the ground. "All right," she continued. "Here." She pointed to a snow-covered peak in another direction. "And what do you see over there?"

Leo looked at the peak and in a second felt with startled certainty that he was in complete communion with the spirit of the mountain, and could therefore achieve any kind of change in it he wished. With the power of a single thought, he unleashed a remote avalanche, which he instantly recognized would have occurred with more force at a later date, perhaps endangering people and livestock in the valleys.

With another thought, he caused a rainstorm on the high ridges, complete with thunder and lightning. He couldn't help thinking to himself, "Hm, got a Zeus thing going on here now!"

He turned to the goddess. A deep confidence came over him, a sense of tremendous capability. He knew without doubt he had similar control over all the other natural forces of this entire world.

"Yes," he thought to her. "I see."

"No, not yet," she replied. "Perhaps you'll do better if we lift the angle of vision."

She pointed to the sun.

With his extraordinary new sight, Leo clearly perceived that the star in this world was actually made of a nearly infinite number of beings of light. They radiated such tremendous intensity of brightness and heat that their physical expression sustained all life in that solar system.

An unimaginable longing to be among them consumed Leo's heart— and in a flash there he was!

Leo's physical body, like those of his innumerable, radiant companions, was a literal beacon of most intensely pleasurable light, love, and joy. He turned to thank his companion goddess lady-friend and mentor, and he saw that she, along with all the other inhabitants of this solar world, had become so effulgent that, even in his own exalted condition, he could not bear to view her for more than a few instants at a time.

The songs, chants, and sounds of their celebration sounded to him like truly celestial music. His ears, refined as they now were, began to nearly ache with pleasure. As he glanced again at the goddess's eyes, Leo felt himself lifted out of his light body at a phenomenal speed. He appeared to be shooting upward in a more fully psychic, energetic, or spiritual form.

Suddenly, he heard what seemed to him the most beautiful peal of heavenly trumpets he had ever heard or could ever possibly hear. Then he felt pressed upward by the current of light so powerfully that all awareness of himself in any limited form or feeling dissolved. In a millisecond, Leopold Stokes was poofed, diffused, vacuumed into boundless mystery beyond all form, all light and darkness, all sense of limitation and fear, an inconceivably blissful joy and potency beyond every kind of time and space.

How long he remained vanished into that mystery, he would never know. At some point he felt himself shooting back into his own bodily condition. In a final flash of radiance, he was back on the plateau in the ordinary world again.

The stellar world of heavenly joy and celebration was gone. It was dusk, or maybe dawn. The immense godlike woman, whose name he did not know, stood beside him. She smiled. He could easily look at her face, though it still had a supernal glow. Neither of them spoke for a long time.

Finally, Leo broadcast a question to her. "Was that what Charley used to call 'the vision of God?'"

She turned to him with a glance of deep tranquility. Her voice resounded around and within him. "It was one of many possible visions of God. A splendid one. This is another. What sight anywhere in any world, Leopold Stokes, is not a vision of God?"

Leo wasn't quite sure what she meant, but he marveled at what had occurred. It seemed to him he could have stayed there on that plateau forever, when he put his hand into the right pocket of his evening jacket—"Still wearing this dang thing through all of this!"—and inadvertently touched the black velveteen jewelry box with Constance's ring in it.

In that moment, a crush of sorrow and longing of a different kind overwhelmed him. If only Constance could be with him now.

And Charley.

And Nan.

Then he knew even that was not what he really desired.

He wanted to be with them.

Where *they* were.

He didn't want to stay in this world. Powers or no powers. Visions of solar glory and ecstatic unity with God, or not.

He just wanted to be back with the people he loved.

The goddess gazed at him. He knew she knew what he was feeling. She told him, "You have experienced a little. And you can do a few things, for now anyway. But you comprehend so very little. And you have transcended even less. In any case, no one stays here forever. And your day and night here are over."

Then the mysterious being laughed. Her laughter rang through every part of his being, at once washing away a feeling of guilt in him and filling him with deep sadness.

She looked into Leo's eyes again. Her expression remained impassive, but now her voice began to sound like a high electronic imitation of... suddenly he recognized who. She sounded just like a salty, God-in-Heaven version of Nan. "By the way, young man, you did fail all your tests. I suggest next time around you find yourself some qualified help on Earth, where you can actually use it.

"Leopold Stokes, bless your heart, you surely are one dang fool cracker, if ever ah seen one!" She flicked a finger at him.

In a flash, he was back outside the hill. He was now lying on another nearby hilltop, barren and exposed to a merciless summer sun. He felt parched. He tried to rise but found he could not. He had no strength in his limbs. Leo seemed to recall having felt this way before, not so long ago. But he didn't have the strength to focus his mind on remembering when, or where. He looked down and saw that, except for his blue silk jacket, he was naked.

Then he knew—there came that feeling of "again" again—that he was dying. Not only that, from the condition of his arms, legs, and torso, and based on how he felt, it seemed to him he must be terribly old. With one trembling, arthritic hand, he reached up painfully to feel his head and his face.

There was no hair on his head—not one. And his face was a mass of wrinkled, wizened, ancient skin.

Leo was glad he had no way of seeing his reflection. He felt, and felt he must look, like he was ninety-nine years old. A hundred and ten. Way old.

Through rheumy eyes—Leo wondered if he had cataracts—he looked around him. The landscape was unfamiliar. Off in the distance, down the hillsides and dozens of miles away, as best he could make out, there appeared to be a city. It was unrecognizable to him, with buildings of many shapes he'd never seen before, sprawling beside a river.

He felt a sudden whoosh of air around his head from above, and a huge shadow flitted past. He looked up. Vultures circled in lazy arcs above and around him.

From below a rise, a man appeared and began walking toward him. Soon he recognized Joseph, who now had the African-American features by which Leo had known him in Stokesland. But he was dressed in the business suit and still wore the stripes of ash across his forehead that Leo had first seen at the border between the worlds—or wherever it was he'd first shown up that way.

Leo tried to shout to him, but the words came out like a croaking whisper. "Joseph, thank God you're here! Am I dreaming or what?"

Joseph's face betrayed no emotion and he did not open his mouth; his voice boomed internally in Leo's mind as before. "No, but you're not exactly what I'd call awake either."

Leo croaked again, "Then where am I?"

Now the yogi smiled with closed lips. "Ah, that, my non-friend, is a whole other question. As usual."

Leo was desperate. He didn't want any more telepathic conversation.

He wished the man would just talk to him.

He wheezed, "Where am I? Where is Stokesland? Ashlin? Cotton County? I feel like I'm dying. You've got to help me!"

Joseph looked away as his voice rang out inside Leo. "I told you that my universe operates on a different scale of time. One hundred and twenty thousand years have passed in the world you call by long-ago names."

Leo bleated, "A hundred and twenty thousand years!" His heart sank so fast and so far, it might as well have just been torpedoed. Leo was beyond despair. "Ultimaya 1.0 promised me that if I found the border between the worlds, all my desires would be fulfilled. Where is Constance? Where is Charley? Where is my life?"

The voice again: "Everyone you ever knew, 'suh,' is long gone. Long forgotten. I told you that you'd have to give up everything to go into the world in the hill. You said you would. You've already forfeited most of it. And now you will give up the rest. Whether you like it or not. And this, precisely, is the ultimate fulfillment of all your desires. For the time being, anyway."

"What are you saying? I don't want to die!"

"You truly are a fool, Leopold Stokes. Don't you understand anything?" Joseph sat down on a boulder, close to Leo's head.

What he said next resonated deeply in Leo's mind, once again from a point in the center of his brain.

"The border between the worlds is not a place. It is a process. It is the transition you call 'death.' If you had a whit of what you call 'gumption,' you would have learned to pass through it while alive. You would have learned to live on its other side, having let go of everything and everyone, most especially yourself as you've known yourself to be, even while you continued to live, and continued—or maybe in your case, began—to love. You could have learned to worship and surrender to and abide in God, instead of exploiting God's gifts to you for your own ends, in this and all other worlds.

"But you did not do that. And you could not do that alone. To do that, you would have needed—what did that Big Lady call it?—'qualified help.' Not a mortal ignoramus like yourself, shrouded in terror and self-obsession. No, you would have needed the help of someone—maybe a whole group of someones—of deep dignity and wisdom, who dare all for love and truth, all-pervasive while alive, walking wildernesses of peace. Perhaps you picked up an inkling that such beings exist."

Leo sighed. He had a feeling this time there would be no bargaining. No negotiations. He resigned himself to hearing out the end of the sermon.

"Now, battered by cravings to get and to have, starving for love and comfort, wanting to be worshipped forever in worlds that are only heartless whirlwinds of dreams flashing by, you have sought your own death more frantically than anything in your life. You have been dying all your life—like everyone else, really—but since you began seeking the border between the worlds, your actual, physical death has been under way. Now it is time for you to pass beyond this body and these worlds altogether. And alone. That, by the way, was one of your very 'deepest wishes.' Good-bye, Leopold—'Mistuh Stokes, suh.'"

Bewildered, forlorn, Leo watched as Joseph rose, pulled a small vial of what looked to be water from his suit, opened it, sprinkled it all over Leo's head and body, closed and pocketed the vial, and then began walking down the hill.

Leo cried out, "Joseph! No! You can't leave me!"

Joseph stopped walking and slowly turned toward Leo. He crossed his arms over his chest, so the studs in the cuffs of his shirtsleeves once again blinded Leo with their brilliance. Joseph's face showed no emotion, but his eyes were hard and fierce as he looked directly into Leo's.

Without his intent, Leo's eyes snapped shut. In his mind's eye, a computer screen shone clearly. On its stark white background, several sentences appeared in black.

"The User has now exhausted all possible fulfillments in this sequence. User conversion and transformation will be required before any future use of Ultimaya 1.0 becomes possible. END SEQUENCE."

Then the screen went blank and disappeared. Leo opened his eyes.

Joseph was nowhere to be seen.

Leo's heart sank. He saw the vultures circling above him in the noonday sun, now spiraling lower and lower, closer and closer to him. He couldn't move. Couldn't protect himself. Couldn't even make a whimper of resistance.

His extremities and limbs started going cold. With the creeping, unstoppable cold came terror, desolation, and remorse. He felt like he'd been tried, convicted, and now sentenced to death. It seemed he really had destroyed everyone and everything in his life just to get what he wished and wanted. And for what? Joseph was right.

Now Leopold Stokes knew he was sure enough going to die. In fact he was already dying. Everything Joseph had said was one hundred percent true. But now there was nothing Leo could do about it.

At long last, Leo's eyesight faded. His body was numb with cold even in the midday sun, so frozen he could no longer feel anything below his chest, and he could only feel anything in his chest because of his labored breathing. He gasped for the last tiny little breaths of his life. Blackness closed in around him.

If he weren't so frightened, numb, and spent, Leo would have wept. But no tears could find their way from his sightless, staring eyes.

He could still hear the wind, and the horrid shuddering flaps of the vultures' wings as they spiraled down, down, closer down, toward their eventual feast. Leo thought, "Oh God, a hundred and twenty thousand years in the future—and I gotta be eaten by vultures? That's it? That is *it*?"

There were no sounds but wind and vultures' wings. Leo felt like he was crumbling to bits, like his stomach was rising to his mouth. His blood freezing solid. His brain fracturing into marbles. His bones and flesh frying into gaseous light.

"It's like what's left of me is turning into dry ice," he thought.

He sighed and was surprised to hear its sound coming from his mouth. Speech was no longer possible, so he spoke very deliberately inside his mind. "Okay. God, I still don't know if you can hear me. Or who or what you are. Or really if you even exist. But if you do...please give me another chance. Please help me. Your Will be done. God, help me!"

He really meant it. Every word. This prayer was real.

He waited.

It didn't seem to make any difference.

Again Leo felt the wave of his own spirit, his own life, rising to break beyond the bounds of everything he had ever known and been. He felt it was going to blow him to the winds, every which way. He fought it back, fought it down, fought it off. Gasped for air. Grasped for life.

But the roaring wave of what felt like his certain end crashed unrelenting into the barrier of his fear, battering and weakening his resolve.

Finally, he could hold on no longer.

Leopold Stokes let go.

He shot with the current of his spirit through dark shapes and sounds, a light flashing past.

Then: nothing at all.

GRATITUDE BEATITUDE

With a start, Leo opened his eyes. He was looking up. A bare white ceiling with a single modest light fixture hovered above him. The light was on.

I'm alive!

The thought crackled like lightning through his mind. He hardly dared move for fear he had no body left after all. But then, with no volition of his own, his lungs sucked in a huge volume of air. It must have been the deepest breath he ever took in his life.

Leo shot up to a sitting position. He was in his old room!

In his old house!

In Ashlin!

Where he had lived before any of this madness started!

In a flash, he could see the old porch outside the window—that wonderfully tiny, cramped, postage stamp of a porch—and the trees and grass of his backyard beyond it.

He took in all the ordinary, simple, little things of his old room: the threadbare easy chair. The knotty pine dresser, from his boyhood. The mirror. The old frayed rug. The alcove and its bare clean desk. The old cotton robe and pajamas he was wearing.

Suddenly about to burst with joy, Leopold Stokes shouted aloud: "I'm alive! I'm alive! Thank God, thank God, *I'm alive!*"

With a chuckle, a very familiar voice replied from slightly behind him,

"Not a bad idea, Stokes. I'd say a round of thanks to your more mortal friends might not be a bad thing either."

Leo whirled around. There, near the head of his bed, was Charley Bass, sitting in Leo's High Point rocker.

"Charley! I can't believe it! You're alive too! You didn't die after all!" Leo leaped from his bed to embrace Charley, but tripped on his robe and fell rolling on the floor. He leaped up again and smothered his old friend with hugs and kisses. "That maniac Joseph didn't kill you after all! It's a miracle! *You're alive, Charley!* You're alive! You didn't die after all!"

"Would you get your sorry-ass butt offa me, Stokes? I swear to God, you're still nuts! Get off me, you madman!"

Charley was laughing but he meant it; he finally grasped Leo by the arms and threw him to the floor.

Flabbergasted, Leo hardly noticed. "Charley! Can you believe this? I am actually alive! I didn't die a hundred and twenty thousand years from now! You didn't get burnt like paper at the border between the worlds! Constance didn't fall in love with Ralph! And I bet Nan's still as old and ugly and mean as ever! Hot diggety! Dang! This is way too good to be true! Somebody must've answered my prayers. Somebody must've helped me out! This is *amazing*, Charley!"

Leo bolted up to his feet and then careened around the room, kissing the furniture, hugging the walls and doors, bouncing and bounding on his bed like a four-year old.

"I gotta give thanks! Thank you, God! *Thank you, God!* Forget you, Ultimaya 1.0! You're history! Thank you, God! Thank you, God! Thank you, God! For my life! For my friend, Charley, still here with me! For this dumb little postage stamp of a house! In this dumb little postage stamp of a town! On this dumb little ping-pong ball of a planet! Thank you for the world, God! Thank you for Ashlin! I'm back! *I'm back!*"

Leo ran and ran, whirling in circles around Charley, shooting out onto the porch and then back inside, shouting at the top of his lungs while Charley sat there laughing.

"Oh, God! I can't believe it! Too good! Too fine! Too simple! Just the old place! Just the old life! Just the old me! *Thank you, God!* Thank you for the bed! Thank you for the floor! Thank you for the window setting there to see through! Too much light! Too much de-dang-licious de-dang-light! Wow! Thank you for the sky! Thank you for the pines! Thank you for the sun! Thank you for Ashlin! And thank you for Charley Bass, the best goldang friend possible on this whole crazy planet!"

Leo leaped ten feet in a bound and threw himself onto Charley's lap, so that the rocker crashed over backward onto the floor and the two of them went sprawling. Charley was so doubled over from laughing, he couldn't get up. Leo was on his feet in no time, kissing more furniture and marveling madly.

Suddenly he shouted, *"Nan!"* He tore out of his room, robe flying around his knees, and stormed down the hallway. Just as he neared the kitchen, he saw her walking in front of him, a broom in her hand.

Yelling, "Naaaaannnn! You're beautiful!" and not missing a stride, Leo hurled himself to the floor and went sliding headlong on the polished wood like a base runner stealing second, only coming to a stop when his outstretched hands smashed into and encircled her right foot.

Nan's eyes bugged out at him in glassy, shocked astonishment. Leo looked up at her. "Naaaannnn! You're here! You're alive too! And you're still old! But you're beautiful, Nan! Goldang it, right from that old gray bun on your head down to the stark perfection of the P. W. Minors on your great old lady feet! I cannot believe it! I just can't believe it!"

Leo pounded his forehead on the floor, drooling with laughter, as Nan shouted at him: "Leopold Stokes, get your hands off my foot! Charles Bass the Third! Ah tell you, Leo's gone mad! He's crazy! Let go of my foot, Leopold! What in the world has possessed you! You are virtual-lay insane! You're scaring me half to death! Don't you go touching me, you perverted maniac! Get off of me!"

She began pounding Leo with the broom while he, chortling like a lunatic, leaped to his feet and gave her a giant hug and a sloppy wet kiss right on the lips. He then went careening back to his room, only to smack square into Charley who was just rushing out the door, aching so hard from laughter that he had to hold his sides.

They both reeled and tumbled and fell onto the bed, beside themselves with hilarity. Leo then fell off the bed onto the floor, where he finally came to rest, still shouting and mumbling incessant thanks to God.

At last Leo wore down a bit, and Charley caught his breath.

"Gotta say, Stokes…best Scrooge impression I ever seen!"

Panting for breath, Leo shook his head vigorously. "No goldang impression, Mountain Man…this is the real stuff. I just…cannot believe I am alive, and back in Ashlin again. I didn't even dare…to wish for this. This is pure, sheer, double D-G Divine Grace and I can't imagine what I possibly could've done to deserve it. No way! Can't believe it."

Leo sat bolt upright, glaring at his friend. "Charley! You gotta tell me right now. What year is this?"

Charley shook his head, smiling, a mock frown on his face. "Come on, Stokes. You gotta be kidding."

"I mean it, Charley! What year?"

"1992, you maniac. What of it?"

"1992? *Incredible!*" Leo jumped to his feet. "I'm back! I'm all the way back! I'm really all the way back!"

He stopped dead and turned to Charley again. "And what day? What day of the month? What month? Come on, Charley, I gotta know!"

"December 17. You've been delirious for a few days, buddy roe. We were all getting a little nervous about you."

"December 17, 1992! I came all the way back! Can you imagine? All…the…way…back!"

Leo's eyes started to well up with tears. He was overcome with so much gratitude he felt his heart might explode.

Sitting down on the bed, he began to weep—soft cries at first, but then longer, louder, more violent ones. Soon he was racked with huge sobs that seemed to come from the core of his being, doubling him over and making his body thrash around on his bed.

Charley stood, straightened out his clothes, righted the rocker, and took his seat in it again. He watched as Leo sobbed out the last little bit of everything he had in him to cry away.

Then Charley asked, softly, "And what have we done with the sorcerer's hat and wand now, Mr. Stokes?"

Leo looked at him, then lifted his bed sheet and blew his nose in it, sounding like a trumpet. "Whew! So, time for another confessional, Charley?"

Charley shook his head. "Maybe you don't need to do any more 'fessing up, Leo. I handled the electronic source of your, shall we say, recent eccentricities."

Leo looked over at the alcove. The computer was gone!

"Charley, what in the world did you do with it?"

"Well ..." Leo's friend was having a hard time saying something. "I... uh...well, Leo, fact is...I—I burned it."

He didn't wait for Leo to speak. "I'll get you a new one, of course. No point trying to turn the clock back on progress! Nothing wrong with computers. Just a 'bad seed,' I guess."

"You *burned* it?"

"You bet I did, Leo. Took matters into my own hands."

Leo looked at Charley with his mouth wide open, shaking his head. Tears sprang to his eyes. One more thing to be grateful for! He was so overcome with the multitude of things he was suddenly thankful for, he was almost forgetting to breathe. He could hardly bear to even think of them all.

"Whoa! Charley, *thank you!*" The words came bursting out of him. "And thank God! I'm actually thankful to God, for the first real time in my life! The first real day of my life!" Leo exhaled, shaking his head again, and began muttering almost to himself. "Gratitude! Beatitude! A multitude of gratitude! I must be crazy!"

Then he looked at his friend intently. "Charley! I gotta tell you what happened. I gotta tell you right now. You just ain't gonna believe it."

"Oh, yes, I am, Stokes. Remember, this here film you're about to roll, I got an advance screening. Couple of 'em, in fact."

Leo spent the next two hours regaling Charley with his story. Charley listened intently, sometimes laughing and sometimes serious. But when Leo started telling him what Joseph had said in his final conversation on the hillside, supposedly many thousands of years in the future, Charley leaned forward, furrowing his brow like he was storing every word in his brain forever. When Leo finished describing his death there, just before returning to life here in Ashlin, Charley shook his head.

"That's amazing, Leo. Just plumb amazing."

"Yeah, I know—some kind of adventure, huh?"

"Well, yes, that too, but I'm talking about what Joseph told you on the hilltop at the end there. That just shifts my comprehension of this whole thing."

"What do you mean?"

"Let me see how to put this." Charley paused for a moment, looking away, thinking. "Well, the more you tell me about what Ultimaya taught you, maybe I didn't have the whole picture on it. Maybe you can't really say it's either good or bad. Maybe, ultimately, it's—" He smiled almost sheepishly at Leo. It wasn't often that Charles Bass III was at a loss for words.

"Let's just say, Leo, that maybe Ultimaya 1.0 is or was a sort of karmic accelerator that ultimately has a very benign influence. Ass-kicking, for sure, but definitely for the good."

Leo asked once more what Charley meant, but Charley said, "Naw, I really need to think it over some more. We can talk about it later."

Before Leo could say anything else, they heard a shout from Nan in the kitchen: "Leopold Stokes! Charles Bass the Third! Y'all's breakfast is on the table and it's gettin' cold!"

The two of them grinned at the shrill sound of Nan's voice and walked to the dining room. They all had a fine breakfast together. Leo punctuated their conversation with frequent shouts of love and joy that sent Nan scurrying into the pantry, fearing another affectionate attack on her person. Still, under her frowns and "don't you dares," she was obviously delighted to see him well and happy again.

But she was nowhere near as delighted as Leo himself.

LETTIN' GO TIME

After breakfast, Nan left to do some errands. Charley and Leo sat at the table, enjoying another cup of coffee. The winter sun sparkled through the bay window onto the linoleum floor, warming the room. Charley reached up to his shirt pocket, found nothing there, snorted, and, shaking his head, put his hand back down on the table.

Leo suddenly noticed. "Charley, you ain't got no weeds on you!"

"That's right, Leo. Cold turkey. And that ain't all I ain't got on me."

Leo laughed. "Hm! I'm impressed. But what do you mean, 'that ain't all'?"

Charley paused, then said solemnly, "Leo, I have decided to chuck everything for the way out."

"What do you mean? Come on, Charley, you got a whole dang chain of stores to run, you ain't going nowhere."

"Wrong on that, buddy roe."

"What're you talking about?"

"Sold it."

"Sold it? You *sold* Charley's Computer Stores?"

"'Deed I did."

Leo leaned so far back in his chair he nearly fell over. "When in God's great Creation did you do that? You never told me you were trying to sell your business."

Charley grinned. "You never asked, Great Sorcerer. Besides, you were just a tad preoccupied, last few times we spoke.

"Remember the first day you consulted me about Ultimaya 1.0, and I told you I'd just postponed a meeting to sign a mighty sweet contract? I put off the close so's we could meet."

Leo said softly, "You did?"

Charley grinned at him again. "Sure did, buddy."

Leo was speechless. Talk about a friend. No businessman in his right mind would postpone a meeting to close the sale of a multimillion-dollar company he'd worked his entire career to build, just to meet with a friend who'd asked for some help but wouldn't even say what it was about!

And what had *he,* Leo, done? He'd been so thick into his own syrup, he never even bothered to ask Charley how things were going, what he was up to. Not even how his business was doing.

Charley went on. "'Course, the whole world did not come to a halt while you checked out to Stokesland. So day before yesterday I got back together with the buyers, big midwestern chain, and we John Hancocked that sucker up one side and down the other. I think it's safe to say I've endowed my spiritual quest and set aside financial security for a couple more generations of Basses besides, should Sarah choose to have a family. If not, well, she won't have to worry. She and any kids she has, they'll have to work"—he smiled—"but they won't have to *worry.* I already had the trusts and such structured, it's all signed, sealed, and delivered."

Charley again reached instinctively to his shirt pocket for a cigarette, then laughed at himself, looked at his empty hand, shook it, and stuffed it under his thigh. He regarded Leo with affection.

"Up till you started coming around half-crazy with Ultimaya 1.0, I have to admit I did not know what in the world I was gonna do with myself. I knew I had to get out of that business or I'd just vegetate and die there, setting in that grungy office like a big hen popping out new franchises, but not really *doing* anything anymore. Then that one day you started ragging me about why didn't I have a guru or a shaman, some kinda mentor, and when was I going to get serious about walking my own talk, and—this was the killer—'you ain't got no gumption, Charley!' That did it. Thanks, old bud."

Leo was still smarting from seeing how selfish he'd been toward his friend. He stammered out, "Don't mention it." Then he thought for a moment. "I still don't get it, Charley. What do you mean, 'the way out'?"

"I'm talking God, Leo."

"How's that?"

Charley stood up and looked out the sliding glass door. For a moment he was quiet. Leo saw the pine needles on the trees outside rustling in the breeze, the sunlight dancing off them like Christmas tinsel. Charley looked at Leo again.

"Well, old bud, tempted as I am to try to make some points to you about your own situation, maybe instead I'll just tell you a little more about where I've been and where it feels like I'm going. And hope that might have some relevance for your own direction too."

Leo felt a wave of irritation pass through him, but he let it go.

Charley turned again to look out into the yard. He was quiet for a time. Then he began to speak.

"All through high school, you know, even when I was being a flat out hellraiser, I was already looking around to find out who'd drawn a bead on what the hell's going down in this life. I mean, I had a stash of Eastern sages in the same closet with my *Playboys*. And I reached the conclusion way back then that there's just no future in investing our hopes and dreams in this life and whatever it can bring us—including people, relationships. Sex. Money. Loved ones. Even kids. The only thing that counts is liberation, in fact, from being ground up in all that karmic stuff of living. Enlightenment. Waking up.

"I mean, that was already obvious to me by the time we went to college. But I knew I also had to live it all out somehow too. I'd tried to go out to that ashram after our sophomore year at State. But I was too young. And the guy running that show, the guru out there—I don't know. To this day I'm not exactly sure what happened. Whatever it was, within three, four months I knew I had to come back and bear down. Create a life. I wasn't cut out to give it all up before I could even really get into life and live it in the usual ways.

"I tried to be 'in the world but not of it,' as the Christian mystics would say. St. Paul, whoever. I tried to live without getting attached. I mean, I didn't want to be off in another world, but I really didn't want to get all bound up in this one, either. So I just made up my mind to embrace ordinary living, marriage, kids, a career, the whole thing, and somehow keep my balance, somehow hold that greater principle close to my heart even in the midst of it all. The God principle, if you want to call it that. The really important thing that nothing else can compensate for, nothing else can approximate. The great freedom. The way out.

"But you know, life…what was it John Lennon said? 'Life is what happens while you're making plans?' Anyway, Ginny came along so fast and grabbed my heart so hard it made my head spin. Suddenly there I am saying vows to her and meaning every word. And then in short order first Sarah and then Josh. I don't know if you remember it, Leo, but we actually had both kids before I even graduated college."

"Yeah, Charley, I remember. We were all kind of blown away. 'St. Charley of the Harley' suddenly becomes 'Father Knows Best.'"

Charley nodded. "Well, not really. Not completely. But then my business, well, like you said, seemed like it just grew up of its own accord all around me. But it also started to eat my energy and my life. Between that and Ginny and the kids, it's like my soul got consumed. I wouldn't say I forgot the call to enlightenment, to getting out of this maze, waking up. But it did kind of go faint in me. And I also lost touch with you and the other folks here in Ashlin. My business just had to be down where the action is, in the Triangle. So did my life. And the years went flying by.

"Stokes, I don't know what to say about it any more—but...well...I fell in love. I mean, the business, it was mostly fun, like a game. I was able to get really good at it without a whole lot of effort and hardly any stress. I wasn't really *invested* in it.

"But Ginny, Josh, Sarah—I got so attached to that woman and those kids, there's no way I could describe it to you. You literally can't imagine. You have to have gone through it, you'd have to know it from the inside, yourself. And sometimes I'd look at my bookshelf and I'd just wonder: Did I go wrong? Was I making a mistake?

"If I was, I knew there wasn't a damn thing I could do about it. I just had to follow it all the way through. That was my spiritual practice. Just living a life. Even though I couldn't make it hardly spiritual at all. Seemed mostly like the opposite of spiritual freedom. Everything all the old sages had warned about. But then..."

Charley sighed. To Leo, he sounded like a dying man, like that sigh came from his bone marrow, from the bottom of his world. The big man was looking down and away, his shoulders slumped, his head hanging. "But then...whew. So soon, so young—suddenly out of nowhere Ginny's got advanced ovarian cancer. And before we can barely catch our breath, it's metastasized. It's in her liver. It's in her lymph nodes. It's every damn where. And she's thirty-two years old? With these little kids? Who really, really, really still needed their mom?

"And me—there I am, I'm making real money. I can afford the best treatments money can buy. Here at Duke; up in New York, at Sloane-Kettering; the Mayo Clinic; we tried it all. Even went to Germany for some leading edge European experimental stuff. But none of it worked. And I was powerless, Leo. I was *powerless* to stop it. I just watched her waste away. I raged. We cried together. But there was nothing I could do."

Charley sighed again, shaking his head. He had said Leo's name but he was in his own world. Leo had never heard him talk this way. He himself was hardly breathing. He didn't want to say a word. He wasn't used to Charley, or anybody in fact, talking like this. It made him seriously uncomfortable. But he didn't want to do anything that would pull Charley out of wherever he was talking from.

"She died in my arms, you know. I'll never forget that last breath. It went out of her. And I'm holding her, I'm crying, I'm rocking her body, and I'm waiting for another breath to go back into her again. It wasn't supposed to just stop like that. I'm waiting, I'm waiting, and it won't happen. It won't go in. Her chest never rose again. She never took another breath.

"She never did, Leo. There was no death rattle. Her life just breathed itself away. Just like that. She was gone. The love of my life. Just gone."

Charley paused. He didn't look up. Leo didn't know what to say, or whether to even try. They were silent.

Leo slowly turned again to look out the kitchen window at the pine boughs in his yard and, beyond them, the pale blue sky of the wintry noon. He thought of how convinced he had been, in the faraway world, that he had long ago lost everyone he loved. And then he remembered how he had died there.

Suddenly it dawned on him: he hadn't just had a deathlike experience. The stark reality was, he had actually *died.* And then he had come back to life, somehow, for who knows what reason. Who could possibly even know? *Thank you, God,* he thought. *Thank you God.*

Charley began speaking again.

"Luckily the kids weren't there. Wouldn't've wanted them to see that.

"I don't know how the three of us got through the days, weeks, months afterward. Somehow we did.

"So there I am, feeling like a walking ghost half the time, but I've got a business to run and I've got these two little miracles, these human cubs. Now they're half-orphaned, being single-parented by a widower with half his heart just bombed right out of him.

"Josh in particular…you know, it's like some piece of Ginny's body and soul lived on in him. It wasn't only that he looked like her. He had almost all her features and almost none of mine, and it was real obvious when he was a little kid. And I loved that! It never even occurred to me to wish otherwise. But it was more than looks. Especially after she died. His way of walking, his way of talking—he wasn't an effeminate kid. In fact he had a tough as nails side to him that was pure male, pure boy, and the older he got the more I saw another hellraiser like me coming up and out— but what I'm trying to say is, he had so much Ginny in him that sometimes seeing her in him, still alive but *as him*...it kind of took my breath away.

"And then that day. Down at Oak Island, a ways north of Myrtle Beach. Renting somebody's beach house for a week. I had to work so hard to try to compensate for Ginny being gone and there was no way I could do it. And it was so hard being reminded of her every day at home, in Raleigh. So we took lots of little family vacations, trying to make surviving easier for all of us.

"I'm in the house on the phone. Some bunch of nothing the office needed to talk to me about. The kids are out on the beach. They're both good, strong swimmers, and for Christ's sakes, there's lifeguards on duty every hundred yards on that strip of sand.

"But suddenly Sarah's slamming in through the screen door, and she's screaming and crying that Josh was way out there in deep water and some freak riptide pulled him way on further out and the lifeguards are trying to bring him in and they can't find him...

"So we rush down to the beach and I just dive in, shirt and cutoffs still on, and swim out to meet the lifeguards who're hauling him in. And they...we get him down on the sand. He ain't breathing. Eyes closed. Limp. No sign of life. They do their mouth to mouth and CPR and all that. They try, they really try.

"But he's gone. Already turning white and blue before our eyes. My little boy. What was he, eleven years old? And now he's gone too."

Another long silence. Charley finally lifted his head and looked searchingly at Leo. It was hard for Leo to meet his glance; it was almost too naked, his friend's grieving heart right there in his eyes, on his face. Leo'd never seen him like that before.

"I could go on, Leo. But...you know. You came to both Ginny's and Josh's funerals. And you and me got back in touch a little more after that. I kept you posted on Sarah. She amazed me and to this day she still does. I keep waiting for signals that she's hopelessly screwed up by these massive losses at such a young age. But I don't know, it all galvanized something in her. I'm sure she'll have some looking at it all to do, some deep diving—I mean just the shock of it all, someday. But it's like she's got the best of both of 'em in her and fundamentally she's fine. Off to school now, not needing a whole lot off of me. She's the one looking after me a lot of the time.

"Sometimes, old bud, really, it's like I've been in an endless bardo of my own. The more Sarah grew up and had a life with her friends and all the stuff she's into, the more the business just ate me up. I think it was a blessing. I sorely needed the distraction. And I'd look at those books now and again, from a distance, shake my head, wonder about it all, and plug back into the grand southeastern expansion of Charley's Computer Stores. As if all that really mattered. And smoking up a storm. If it wasn't for Sarah and the fascination I have with the silly tech stuff, I could've just walked off a cliff somewhere. So I suppose smoking was my way of saying to God, to life, 'Okay, I'll hang on in here on principle. Take care of my little girl. Do the world a little good, computer nerds at least. But there's a whole part of me that's just done. Screw it. Who cares. It's all flying by anyway. Like this cigarette smoke in the wind.'

"And I just kept going along like that, Leo, till that day when you busted me. You and Ultimaya. And, 'Bass, you ain't got no gumption.'"

Charley seemed like he was easing out of the intense feelings he'd been having. Leo found he could breathe again. He exhaled out loud. Then he felt he should say something after Charley's outpourings.

"Well, Charley, good Lord...I don't know what to say...I don't think 'you're welcome' is exactly what's called for here, but..."

Charley unconsciously reached to his shirt pocket for a pack of cigarettes, then snorted in amusement and shook his head again on finding it empty. *"He didn't do that the whole time he was talking,"* Leo thought. "Didn't reach for a single weed."

Charley eyed him. "I don't reckon I've ever shared much of that with a single other human soul, Leo. The only reason I did it today with you is, I want to somehow send you smoke signals about where you're going, now that it seems like Ultimaya is out of the picture and you're back in good ole Ashlin.

"I mean, you're thanking God or Life or whatever like crazy for bringing you back from there to here. Well, hell, Leo, I'm glad to see you back too. I can appreciate what you feel. And I'm not gonna launch into another sermon.

"But I just have to appeal to you to take a closer look. I know what I gotta do. And it's something I gotta *go* and do somewhere mostly away from here. I just know it. So if there's anything *I've* got to say to God or Life or whatever today, it's a prayer that you will somehow get with *that* program. Now that you've seen what Ultimaya showed you, Leo, I also think it's time for *you* to to wake up out of the game of charades here. Please don't just take the next shot of anesthesia in good old Ashlin. Not after all you've seen. 'Cause sooner or later it's all gonna be gone again. You, me, Constance, the slats out there on the porch, the breeze rustling through the pines, the bank, Nan…the whole show."

Leo was getting agitated again. "I don't know, Mountain Man. Seems like you're just getting into your negative rap about life and the world again. I mean, I don't mean any disrespect about Josh and Ginny. And you're right, I can't possibly know what you've gone through, with them dying and all. You know that."

Charley nodded.

"But it's like something has colored your lens on life a deep dark shade of gray."

Charley shook his head, looked up, and smiled. "Whoa now. I'm not just moaning and groaning here. I'm drawing on about five thousand years of the best wisdom the world has ever produced—wisdom that just doesn't happen to jibe with the modern West's whoop-it-up cheerleading about how great life really is or soon will be for everyone. The *Bhagavad Gita,* the great Buddhist sutras, all that ancient perspective isn't just negative about life. But it's not a bunch of naive romance about it either."

Leo stood up and started pacing. "Charley, I never read the—whatever—'Bog-and-God Geeter.' I wouldn't know a 'sutra' from a suit. And I don't know if I trust anyone who lived in a very different world thousands of years ago to tell us what we oughta do and how we oughta live right now."

"Fine, Leo, but how do you know Ultimaya's not in temporary remission in your own nervous system? Like some virus that can come out whenever and give you shingles of the brain, or whatever just happened to you these last few days. You don't rightly know. And you can't!"

Leo snorted. "Well, shoot, Charley, that's right. I don't know, and I can't. But dang it, *I'm here!* And I can't imagine dropping my whole life for some highfalutin quest to not have to be a human being after all."

"Come on, Leo! My, my, how fast we forget!" Charley rolled his eyes. "Back in your future world you were begging for help from anyone and everyone! Now you sound like Burt Reynolds after he gets back to the beach in that movie *The End.* You've already renegotiated your contract. You're cool."

Leo didn't say anything but eyed Charley with a sullen stare. He sat down again in his chair and crossed his arms in front of his chest. Then he leaned back and propped a foot up on the table, the sole of his shoe facing Charley square on.

Charley waved a hand dismissively. "All right, never mind all that. Let's look at something else here, Stokes.

"I think everybody's hard drive took a couple of whacks from your Ultimaya trip, buddy. Lookit: I had all these conversations with you in the middle of it. I actually saw that black guy, Joseph, and that Bentley in my parking lot. Saw the ring too. So I actually physically experienced some of your Stokesland reality. But when I talked to Constance—"

"You talked to Con?"

"Yeah, I did. You had Nan and me wigging out, Stokes! I needed all the data I could get to try to figure out where you were disappearing to. So I just asked Con if she'd by any chance heard from or seen you. She said no. Hadn't heard from you in a month."

"Dang, Charley! Why'd you go fumbling around in my affairs like that?"

"'Scuse me, 'Mistuh Stokes, suh!'" Charley's eyes flashed and his voice was ragged with controlled rage. "Far from 'fumbling around in your affairs,' I do believe you employed me as a pro bono consultant in your attempt to reconfigure the entire universe to your precise specifications!"

Leo glared back for a moment. Then he relaxed and awkwardly grinned. "Oops. I do believe you're right. Sorry. Go on, Charley."

"Thank you, Mr. Stokes." Charley let out a long deep breath. "All right. So that's me and Con. Nan, on the other hand, *swears* that Constance came by here to see you and tried to have a conversation with you. Says she let her in the door, remembers what she was wearing, all kinds of stuff. But Constance says no way, that just never happened. She was so hurt she even went out of her way to avoid driving past both your house and the bank." He paused, shaking his head ruefully. "You really got a way with women, Stokes, I tell you what. To this day, I just don't rightly know what makes her hang on to you so."

Leo squirmed. Charley's story was confusing him, and he was starting to sweat. He'd assumed it'd be possible for everyone to make sense of his last several days, and he would just be able to plug back into their shared world. Just about like nothing had happened to him—or them. But now it seemed whatever actually had taken place, no one could make sense of it. Or even agree on what happened when.

"Now, I know very well you and me met in my office the last time just two days ago. But Nan swears that you've been lying in your bed delirious for three solid days, Stokes! Sweating like a horse on a plow at high summer noon. Says you didn't go anywhere and the only lucid moments you had were the ones she overheard with Constance, and one conversation she had with you, which she absolutely and in one hell of a huff refuses to tell me about. Says, anyway, she's been worried sick, old Doc Ainsworth's been by here once a day—yep, I called him, he confirmed it. Says he was on the verge of hospitalizing you. He was even wondering whether you might be heading someday to Dix Hill."

"What? You gotta be kidding me! The loony bin in Raleigh?"

"Hey, you been outta your mind, bud. And not exactly quiet either. Ainsworth was grasping for sanity straws from you. Said he was relieved at least to hear, through Nan who'd kept him posted, that when Constance visited you, even though Nan couldn't hear what y'all said, it did sound to her like a sane conversation.

"But oops—please recall: Constance says, no way; that discussion never happened."

Charley looked hard at Leo and cleared his throat to make a point. *"You're welcome, Leo."*

"Thank you" couldn't come close to Leo's lips. He looked away, feeling like he'd been punched in the gut. His world was spinning again.

Charley went on. "Anyway, by your own account you have not been in this house for a minimum of—what was it?—a hundred and twenty thousand years." He laughed. "So I don't think we'll ever straighten out what actually happened here—or wherever. Bunch of halfway worlds in collusion." He tilted his head to one side, pondering, then laughed again. "If old Velikovsky only knew the half of it—"

"Vello who?"

"Never mind. So all of us got a complimentary Zorro slash from Ultimaya—we each wound up with a big *U* carved into our memories, right there in the hard drives. And how do you know you ain't gonna get catapulted right back into that insanity again someday?"

Leo felt his heart sink even more. His gaze fell to the floor. He'd exhausted himself physically, running around thanking God and everyone and everything in sight for him being here back home again. Now the real-world reality of what'd happened here at home while he was wherever he'd been, was crashing in on him. "I—I don't. I don't know it won't happen. I don't know squat. That's the truth of it. And...yeah, I'm—I'm pretty scared. Now that you put it all like this."

Charley leaned forward across the table. "Well, so am I. Not so much for you, or that what's happened to you could happen to me. I'm scared of being stuck in this machine of a life. 'Cause, to get right down to it, what happened to you ain't that far off of what's happening to every one of us. All the time!

"What I mean is, I'm not a whole lot better off than you. But I know I gotta focus, and I gotta get help. I was telling you to track yourself down a guru, or a shaman, someone with some serious expertise to help you unravel yourself out of those wacko worlds you were prowling. But I should've been talking to myself. Maybe I was.

"So this time around, I gotta go for it and not let up. Chucking my Winstons is the least of it. I'm doing something far more deadly than smoking, Leo, and I'm doing it full on, all the time. So's just about everybody else on the planet. Same boat. Same machine—same program. I've got to find my way out of *that.*"

Even though Leo was feeling pretty defeated, that whole line of thinking from Charley made him bristle again. But he didn't let on in his tone of voice. "I don't know, Charley. Sounds kind of sixties romantic to me. 'Flower Power Bass the Acidhead rides off into the sunset to play Zen-ist.'" He grinned, thinking, *Shoot, that's the kind of play on words Charley himself would say.*

If Charley noticed, he didn't show it. He stood and began pacing the room. Leo watched him, mute. He didn't want to hear a word of what Charley was saying. He couldn't exactly refute it. Some of it rang sort of true. But he felt dazed, like all his insides were somehow swamping together and draining toward his feet.

Yet something else was stirring inside him too. What was that phrase Charley'd had for him when they were kids? Leo couldn't remember it. But he felt the mood of it starting to rise up in his gut.

He looked at his very large friend, now standing at the kitchen window. "Charley, didn't you already try that, way back when?"

Charley pursed his lips and nodded.

"So what's different now?"

"I don't know. Less tread left on my tires," Charley said. "More school-of-hard-knocks smarts branded into my brain by living a life. But yeah, who knows if I'm gonna pull it off now? Hell, I only stopped smoking two days ago.

"I do know this—it's lettin' go time for this boy. I gotta somehow explode for the God that's all about freedom from this dream machine. And I know in my bones I won't do it if I don't get to see the real freedom light radiating like a divine dynamo in somebody or somebodies right in front of me. I gotta get my desires upgraded, my whole 'dynamic wish-field' reconfigured inside and out; it's like my whole body's gotta get magnetized to God. Nothing else has the power to blow me out of the machine. I know it in my bones."

Charley was still looking out the window. Leo eyed him, shaking his head. He wasn't buying Charley's sermon this time. Not anymore. He couldn't think of anything to say at the moment. But he still felt that volcanic thing coming up in him. And this time it wasn't going to be stopped.

Charley sighed, and looked again at Leo. A scowl came over his face.

"So come on, Leo. You got the picture. You owe it to yourself—hell, man, you owe it to Nan, you owe it to Con, you owe it to everybody to begin to live on the basis of what you've seen. Performed, in fact. You just starred in one of the wildest instant-karma theater pieces I ever heard of!"

Leo was ready to talk. He started out slow and easy; he didn't want to show too many cards too fast. "I don't know, Charley. What do you want me to do? Who do you want me to be? I don't think you appreciate what it means to me to be out of that—that—whatever it was! Even if it's just for now. I don't think you get it. I mean, right now, just to see that sorry old pine porch of mine out there with paint flaking off the railings, I feel like I'm in paradise or something. I'm not ready to throw all this away. I'm not."

He'd been heating up for a while, and now Leo felt himself turning red. *The Leo-nuclear weapon. The L-bomb.* Right! Those were Charley's names for when he uncorked. Leo wasn't ready to blow up yet, though. He wasn't sure he even should, if he really wanted to back Charley off once and for all.

But he didn't mind letting out a little heat.

"Why in God's good Creation am I apologizing to you? Yeah, thank you for all your help. Fine. But that's it! I could care less about all your metaphysics, Charley. I'm setting here feeling like I'm finally ready to be a decent human being. Here, in this humble little town, with my humble little townsfolk, and my humble little bank, me and my humble little Nan and my humble little Constance. Humble little me!

"I'm no big deal. You got it right. No saint. No monk. Shoot, I'm finally ready after twenty years to embrace a woman who's never stopped loving me the whole time—and you're telling me to give her up? To give all that up? No way!

"I'm not ready to chuck these people—the bank—these ole redneck farmers trying to rassle a living out of this hardscrabble clay. They're my folks, Charley. They need me. I'm not ready to go find someone who's supposedly gonna help me get free of this deadly 'dream machine.'" He lowered his voice. "I actually wanna stay right here in the dream. For as long as it'll last me."

Leo paused. For once Charley was quiet and listening.

"I'm not ready for spiritual liberation, C.B. III. I just got here. That don't mean I'm refusing to live on the basis of what I've seen. I think I've got a lot to learn about love instead of want—about give instead of get—

about being with other human beings. And I'm just grateful I got a clear shot at it right here, right now.

"I thought that first morning I woke up in Stokesland was like Christmas Day. That was nothing compared to how I feel right now! The simple things I have, the everyday folks around me who love me and I love them—no way I'm gonna up and leave it all. No way, Charley! No way."

Leo's big friend was silent for a few moments. Then he spoke calmly. "I'm not saying you have to do what I'm doing, Stokes. Fine, you stay on and try to make it all work out. Who knows, maybe you and Con'll get down to it at last. That'll be a society page occasion, all right. The whole county'll turn out to clap and cheer for that one. And if you want me to, I'll be your best man. Wouldn't miss it for the world!

"But what I am saying, old bud, is, think it over. Don't forget this conversation while the wheels of ordinary living keep on turning, all around and inside you. You're like Frodo back in The Shire after the whole big adventure of power—you know, the hobbit, right? *Lord of the Rings*?"

Leo shook his head.

Charley chuckled. "Right. You don't know. By the way, just to set the record straight, while you were lost in the magic realms beyond Stokesland, whoever showed up in the far future and got torched by your Joseph IBM-Ananda friend, it sure wasn't me! At the time I was down here putting two truckloads of green dream money in the Cotton County Regional Bank. That's part of why I came up here from Raleigh. Ernestine set me up the special accounts and trusts right here. I just shoveled a few cool mil into your dream bank, Leo. In part so you can keep on taking good care of your everyday folks."

Leo was taken aback. He muttered, "Well, I'm...I'm pretty sorely in your debt, Charley."

Charley nodded. "Well, maybe so. I'm in yours too. You ain't Bob Jackson, and that's a good thing. You and Ernestine—I can trust y'all. But let's not drift. You may try to tie your life down here in 'humble little

Cotton County' and be a Good Samaritan for the rest of your days, and then what? Zap! Exit visa! And then right back into the karmic accelerator. The bardos, buddy. The after-death madness. The kind of scenes you just came from! When that day comes, you won't wake up here again in your old bed. And wherever and however you *do* show up, you will want to have something else altogether going on, that can be your rudder in the bardo storm."

For Leo there was something exhilarating about having a spiritual argument with Charley at a time when he, Leo, finally had some kind of experience to bring to the table. Even so, his blood was still about to boil over.

Charley was thinking, then spoke. "You know something, maybe that program really is, or was, an 'ultimate form of Maya.' Maybe the ultimate form of Maya points you to the need to get free of Maya altogether. Maybe the ultimate set of illusions leads you to find someone, some practice, some way to go about living that can trustably take you beyond illusions, beyond this whole game, the whole machine of life and death as we know it."

Leo let out a long, frustrated sigh. "But what about other people, Charley? What about improving the world? 'Love your neighbor' and all that?"

Charley grinned at him. "Sure, Leo, you can try to fix this place up a tad, but you're only going to get a bus stop so clean! This world is no destination. So yeah, it's good to do good things, good to be kind. But all that is secondary to getting your ass free of the dream even while you're in it. Making that your top priority is gonna do the whole world and everyone in it a lot more good than trying to do good deeds while you're still entranced and mummified.

"Though, again, I must say how deeply moved I am by your sudden altruism, Stokes!"

Charley looked at Leo with his eyes dancing. He tried to keep from cracking up. But he couldn't. With a huge guffaw, he spluttered into uncontrollable laughter, and couldn't stop.

Every time it seemed like he was quieting down, he looked at Leo again, tears streaming down his face, and his huge laughter started up again.

Leo was not amused.

Latchin' On Time

T he more Charley laughed, the redder Leo felt his face get. Finally, he too could no longer hold back, and he erupted. "Since *when,* Bass, did you corner the market on being able to change? Maybe I got something outta this whole thing that you can't see yet! Maybe I'm gonna be a different man. Maybe, just maybe, I already am one! How in tarnation do *you* know? You don't know. You don't know at all! You've been doing all this high and mighty preaching—bardos this and karma that—*now you listen to me, 'old bud'!*

"You don't know what's on my mind. You don't know how I feel. You don't know who I help. We've been living in different worlds half our dang lives, Charley. I don't presume to know the full scope of your life. What gives you the dad-gum gall to think you know about mine?

"Know what? Something's just starting to percolate in me, and I know it as strongly as all this stuff you know about masters and waking up and so-called spiritual freedom—speaking of dreams, a pipedream if I ever heard one! I didn't know this thing before, and maybe I couldn't have, but I do know it now—in *my* bones!

"And this is what it is, my friend. You live on a pretty rarefied plane, but I still got red clay squishin' up between my toes. I may wear a suit in the bank, but the work I do puts dirt under my fingernails. I'm connected to the goldang earth in a way you ain't even close to. I'm connected to the people who live it and till it and make it sustain us. And I'm pretty dang certain that for people like you to have the luxury of finding your God that helps you wake up, people like me are gonna have to get and stay in touch with our God that keeps it all going. And every now and then, shows us a little mercy and eases up on some of the pain."

Leo took a breath. His nostrils were flaring. He could barely look at Charley without feeling the red climb up his neck again. Charley was looking down.

"Look here, Bass, even if you do take off and find your 'way out,' somebody's gonna have to hang in here. I may not be the Mother Teresa of American finance, and no, I ain't read all those weird books and fine literature you can't help popping off about. But I read the news. I watch CNN. I smell the pollution. I see what's happening to the soil and the water. I see it in the drained and dog-tired faces of the farmers trying to dodge foreclosure year after goldang year.

"And you don't know what I do, what steel rods of government regulations I bend and what rules of my own risk management I break just to keep those boys on their tractors. You don't have a clue. So it might be to your advantage to shut your *dang mouth* about me and my altruism!

"Shoot, Charley, even so's you can go do your romantic thing for 'freedom from the dream,' somebody's gonna have to stay here and make sure Cotton County Regional keeps those trusts of yours strong and secure. So my bet is, for a few privileged people like you to go find a way out of this hardscrabble life, a whole bunch of other folks like me are gonna have to stay right here in place—wherever we are!

"This world may be 'halfway' and it may be a 'bus stop' in some highfalutin, big-brain spiritual way of seeing things, but it's *home,* Charley. For us. For our children. For life. And we got a lot to do to keep things going and move them along, make things right or righter where we can.

"So don't go pulling spiritual rank on me, Mountain Man. You got your thing to do. Go! Do it! Your money's safe here. Send a fax to Ernestine any old time; we'll wire you what you need.

"Meantime, I got my own thing to do. It's real different from yours—but it's real important too. It's lettin' go time for you—fine. But it's latchin' on time for me, like I ain't never latched on before. And maybe, just maybe, you need me to do my thing as much as I supposedly need you to do yours."

The two men gazed at each other in silence for a long time. Leo realized after a couple of minutes that his lips and teeth were pressed together so hard, they were starting to hurt. Without looking away from Charley's eyes, he relaxed his jaw.

Charley's expression betrayed no emotion, no response one way or another. But Leo knew his old friend couldn't dismiss or ridicule what he'd just said.

Finally, Charley grinned and looked off. He laced his fingers together and stretched his arms above his head, then put his hands behind his neck and leaned back.

"Been awhile since I saw the old 'L-bomb' detonate, Leo. Not bad, old bud, not bad." He paused. "Look, Leo, I...you're right. I stand corrected. I didn't mean to patronize or pull rank. And honestly, well, I'm...I'm real happy to hear you talking this way. Maybe, just maybe, there might not be a contradiction between what you're saying and wanting to do and what I'm saying and talking about doing myself."

Leo rolled his eyes and snorted. Charley shook his head.

"Naw, now listen, I said 'maybe.' Let's hold that possibility open, okay? Meantime, whatever you choose to do in your life, buddy roe, just don't lose sight of the vision you got on your Ultimaya ride. You just got a look at something that's deeper than this world. It's the substratum, the bedrock under the mud. You just fell into the crack at the bottom of the universe, Leo. And that crack'll never close back up on you, no matter how much good old Carolina clay you got squishin' up between your toes!"

Leo did not meet Charley's glance. His body was rigid. He neither denied nor acknowledged what Charley was saying. Charley sighed, then suddenly grinned and laughed.

"'Course, ain't no way you can just forget it. Talk about a crack in the world: you told Nan to spontaneously combust—and she actually did! Reading about that kind of stuff is one thing—actually willing it and then seeing it…nah, you won't forget."

Charley forced another laugh. Leo could tell he was trying to relieve the tension that, like smoke from a bad cigar, was still hanging between them.

There was another long silence. Charley reached again to his shirt pocket, absently, then put his hand on the table. He gave Leo an affectionate smile.

"Well, Ultimaya 1.0 took you to the water, in its own bizarre, bi-Zorro way. And if it couldn't get you to drink, I sure can't. I was just looking for a little companionship along the path…guess I'll have to find it elsewhere."

Leo smiled back wanly. "Could've cut through a lotta angst here, C.B. III, if you'd just said you wanted the pleasure of my company to begin with."

Charley shrugged. "Maybe so." He gazed at Leo quizzically, a smile playing at the corners of his mouth. "So, are you really gonna try again now with Constance?"

Leo nodded. "Yep, think so. In fact…I think I better get on over there right now. I got twenty years of being an idiot to make up for. I sure wish I still had that ring."

He suddenly looked down the hall toward his room and, without a word, got up and walked down the hall. Charley looked at him uncertainly, then stood and followed him. Leo opened the bedroom door and they both stepped in.

Leo could've sworn that when he had first come to in the room, back home after his strange journey, the space where his computer had once been on the desk was bare.

But now, in its place, folded neatly in half, lay the blue silk evening jacket. Almost like it had been there the whole time. Like it belonged there.

Charley asked, "What is it, Leo?"

Staring at it, Leo replied in a whisper. "Charley, I never had that jacket before Stokesland. I wore it the night I kissed Constance good-bye on the driveway there. I wore it when I came down to Raleigh with Joseph to see you. I wore it on the trip to the border between the worlds. I wore it…into the other universe. I was wearing it when I died in the future. Matter of fact, that's *all* I was wearing when I died!"

Charley was standing by his side, just behind him. He whispered back. "OK. Amazing. Something else?"

"Don't you remember? I told you, I carried the ring with me in the right side pocket, the whole time."

They looked at each other. Charley gestured toward the jacket.

A little unsteady, Leo walked to his desk. He picked the jacket up by the back collar with his left hand. It was certainly real—as real as anything else in this world.

A wave of relief and awe rushed through Leo's whole body and flooded his heart and brain as he stood there looking at the jacket, holding it up for a long minute. He thought, "That whole thing—*it wasn't just a bizarre dream!*"

He turned the garment so the right pocket came into his view. He looked at his friend. Charley was looking at the pocket, eyes wide.

"Whew!" Leo took a breath and exhaled. Then, with his right hand, he reached into the pocket.

The little velveteen box was there!

He pulled it out and held it up. "Look, Charley!" Leo whispered, trembling with excitement. "It's still here! *All right!*"

Without another word, Leo strode to the bed, laid the jacket out on it near the wall, and sat down on the bed. Charley pulled the rocker nearby and took his seat in it. The two of them looked at the box in Leo's hands. They were both grinning.

Leo hardly dared to breathe as he cradled the little box in one hand and opened the lid with the other.

There it was! The ring shone forth in the black velvet interior of the box, as lustrous and elegant as ever.

Leo whispered again. "Same ring, right, Mountain Man?"

"Sure is, Leo. Never seen anything like it before. Amazing—even to me."

For a few moments, they just sat there gazing at the gem. It was truly dazzling. Then Leo closed the box's lid and stood up. He turned and faced Charley.

"Well, what do you think? Ain't that a sign it's right for me to go see Constance and win her back?"

Charley laughed. "Who knows? I'm no expert in that field. But that sure as hell is what you're intending to do, right? Sign or no sign? Ring or no ring? Right?"

"That's right. So guess I better get on with it, don't you think?"

"Guess so, buddy roe. Give me a call. I'll be down at the office on into the evening, catching up on some stuff. I'd like to hear what happens. And tell Constance I said hey."

"Will do."

Charley rose to his feet. They looked at each other, laughed, and embraced. Then for a moment they just held one another's shoulders, looking each other square in the eye.

Charley grinned. "Bless your heart, Stokes. You are one piece of work, all right. And I am proud to be your friend."

Leo grinned back, then bolted over to his closet to change clothes. "Gotta get a move on, Charley! Time to latch on here, for sure. And play a little Santa Claus! Catch ya later!"

THE "U" SLASH

Leo heard Charley saying good-bye to Nan, who must've returned while he and Charley were contemplating the ring. He threw on decent street clothes and splashed on some cologne. At the last minute, Leo decided he just had to wear the blue silk evening jacket, however weird it might look. He thought, "Shoot, Con never saw me in something like this before, except in Stokesland, which doesn't count. But I can't not wear it. Just like I can't not give her that ring."

He tooled over to her house in the old gray Lincoln—enjoying its age, its familiarity, and the fact that it was not a Bentley and there was no chauffeur in sight—and pulled up in Constance's driveway. Walking up onto her porch, Leo suddenly realized he hadn't even called to ask if he could come see her. A fit of nerves hit him: "What if she won't see me? What if she hates me now? What if I don't mean anything to her anymore?"

He tried to shake all that off. "Come on, Stokes," he whispered to himself. "Get with it! She loves your hide, boy. Let her know you love her too—and she'll want that ring on her finger in no time!"

He rang the doorbell firmly, then waited, turning to look back at the street now dappled by afternoon sun filtering through the trees. He found it hard to believe that all this was just a "halfway world."

Thinking about everything Charley had told him, about what he went through with Ginny and Josh, made Leo grimace and shake his head.

"Never seen that man uncork like that before," he said to himself. "No wonder he's so down on this world and this life."

He looked at the lovely winter's day. Serene, clean, small-town street. Maples and sycamores naked to the breeze, waiting out the cold. High cirrus clouds scudding over the pines in the distance. Couple of kids playing in a yard. Now and again, a car, a dog, a cat.

"This is real," Leo thought. "This is life. Families loving each other, working out their lives together. Life is tough sometimes, for sure. But it's not just a bunch of bad karma. There's nothing human beings can't work out if we set ourselves to it. It ain't just a machine of action and bad reactions, everything repeating itself and tying us down like Charley was yakking about. Truth is, that boy is still so stung by losing Ginny and Josh the way he and Sarah did, he never really got back to the land of the living. That's the lens he's looking through. And that glass is *way* more than half empty.

"I should've told him that today. I mean, I brought it up, but I let it slide. Next time I'll bear down on him. It's a painful truth, but dang it, it is a truth. Naw, this *is* the real world. It's good. It's true. It's basically okay. What could something like Ultimaya possibly have to do with this? *That* was the bad dream. Not this."

He heard the door opening behind him. Constance peered out from inside the screen.

"Leo!" she exclaimed. "Well...I must say I wasn't expecting to see *you* standing out here." Her green eyes were wide with surprise as Leo approached the door.

"Well," he said, "I suppose we can stand on either side of this screen and talk. But it might be more comfortable setting down somewhere. Don't you think, Con?" He grinned at her, feeling mischievous and a little bashful at the same time.

"Oh, I'm sorry! Come on in, Leo. Lordy, you took me so by surprise I forgot to invite you inside."

Constance blushed, and the sight of it only thrilled Leo all the more.

He was drinking her in like he never had before—ever. He couldn't believe it. Finally, after all this time, he knew for certain that he was in love with Constance Cunningham.

And today was the day to let her know it. In no uncertain terms.

Still, as they walked into her living room, Leo felt the tension in her. He knew she was still hurting after the way he'd ignored her for the last month—capping about twenty years of him holding her close for moments, sometimes weeks, then pushing her away for months, even years. He really understood now that he had hurt her badly. Looking at her as they silently sat down, it made him wince.

Even so, he couldn't take his eyes off her. She just looked delicious to him, voluptuous and sensual, vulnerable, sweet. It was all he could do to keep from grabbing her and kissing her like crazy.

"Con, you look fantastic. Absolutely fantastic."

"I *do,* Leo?" She grimaced and shook her head. "Lordy, I feel like a wreck. But I am really glad to hear you're okay, Leo. You know, you had everybody worried sick. I mean, just worried sick."

They sat next to each other, though not too close, on her couch. Leo felt awkward, and he knew she did too. But she seemed genuinely glad to see him.

She got up and put on background music—Pachelbel, of all things, which, given what had happened in Stokesland, Leo found amusing but a little unsettling—and brought out some crackers, cheese, and apple cider. Leo decided he'd best settle in for the long haul, to get to the moment when he could spring the question and "the sparkler."

"Y'know, Con, while I was sick I had a lot of time to do some thinking—even though I was delirious half the time." He smiled. "And I was trying to remember exactly the first time we met each other. Was it at the homecoming party, my senior year?"

"No! Absolutely not, Leopold Stokes. It was at my parents' house where you came to pick me up and take me to the homecoming party, your senior year. And, *excuse me!* We didn't just run into each other there—*I was your date!*" She bugged her eyes out at him in mock anger. "And I was just a lowly little sophomore! I wouldn't have even shown up that night if you hadn't brought me with you." She giggled. "My, but that was a long, long time ago."

That was enough to break the ice. They snacked and laughed and reminisced for a while, about all the exploits of Charley and his crowd, and how the two of them, Leo and Constance, had almost but somehow never quite gotten together till years later.

At some point it was natural enough for Leo to bring up what a heel he'd been over the last month—and then some!—and to apologize.

"Con, I'm not kidding, and I'm not just trying to be nice. I've treated you real bad. I didn't do it maliciously. I…I guess I was just afraid, darlin'. But I did it. And I know I hurt you real bad. I know I did. And believe it or not, lately I have learned some very big lessons about how to live my life. And I want us to have another chance. I am truly sorry, Constance. Can you forgive me? And give us another shot at it together?"

Constance had been listening with a sweet but tense smile on her face. When he finished, she broke down and cried, and Leo took her in his arms and held her.

Soon enough, she was laughing again. They continued to reminisce, talking and gossiping about all kinds of people and times, Leo occasionally kissing her face and her hair and caressing her neck and nose and chin, her arms, her shoulders, just delighting in being with her.

When Pachelbel's *Canon in D Major* began playing, he felt it was time to make his move. "Same as in Stokesland," he thought. "No way to listen to those strings and not have a heart full of love."

"Con?"

"Mm?"

"I got something important I want to talk to you about."

"Why, Leo, I was under the distinct impression we've been talking about important matters all day long."

Leo was stunned. That's what she had said in Stokesland too.

"Yeah, that's true, but this is, uh, something of another order of importance."

"Am I perhaps underdressed for the occasion? Or maybe I should walk upstairs and back down, so I can make a proper entrance first?" She giggled and snuggled up closer to him.

"Naw, now Constance, I'm serious about this."

"I know you are, Mr. Stokes, and I'm teasing you because I'm enjoying myself a whole lot today. I'm enjoying just being with you here, more than I have in a very long time. So I don't know if I want to get all bankerly serious. For all I know, you're going to pull out some spreadsheets or something."

Leo was starting to get disoriented. Again, this was almost to the word what she had said in Stokesland. What in tarnation was happening here?

Aloud he said, "Con—"

She placed a fingertip firmly on his lips to shush him, smiling playfully. "Yes, Leo? Cat got your tongue?"

He pulled his left arm from around her shoulders to remove her finger. "Dang it, Constance, I mean it. I want to talk about us. I want to tell you something you've been waiting a long time to hear me say. Now I'm ready to say it, and you're playing games with me."

She became quiet. The violins of another Pachelbel piece filled the room with a depth of feeling so tangible Leo could almost taste it. He sensed the time had come. After more than twenty years, the time had come.

He leaned over and whispered in her ear.

"Constance Cunningham…I want you to be my wife. I want you to marry me. Will you marry me, Con?"

Constance did not turn toward him but sat quite still. Leo felt flustered, still disconcerted by the way the conversation seemed to be repeating the last one that had happened while he was apparently, at least to everyone else, lost in his Ultimaya delirium.

"Oh, heh, heh—I almost forgot," he said. A little nervously, he fished around in his jacket for the small black box. "Here it is, hon, that knuckle-sparkler I've been teasing you about practically since we were in high school." He opened the box to reveal the extraordinarily brilliant and beautiful diamond ring.

Constance turned to him now, and when he saw her expression, Leo's heart sank. There were tears in her eyes. But they weren't tears of joy and love and gratitude. They weren't tears of delight. Love, yes, but—pain. *Just like in Stokesland.*

"Why, Leo? Why have you waited so terribly long to ask me? Didn't you know how much I love you? Didn't you know I'd just about given up that you would ever accept my heart?" She stopped and sighed.

When she spoke again, there was fire in her eyes. "What am I supposed to do now, Leo? What am I going to say to Ralph? What am I supposed to do about what I've started to feel for him while you've kept on giving me the message to forget about you? Just what am I supposed to do, Leo?"

Leo felt—again—like he'd been harpooned in the solar plexus. It took him a moment even to get out that same single word. *"Ralph?"*

Tears were streaming down Constance's face.

"Leopold Stokes, don't you dare play dumb with me! You know very damn well that Ralph Honeycutt and me have been—well, consoling one another, just spending time." She sighed again and shook her head in dismay. "I declare, Leo, I've been so happy with you today. This is the first time I've truly enjoyed myself since Helen's accident. Between that and you being such a 'dang mule,' as you would say, I had just begun, finally, after all these wasted years to…to give up hope.

"And Ralph has, well, he's just been there for me, and me for him. We haven't said anything about it. But people are aware, a few anyway. Nan Creech has talked to me about you and Ralph a half dozen times at least. Every single time she's told me she was gonna get on you about getting on with it with me, if you truly want me."

"Ralph Honeycutt? Helen? *Accident?* Don't tell me, Constance!"

In a rage, Constance pulled away from him, crossing her arms over her chest. "I just cannot believe you, Leopold Stokes! I can understand these last few days, you being sick and all, but what about the last month? I have not failed to warn you—for a lot longer than that. I have not failed to plead with you to take me and my love for you seriously. What did you expect? I was going to wait forever? I feel guilty enough about Ralph—Helen being in a coma and all."

Constance turned away from Leo and shook with deep sobs for several minutes.

He felt so devastated, and so convicted by the truth of everything she was saying, that he didn't feel he should even touch her.

She kept crying.

He just sat there.

Finally, Constance calmed down. She got some tissues, wiped her face and nose, and dried her eyes. Without turning back to look at him, she continued.

"Helen is my closest friend. I feel so bad about her, and about him too, and about you—I declare, Leo! Really!"

She whirled around, imploring him with her gaze. "What did you expect me to do? I was the one who found him there hugging her and crying after that stallion kicked her teeth in and trampled her. And this whole month you never had any time for us—not for me, not for him, not for her!

"You acted like you didn't even know it happened. I understand that you never knew Ralph very much. He didn't hang out with you and your whole smug and uppity crowd. But you could've come around for my sake, Leo! Instead of giving me the cold shoulder, just 'cause I don't want to be alone and rejected for the rest of my life!

"Well, that man's got a heart in his chest, Leo. I love you, you know I do, but I love him now too. Most of all, I love her. I have got to devote myself to helping Helen come back to life, if she ever can and will.

"I don't know how I love him. If Helen does wake up, I am certainly not going to announce to her that Ralph and I have fallen in love. But I can't become engaged to you with all this going on. It's too soon...it's not real...I just can't."

Constance looked down at her left hand with its ringless ring finger and spoke more softly. "It's a beautiful ring, Leo. Seems like it almost shines of its own light. It's just exquisite. My whole heart wishes I could take it. But I can't. Not now. Maybe later. I don't know. I have to think it over. I need to feel you're serious. And I just need a little more time. You have got to respect that in me, Leo. You know you do."

He didn't show it, but Leo was dumbfounded. The history of Stokesland. Repeating itself in his real life. He remembered Charley's comparison of Ultimaya with Zorro, who left Z-slashes behind him with his sword. Now here was this whole cluster of repetitions with Constance—refusing his ring. Helen. Ralph! *Talk about a U-slash!*

Leo stammered out a reply. "Okay, Con, I—I understand...what you're saying. I can't blame you, though...I surely hope you'll come my way in due course. And honestly, I didn't know about Helen. Somehow managed not to hear a word about it. 'Cause of all the bad blood between me and her daddy, nobody even mentions them to me any more, Con—not even you! But I'm sorry. I'm really very sorry. You'll have to let me know how I can help, okay?"

She nodded, without looking at him. They sat quietly awhile longer. Constance leaned back toward him, lifted his arm up from his side and wrapped it around her shoulders, and snuggled back against him. But something had changed now. After a few moments she rose and looked down at him.

"Leo, you only just got out of your sickbed today. Don't you think you ought to go home and rest?"

He smiled. "You're not trying to chase me off, are you?"

"No, I am not trying to chase you off. But, well, it seems like we do need a little space now. Don't you feel that's true, Leo?"

"I don't want to feel that. But yeah, I guess so." He stood up and embraced her, kissing her softly on the lips. She responded, but only a little. He pulled back just a bit and looked into her wet green eyes. "I love you, Constance."

"I love you too, Leo," she whispered. "I just don't know how *much* I love you anymore. Or maybe I don't know quite *how* I love you anymore." She bit her lip and looked aside. "No, that's not it. I mean…I just don't know anymore, Leo. I just need time. That's all."

She led Leo to the door and walked him out onto the porch. "Will you give me a call tomorrow?"

Leo's heart leaped in his chest. "You bet," he replied, smiling at her. He walked Constance down the steps. "I definitely will. Thanks for asking."

She smiled back and gave him a little wave.

THE KARMA YOU DESERVE

s he drove the old gray Lincoln back to his house, Leo tried to put his finger on exactly why he felt so...well, rotten. Constance had, after all, come close to assuring him she would accept his proposal eventually. Mostly she just needed time.

Then why did he feel so rancid about it all?

Well, for one thing, Helen.

This was more than repetition. This was more than what Charley would call a little "karmic lesson." She really had been kicked and trampled and now was fighting for her life. Gorgeous woman, vibrant, still young—nearly dead, from a horse gone berserk. What dreadful news.

It didn't make sense to Leo that he'd somehow not heard the news. But what he really couldn't figure was why did *he* feel guilty about it?

It was as if his experiments with Ultimaya had caused her accident, when in fact both the accident and her falling into a coma, according to Constance, had preceded his adventures with Ultimaya 1.0 by at least several days.

Clearly, he must've picked up somehow on what was already happening with Helen. He wondered, "Is this what happens to psychics? Never thought there was anything to all that. But now I don't know what has anything to it and what doesn't."

As he pulled into his own driveway, Leo had to admit to himself: he was spooked. Something about this whole incident—now, sure enough, in his real world, the actual town of Ashlin with its whole cast of real-life characters—something about it all just reeked of Ultimaya. That, more than anything else, was what was getting under his skin.

Talk about events repeating themselves, actions and underside reactions—this last conversation with Con was weird!

Was the evening he'd had with her in Stokesland just some kind of dream premonition of this talk they'd had now in what he could only know as real life?

Or was this just some kind of flashback on *that?*

He had no idea. "The one thing I do know," he thought, "is this is all weird. Nasty, gruesome, strange, and flat-out weird."

He looked out the car window. He'd been sitting there for several minutes with the car no longer running. He shivered. It was getting cold.

Leo entered the house in a foul mood. Nan was in the kitchen, and it was nearly dinnertime. "Leopold Stokes! Your dinner's on in about three minutes! Don't you be late, hear?"

"Okay, Nan."

Washing his face and hands didn't relieve his mood even a little. As soon as they sat down to eat in the dining room, Nan immediately noticed.

"Something disturbing you, Leo?"

"Well, Nan…tough conversation with Constance."

He told her what'd happened—more or less. Nan was all ears, and he could feel her sincere concern. He could see it meant a lot to her, his relationship with Con. Nan's pledge to his dying mother was at stake here too.

But, thankfully, she didn't get shrill about it. After he finished his story, all she said was simply, "Bless your heart, Leo. Bless both your hearts—you and Constance both. I surely hope y'all can work it out. I personally think y'all would make a very lovely couple."

They sat eating in silence for a time. And, for a while, all was calm, though there was a pall of sadness in the room.

But the longer they sat, the more Leo could sense a tirade building in Nan—like magma in a volcanic dome. He laughed inwardly. "Hm, must be what I'm like, in miniature. An 'N-bomb.'" He didn't say anything, just continued eating quietly.

Finally, she could hold back no longer. "Well…can't say I personally did not try to warn you, Mr. Leopold Stokes. But you would not hear a word of it. Not a single word."

Leo looked at Nan in amazement.

"When did you do that, Nan? And where?"

"Why, right here! Right here at this very table. The other day, before you got so ill we had to put you to bed."

"And just exactly what did you tell me, Nan?"

"I beg your pardon, Mr. Leopold Stokes! How dare you give me the third degree! I'm the one who's been trying mightily against your stubborn opposition to get you to take this woman's hand—for years now! *I'm* the one who, if you will kindly recall, promised your own momma I would see to it that you found yourself a suitable bride and carried on the Stokes family name! *I'm* the one who—"

"Whoa, whoa, whoa, hold on a minute, Nan! I understand all that. I appreciate your concern and your help. All I asked is a simple question—just exactly what did you tell me the other day?"

"I tried to tell you to be aware that Constance was going through a change of heart, owing to some heavy burdens on her soul, with her poor friend Helen's accident and feelings she was having about Ralph Honeycutt. I tried to tell you about all that. But you were so full of your own notions about her that you just brushed me aside."

Nan put down her fork. She wouldn't even look at Leo.

"You actually told me, Leopold Stokes, that Constance Cunningham would be happy to wear a pop-top from a soft-drink can just to be engaged to you! Talk about arrogance. My, my! You know that Bible saying, 'Pride goeth before a fall'? I do believe, young man, you may have just proved that point—mightily, I might add!

"Well, at that point I just simply gave up. There is only so much a body can do if someone is simply intent on ruining his entire life beyond repair. And now you're finally fixing to learn your lesson. Well, that's a fine how-de-do, Mr. Stokes, but I—"

Leo could not handle another word. "Nan! That's enough. I got the message! Okay?"

But now that she was rolling again, Nan was not to be stopped. "No, sir! It is *ab-so-lute-ly* not enough! It's high time you shut your own mouth and listened well to your elder on this issue. It's high time you began to listen to a family friend who shares a woman's sensitivity and feelings about these very delicate matters of the heart. You've been walking all over that poor woman most of your born days, Leopold Stokes. And from my point of view, if she walks out on you now, it'll be exactly the karma you deserve!"

In a huff, Nan rose from her chair, slammed it up against the dining room table, and stormed into the kitchen.

Leo watched her, the blood draining from his face. When she had ceased stomping about, he shouted to her, "Exactly the *what* I deserve?"

Nan shouted to him from the sink, "You heard me, Leopold Stokes! *Karma!*"

Leo walked to the kitchen door, fuming. "Just exactly where did you come up with that one, Nan? 'Karma' is not a word you'd have picked up from *Reader's Digest* or your church hymnal. Where the hell did you get that idea?"

Nan still wouldn't look in his direction. "Don't you swear at me, Leopold Stokes! How I develop my vocabulary is my very personal business, and surely none of yours. But if you must know, Charles Bass the Third told me about it today while we were waiting, and hoping, and just praying to the dear Lord for you to *have good enough karma* to recover from your delirium—*and* your delusions of grandeur!"

"*Charley!* Goldang it, Nan!" Leo exploded. He was so furious that he hauled off and smacked the dining room door with the full force of his right fist—and then yelped, fighting back tears from the pain in his knuckles.

Terrified, Nan ran into the pantry and slammed the door behind her.

Standing there looking at his damaged knuckles—he'd hit the door so hard he broke the skin, and his hand was about to start bleeding— Leo laughed out loud.

"Repetition. Again! I can't believe it."

He laughed and laughed.

Then he shouted into the pantry, "I apologize, Nan. Don't worry. My fault. I'm not angry at you."

He heard no reply.

ULTIMAYA'S OTHER NAME

Still chuckling, and leaving Nan to her own devices, Leo turned and walked into his room. Without so much as a thought about it, he went straight to his phone and rang Charley Bass in Raleigh. Sure enough, Charley was still in his office, like he said he'd be.

"Oh, hey, Leo. So what happened?"

"You can probably guess, Charley." Wrapping a handkerchief around his bruised hand and wincing, Leo proceeded to tell him all the details of his spooky, U-slashed visit with Constance and his aggravating conversation with Nan. "But can I ask you one small favor, Mountain Man?"

"What's that, old bud?"

"Can we skip the comparative religion course for my housekeeper? I mean, really, that's all I need, Nan lecturing me now about karma!"

Charley burst out laughing. "Hey, bud, till you show some early warning signals of noticing how karma operates, somebody's gotta give you a foghorn from time to time!"

Leo laughed. "Well, all right. If she's gonna yammer at me, better that than her usual sermonette."

He paused, and thought of Constance. The rotten feeling from their meeting welled up in him again.

"But, hey, Charley, I don't get why Con's gotta hold out on me. I mean, *Honeycutt?* Shoot, Helen's still alive. It ain't like Ralph is exactly available."

Charley chuckled. "Well, glory be! Sounds like Con's got you nervous, Stokes. For once! It may piss you off, but to me this is one of the first signs of plain old guts in this lady since high school. She's trying to work out something bigger than she is.

"And you meantime—Earth to Leo! You're not even close to feeling her situation. I mean, come on. Even without the Ralph business, having her lifelong best friend in a coma? With her teeth kicked in?"

Leo thought about Helen, and for the first time that day he vividly remembered their delicious lovemaking in that bedroom...wherever they'd been. The memory made him squirm inside. He didn't even want to think about it.

Charley continued. "I bet you that's probably what Constance wouldn't tell me about when I talked to her. I mean, the whole thing with Helen and now Ralph. Well, I've hardly spoken to any of y'all for years, except you. Kinda makes sense she wouldn't go there with me. Today is actually the first time I heard of Helen's injury, myself. My ancient flame. Hm."

Charley sighed. Leo waited for him to go on.

"Con probably does need a little space and time on that account alone. She's got her needs too. Unpredictable for a change—shoot, Stokes, Con is a *woman!* So you want her, you're gonna have to go after her, buddy. But hey, maybe it's time. Maybe you're both ready to get down to a real adult love relationship. At last."

"Well...I feel I am, Charley. I guess it's just hard for me to accept she might not be."

"Yeah, but in addition to whatever she's naturally going through, Leo, you also ain't outta Ultimaya's grip yet. I don't think so. I mean, Con telling the whole story near on verbatim, same as she laid it on you in Stokesland...sounds like signature, vintage Ultimaya to me. Yessir: calibrated, machine-tooled karma. Karma is just not usually so black-and-white and if *a* then *b*. Ultimaya makes it so you'd have to be a mule headed fool not to notice the repetitions and consequences." He paused. "Guess you were the ideal mark, Stokes!"

Charley laughed. Leo didn't. For a moment neither one spoke.

"Whoa!"

"Whoa what, Charley?"

"Something just dazzled me for a minute there." Charley snorted, laughing. "Can't believe it never occurred to me before now."

"What's that?"

"What you just got treated to was only Ultimaya *1.0,* Leo!"

"And? Lay it on me, professor."

"'One-point-oh' means this was just the first release of the Ultimaya program. That means there could be Ultimaya 2.0, 3.0, and so on, down the line. Who knows how many different versions might show up in the future? And who it might affect? And how?"

Leo started feeling uptight. "Whew. That's kinda scary."

"Well, yeah! But hey, anything that can set a human being as straight as old Ultimaya's set you is bound to be a little scary, no matter what the delivery system."

Charley broke himself up laughing. Leo's chuckles were a tad quieter.

"Grabbing you by the shorthairs of your soul the way it did, and maybe still is, Ultimaya 1.0 has been a kind of primer. Almost too simple, symmetrical, like a game, a hi-tech, real-life Cliff's Notes on how reality works. But maybe we ain't seen nothing yet, old bud. God only knows what kinds of mucking around with human karma that program might get into in later releases! I mean, it's more like an operating system than like an application."

"Translation for the techno-dummy here, Mr. Bass?"

"Well, on your machine, most of the programs were what we call 'applications.' The main one they all rode on was the 'operating system.' That was MS-DOS in your laptop. By being plugged into that operating system, you could then do word-processing, or work on spreadsheets, do telecommunications, and so on. That is, if Ultimaya would've let you!

"Anyway, Ultimaya might turn out to be a basic background or operating system for all kinds of further developments. On the spiritual side alone, the possibilities are endless."

Leo was quiet. *This man is deep,* he thought. A feeling welled up in him of how much he respected Charley and treasured their friendship.

"You know a lot, don't you, Mountain Man?"

Charley didn't reply right away. When he did, his voice was soft. "Fact is, apart from all the tech stuff, what do I really know? Ginny and I worked out a whole lot between us, on a human level, but in the big picture...who knows? I've read a lot of spiritual books, made a few forays into the real thing years ago. I've tried to keep my eyes open since and I've done a patch of noticing what's going down here while the dreams, American and you name it, have been crumbling around us. I mean, this little recession we're crawling out of is the least of it...

"But what good'll all that do me in the bardos, Stokes? Most of what I do know is still in my head. Nowhere near my heart and guts. So, I've got to do what I am about to do."

There was a long silence.

"Charley...did you mean it, if me and Con do get together? Being my best man?"

"'Course. If you'll get on with it, y'know? I can't make guarantees for another two decades down the line!"

"Great. Thank you. Don't worry, I'm on it. Though, it does depend on that unpredictable woman Ultimaya helped me figure out I really am in love with. Talk about a U-slash!"

Charley laughed, but Leo just sighed. He felt like he suddenly had a mountain to climb. A real steep and icy one.

"Where you gonna go, Mountain Man?"

"Don't know. I'm checking out some options."

"You'll stay in touch?"

"You bet. Hey, that's getting easier than ever. Brave new world."

Then Leo remembered a final request. It'd been on his mind ever since he drove away from Constance's house that afternoon.

"Charley, I think I gotta bring some spirituality into my life too. I mean, you're right, Ultimaya practically branded that need into my soul.

But I can't do it like you. I've gotta stay here, do my thing here. No matter what happens with Constance."

The thought slipped through his mind that maybe he could somehow help Helen, or help Con help Helen, come back to life. Then it hit him again: he wasn't sure how he'd handle it if Helen did revive.

He kept talking.

"God gave me my life back *for* something, Charley. Somehow I have to make it about God. And I don't mean the Job Hawkins–Strap Rock version of God. You know that. On the other hand, your spiritual stuff is brand new to me. I don't get it. And I feel the place I need to start is right here where I've always been. I'm a baptized Christian and to be honest I don't have a clue what that really means. I want to find out. But, whew... let me see if I can get myself to say this thing. It's kinda hard to...uh... you with me?"

"Right here, Leo."

Leo was surprised to feel tears welling up. "Whew, okay. I'm...I don't know where this is coming from." He sniffed back the tears.

"That's that U-slash, buddy roe. Maybe Ms. Ultimaya's other name is...God."

Leo broke down sobbing. This had never happened to him before. He hadn't known he could ever even have such a feeling. The tears and sobbing came from somewhere inside he couldn't fathom or put a name on.

Charley stayed quiet.

After a time, Leo pulled out a handkerchief, wiped his face and eyes, and blew his nose.

"Okay. Here's the thing. I'm starting to see that life's supposed to be about God for *God's* sake, rather than about God for my sake, or just about me with no God in sight. And it's supposed to be about God for *other people's* sake—for *life's* sake. Does that sound right?"

"Yeah, buddy. Righter than rain and sunshine both. And sounds real Christian, too, by the way."

"Well, given my track record right up through this afternoon at Con's, you're right, I—I need help. I need...I need more grace, Charley. I need some kinda higher wisdom. All that stuff about shamans and masters and whatnot, gurus, just goes right over my head. I need something to help me make sense of all this in the here and now, with my feet on the only real ground I know. It's all pretty new and strange."

"I understand, Leo. Believe me, I do."

"Well, then, do you think maybe—maybe you could lend me some of your books about it all? I ain't exactly your bookworm type. But I gotta start somewhere. Something simple and plain. Basic. That'll help me get into my own spiritual roots."

"Of course." Charley was obviously surprised. "Hell, Leo, I'll give some of 'em to you."

"Thanks, Mountain Man."

Charley was quiet for a few seconds. "Y'know, Leo, ever since I left you this afternoon I've been mulling it all over again. You really nailed it there—you gotta do this thing your own way. They say in the old texts, one of the secrets of spiritual growth is to find your own particular path. So I get that you got your own path to find and walk. And I am in no position to tell you what it should be."

Leo was stunned. "Well, thanks, Charley. Maybe I ain't a total spiritual dumbass, after all."

"Well, Leo, maybe you ain't. Everybody's got a blind spot, including me. And you definitely helped me take a look at some things I wasn't seeing too. In me."

That prompted Leo to say something else—something he felt was a little risky to bring up. He'd thought of it earlier in the day.

"Charley, before you up and disappear on me, while we're working this particular row to hoe, can I mention something else? About you?"

"Well, uh, yeah sure, Leo. Fire away."

"Well, this isn't easy either, but...I just keep getting the feeling that your particular way of seeing things—as wise and well-informed as it may be—just might be seriously colored by the tragedies of your life. Losing Ginny. Losing Josh."

There was silence on the line.

"Charley, I don't know if there's any truth to this. I just have that feeling. And I can't imagine what you've lost. Or how deep a hatchet it sank into your heart and soul—"

"It's okay, Leo." Charley's voice was soft and quavering, but clear. "Go on."

Leo pulled the phone from his ear and looked at it. This was new territory but it seemed the risk was paying off.

"All right, then. It's like you're angry at God, Charley. It's like you haven't forgiven life for taking Ginny's and Josh's lives away from you. And that deep, horrible loss has maybe colored your whole philosophy. You said yourself, it's like you've been in an endless bardo ever since.

"So, yeah, there's a side of me staying here in Ashlin that has a whole lot to do with how I know I gotta live my life now. But there's another part of how I can't do it your way that—well, it's because I can't believe your picture of reality. I don't buy it, Charley. And I can't."

Charley's voice had an edge. "Yeah, Stokes, I get that you've got to find your own way. But my basic take on things was intact way on back there, decades ago—way before I met Ginny, way before Josh was even born."

Leo felt a rush of intensity rise in him and didn't hold back. "Dang it, Charley, *something changed in you* after Ginny and Josh—and you're not copping to it. That whole dark, hopeless, depressing thing about the relentless machinery of it all...that wasn't there in you before, Charley. A spark of life just went right out of you and it ain't come back. And that dark hole in your heart colors how you see everything from the inside.

"You really need to take this in, my friend. 'Cause wherever you go and whatever you do on this big quest of yours, to me, this thing is like a ball and chain you're dragging behind you. It's karmic, man. And it's gonna drag you down and hold you back."

Leo was startled at what had just come out of his mouth. But now he knew he had to just stay quiet and let Charley react however he would. Talk about a negotiation!

More silence.

Charley sighed audibly.

Then he said softly, "Well, well. Guess who got grabbed by the shorthairs of the soul now?" He sighed again.

Leo felt like he'd stepped off a cliff in their relationship that he hadn't even known was there. Like they both had, and now they were in some kind of free fall.

Charley went on. "That's deep, old bud. Coming at me from a direction that—well, it was in my blind spot. I'm gonna have to really chew on it and digest it."

His voice regained some strength and energy. "Kind of confirms something about you though. Talk about karma, there's another word from ancient India: *dharma.* It means 'what sustains.' With a capital *D* it means the ultimate truth, the big Law of life, the real teaching and story about reality. But with a small *d,* dharma is each person's lot and role in life. And the big point is, everybody's dharma is unique. No one's is the same as anyone else's."

Leo smiled and continued listening. Charley Bass was just born to preach.

"Even though it was about me personally, what you just said might be some big 'D' Dharma. I'm gonna have to work with it for a spell. But I'm getting that, even to be able to say it, you must really be plugging into your own small 'd' dharma. 'Humble little Ashlin' and all that.

"Maybe all that ain't so humble. Maybe it's your unique way of serving—serving others, serving life. And yeah, serving God. Maybe your calling is just to be a beacon of good in your little town. Which, when it gets into the real realm of the human heart and soul, ain't so little after all, is it?"

Leo was so touched to hear Charley acknowledge him this way, he couldn't speak.

Charley went on. "What you're saying about wanting some of my books—makes me feel like I can really go, wherever my path is gonna take me. Great teachers there in those books. Plenty of real deep Christians too. Then again, they had their own dharmas, their own callings, in their time and place. We still gotta work out ours."

They fell into another silence. Leo, his eyes moist, felt an unspeakable sorrow of imminent parting flood the space of their friendship. He knew it was a good thing, not a bad thing. But it still felt like water silently but unstoppably rising in the cabin of a submerging cabin cruiser. With two people in it, and at least this stage of their friendship about to drown. And no possibility of escape.

It was just the way it had to be.

Leo blurted out, "Charley, you truly saved my life. I love you like a brother. I'm gonna miss you. I'm gonna miss you real bad."

"I love you too, old bud. So much it makes my heart ache. And yeah—me too. This is gonna hurt."

Silence again.

"Thanks, Charley. Take care. Talk to you later, my friend."

"Later, buddy roe. Later on."

And so concludes, at least for now and for all we know, "the trouble with the wishes of Leopold Stokes," the first release—1.0—of Ultimaya.

Acknowledgements

Ultimaya 1.0: The Trouble with the Wishes of Leopold Stokes owes much to many.

First, I happily acknowledge the Divine Feminine herself, in so many traditions simply known as "the Goddess" or "the Mother." As strange and crazy as it may sound, the One Whom I've come to call "the She-Mystery" first danced into my heart and soul in ways that have transformed my life by coming to me in the inspiration to write this very book—and as its title "character." That was over twenty years ago.

She didn't stop there either. But…that's a whole other story.

This story, *Ultimaya 1.0,* benefits from the diligent, passionate researches of billions of men and women in the global laboratory of being and becoming that has produced all our spiritual, intellectual, and artistic cultures. I'm especially grateful to two modern spiritual adepts who were my most important initiators and teachers, the Indian sage Bhagavan Sri Ramana Maharshi (1879–1950) and the American-born avatar Adi Da Samraj (1939–2008). In particular, those familiar with Adi Da's teachings will no doubt see his distinctive footprints here and there in the sands of this fantasy.

The novel also owes much to so many storytellers, cultural interpreters, myths, and legends—from the nameless weavers of olden tales such as *Aladdin and His Magic Lamp* to the good Mr. Dickens; from the worldwide shamanic tradition forward to Lewis Carroll, C. S. Lewis, J. R. R. Tolkien, C. G. Jung, Joseph Campbell, Olaf Stapledon's *Star Maker* and Walt Disney's *Sorcerer's Apprentice*; back to the ancient *Tripura Rahasya: Mystery beyond the Trinity* and the medieval *Tibetan Book of the Dead;* to many other histories, scriptures, fables, fairy tales, morality plays—*Pilgrim's Progress* comes to mind—and more.

I am also deeply indebted to many individuals. Among the early supporters and helpers who made its original version possible in 1990-92, only a few remained in my life in any active way, and some do today. Of course, there was my father, Murray Bonder. From the beginning of my writing this book to the end of his life in early July 2011, he was its great champion. My mother, Anne Bonder, gave me great encouragement and help in so many ways throughout our lives together. She died in 1996. My beloved sister and only sibling, Ellen Bonder Lohr, has also supported the project wholeheartedly. Karen Peoples remains a dear friend, and Marcia Cohen, an abiding, heartful presence.

Of the others whom I thanked in the original acknowledgements pages back when I first wrote the book (1990-92), some have also died. One who deserves special mention was the late Oscar Collier, who became its enthusiastic literary agent until I decided not to publish the story in its original form. (See "Author Q&A" starting on page 280.)

Many who were so helpful back in the early 1990s I presume are still involved in the spiritual school of my former teacher Adi Da. There's a delicate politics of spirituality in situations where a once central participant has departed from a once shared path. As they might not appreciate being named here, I'll refrain from mentioning people who were then in that community who gave me both material support and encouragement on this project. To those who do someday read these words, please know I remain grateful.

Coming to this side of the millennial divide, I'm also grateful to many people.

First and foremost, my wife, Linda Groves-Bonder—to me, the most wondrous human embodiment of that She-Mystery I've ever encountered, and my beloved partner, dearest friend, and companion on the path of living every single day. "Soul mates" barely begins to point toward the richness of our unity, our dance.

Also, my late father's wife, Carol Bonder, truly the love of his life, who has been such a steadfast, kind, and caring anchor to our whole extended family. A natural embodiment of Southern grace, Carol delighted in the story and its characters from early on. Her response helped assure me it might be well received in the lands of my later childhood and youth—North Carolina and Tennessee—and elsewhere south of America's Mason-Dixon line.

Friends and colleagues who support Linda's and my work financially have made generous donations that have directly or indirectly facilitated the book's publication and promotion. Our heartfelt thanks to: Leslie and Geoff Oelsner, John Morrison, Sandra Glickman, Hans and Jackie Jonassen, Chris Stewart, David Mitchell, Dan Altman, Lynn Taylor, Andrea Bruecks, Rod Taylor, Marty Cooper, Jed Bentley, Mark Taylor and Vera Angelico, Allan Morelock and Gena Netten, Ardith Dean, Steve Beckett, Stephen Sweet, Gina Anala, and Gayatri Schilberg, and others who prefer to remain anonymous.

Deep gratitude also for the support of John Records, my dear friend and a master in both kinds of "real worlds" (www.johnrecords.com); my coach and confidant, Pamela Melton (www.intimate-transformations.com); and David Lesser, Linda's and my informal yet essential business development advisor (www.executiveconfidant.com). I'm also grateful for the encouragement and wise advice I've received from founder John Eggen and my coach Lorna McLeod of The Mission Marketing Mentors program (www.missionpublishing.net), and from author's champion and coach Tom Bird of The Tom Bird Method (www.writeyourbookin8days.com).

Stephanie Marohn (www.stephaniemarohn.com) anchored the text with expert copyediting, helped me solve some typographical issues that had nagged at me all through the years, gave me deft editing suggestions that I feel have improved the book's tone and texture immensely—and generally classed up the story's telling all around. Since receiving Stephanie's contributions I have made substantial changes to the back matter and added two entirely new sections to it, the "Reading Group Guide" and "Author Q&A."

Genie Raff, the incomparable manager of Linda's and my virtual office and such a dear heart, helped with organizing and formatting the manuscript. Our clients and friends Liz Stevenson and Arthur Gillard did a careful proofreading; Liz provided additional formatting help and an extra editorial look at parts of the book that I reworked later. Then, when the book was laid out for its print edition, we enlisted Robin Quinn (www.writingandediting.biz) as a professional proofreader to make sure everything was intact. But Robin also offered such superb, detailed, final polish edits to her proofing sample that I couldn't resist having her give the whole book one more run-through.

Finally, a team of generous volunteers convened for an "Ultimaya Proofin' Barnraising." Lynn Taylor, Louise Herschelle, McKay, John Morrison, Jane McGillivray, Sean Arnold, Amanda Gustafson, Tyler Keith, and Jordan Paige each either read through the whole book or did a fine-toothed comb proofing on a specific section.

Each of the editors and proofers has contributed as much as possible to the text in the particular moment she or he added to its development; many thanks to each and all.

Gaelyn Larrick (www.artservingspirit.com) designed the book's inspired cover, a work of art; Linda and I couldn't be more pleased with it. Deborah Perdue (www.illuminationgraphics.com) created the elegant interior design and laid the book out in its print format. Patricia Bacall (www.bacallcreative.com) converted the text into ebook formats and set up everything we needed for its optimal electronic distribution on Amazon.com and elsewhere. The folks at our printer Lightning Source (www.lightningsource.com) have helped us get a beautiful printed edition onto bookstore shelves and into readers' hands, as well as providing easy access to excellent distribution through Ingram. And I am grateful to Elaine Wilkes, creator of the online course *How to Get Your Book into Stores*, for a superb collection of practical marketing resources and her kind generosity in making them available (www.getyourbookintostores.com).

A team of Linda's and my clients have generously volunteered time and expertise to help us bring the next forms of our spiritual offerings into the world, and that includes the publication and marketing of this novel: John Morrison, Gina Anala, Michael Schwartz, Bryan Hudson (a she!), Hans Jonassen, Amanda Gustafson, and Gena Netten.

Stephen Dinan of The Shift Network gave me a big infusion of encouragement and support, and a juicy endorsement. A golfing friend, Mike Hatfield, CEO of the hi-tech company Cyan, Inc., has also written helpful words about the story. He was one of the first enthusiastic readers who signaled that the book can reach a broad audience beyond those already intensely interested in spiritual ideas and practices.

Linda's and my deeply kindred teaching colleague Robert Augustus Masters, himself a writer of legendary finesse, offered along with his appreciations a crucial insight into a specific weakness in the story. Truth be told, I had tussled a bit with that section of the book but had given up trying to correct it further. Robert, however, also made a suggestion for how I could improve that passage which had never occurred to me. I've gratefully followed his recommendation, as much as I could; if the tale benefits, it's due to him.

I am also indebted to Gena Netten, a former brand and marketing manager at the Educational Testing Service, and to Susanne West, an author and professor of psychology at John F. Kennedy University, for their early words of praise and enthusiastic support.

Monika Mitchell, CEO of the increasingly acclaimed website Good Business International (www.good-b.com), for which I write a blog called "The Spirit/Money Split," contributed the final comment we were able to insert in the first edition. In our era when the greed of bankers and other financial and commercial professionals has had shocking consequences for the whole world, I'm honored she would call it "required reading" for such folks. The book's protagonist, Leopold Stokes, came to my mind as a banker long before anyone could have imagined the devastating events of the last several years.

Linda and I are also thankful to the following folks, participants in the Waking Down in Mutuality spiritual work I founded or people on our mailing list, who purchased the book well before its actual publication: Amy Conger, Sandra Glickman, Chris Stewart, Gary Rich, Andrew Ward, Bruce Atkinson, Liz Kennedy, Rosemary Read, Nick Nielsen, Tyler Keith, Pat Keating, John Morrison, Marc Hanlan, Cielle Backstrom, Charles Dudas, Duncan Herring, Jackie Jonassen, Jim Mathis, Arthur Gillard, Tara Bowers, Barbara Witney, Dorian Schiller, Ruthie Hutchings, and Craig Powell.

Ultimaya 1.0 is the most sheerly fun book I've ever written. My special gratefulness again, then, always goes to that mysterious Spirit-presence who animates this story: Ultimaya herself.

About the Author

Born in New York City in 1950, Saniel Bonder moved with his family at age seven to the small town of Smithfield, North Carolina. A Harvard B.A. in Social Relations and an Honorary National Scholar, while in college Saniel began a spiritual quest that became the focus of his life. His quest benefited from both Western and Eastern trainings and culminated in a great awakening in 1992, after which he began teaching others.

His passion has been to democratize spiritual awakening and help everyday people integrate it with all aspects of ordinary living. In the mid 1990s, Saniel began developing what is now the international Waking Down in Mutuality transformational work. To allow the work to achieve fully democratic, mutual governance, starting in 2005 he willingly turned over its formal control to colleagues he had originally trained. He and his wife Linda Groves-Bonder remain active teaching leaders in the growing Waking Down community network (www.wakingdown.org, www.awakenedmutuality.net). They are also founding members of American philosopher Ken Wilber's Integral Institute.

Saniel's books include *Waking Down, Healing the Spirit/Matter Split, Great Relief, The White-Hot Yoga of the Heart,* and a novel converted from a play, *While Jesus Weeps.* He and Linda are coauthoring a flagship new teaching book with an accompanying multimedia series, *The Human Sun: Radiant Gateways to Your Awakening, Wholeness, and Unique Purpose* (forthcoming 2012). They co-present the book's core teachings on a 2-DVD set, *Awake and Radiant: An Invitation to Your Direct Conscious Embodiment* (www.TheHumanSunSeries.com, now available).

Other forthcoming books by Saniel include *The Seven FundaMentals of Honest Swing Golf,* on golf's "mental game," and *The Spirit/Money Split Strikes Again!,* from his blogs at Good Business International, www.good-b.com, on the hidden sources and deeper implications of recent financial-economic events. He also enjoys playing flutes, and has a CD of solo tunes, *The Nectar.*

Saniel and Linda are now founding Human Sun Institute, www.humansuninstitute.com (site under construction), as a globally active institution to "awaken and empower leaders for the third millennium." (See "Author Q&A," p. 287.) They live in the countryside near Sonoma, California, with their highly sentient cat Hercules, surrounded by vineyards, pastures, horses, and lots of birds.

For a free four-session audio introductory course on Saniel and Linda's work, visit www.heartgazing.com. For information on their offerings, including customized programs and retreats for individuals, couples, groups, and corporations, write them at info@sanielandlinda.com. You can also get more information on their own work at www.sanielandlinda.com, and on the Waking Down in Mutuality network and offerings at www.wakingdown.org and www.awakenedmutuality.net. And, see Saniel and Linda and many other Waking Down teachers on YouTube video clips.

Reading Group Guide

1. Ultimaya 1.0 addresses age-old questions about the purpose of our lives and how we should live. One perennial quest since the dawn of our humanness has been to figure out how to fulfill our desires for the material or tangible things of life, such as wealth, sex and love, health, success, knowledge, sheer pleasure, fame, and so on. An often conflicting quest has been to achieve spiritual freedom, wisdom, enlightenment, salvation, or liberation—often described as emancipation from bondage to those other "worldly," materialistic attractions and pursuits.

How do you see these quests and their values appearing in *Ultimaya 1.0*? Which character most exemplifies each one of them? Summarize the value systems of each of the two main characters, Leopold Stokes and Charley Bass. Does either of their worldviews and value systems "win" in the end? If so, which—and how? If not, what happens instead?

2. Which of these two primary orientations to life most characterizes you, or has the most influence on your day-to-day living? As you read or listened to the book, did you have any moments of strong self-recognition where one or another character was voicing or living out attitudes that you identified with in yourself? If so, describe at least one of them.

3. How would you describe Leopold Stokes's relationships to each of the primary women in his life? Does Leo grow in his appreciation for each of them through his ordeal and journey? If so, in what ways? If not, what do you feel he is missing or failing to understand even as the story ends?

4. Based on what you know of both Leo and Constance, what do you think is the likely future of their relationship in the possible aftermath of *Ultimaya 1.0*? And, what would you personally prefer to take place between them in their possible future, if anything?

5. At different times in the book, Charley Bass, Leo's computer mentor and longtime friend, gives a bit of a sermon about his take on the mysterious computer program Ultimaya 1.0 and Leo's relationship to it. Does Charley's view or appreciation of Ultimaya 1.0 change at all in the book? If you think so, give examples of how, and why. In what ways, if any, did your take on Ultimaya 1.0 change over the course of the book? How do you feel about the program now? Do you think it was a force for good in Leo's and others' lives, or not? Explain.

6. One of Charley's primary ways of describing the effect Ultimaya 1.0 seems to be having on Leopold's life is what he calls "calibrated karma." Another of the key points he tries to bring to Leo's attention more than once has to do with the notion of "halfway worlds." How would you define each of these phrases? Do you agree with Charley's understanding of them? Do you agree with what he's trying to persuade Leo to do about each of them?

7. How did you find yourself responding to Leo's choices and actions in his interplay with Ultimaya 1.0? Did you ever feel he was on a right track? In contrast, did you ever feel he was in effect driving himself off a cliff by over-reacting and trying to command the program? Give a couple of examples of how Leo's choices struck you and what you felt at different moments of his journey.

8. The engagement ring that Leo acquired in Stokesland and wanted to give to Constance Cunningham, his longtime-sometime female companion, becomes an object of very special meaning to him throughout the wilder, more bizarre parts of his journey and afterward. What does the ring symbolize to Leo? What does its value to Leo tell you about what matters most in life to him, and how he relates to the people around him, especially Constance? Do you have any objects in your life that have similarly strong meanings to you? If you do, describe one or two, and explain their value and meaning for you.

9. Leo has the experience several times in the book of realizing that he has misinterpreted, misunderstood, and failed to appreciate other people in his life—both in Ashlin and in Stokesland. What turned out to be the relationship between Joseph, the African-American chauffeur, and the man Charley referred to as "IBM-Ananda" in Leo's dream-visions of the future? How does Leo later realize he was holding stereotypes about Joseph earlier in the story, or about Chatsworth the butler? Did his experiences show you anything about your own possible tendency to objectify others and to see in them stereotypes rather than actual persons?

10. Leo and Charley undergo several shifts in their understandings of one another and their relationship. Describe at least two of these shifts previous to the final chapter. Do you feel these were plausible, real passages in these characters' development? What if anything rang false for you?

11. At the end of the story, what do Leo and Charley discover about their relationship and their likely immediate future as friends? How did that discovery make you feel? Do you think it likely that Leo and Charley will each fulfill their particular dreams, goals, and intentions? What did you hope for each one of them as the story ended? And what, if anything, do those hopes for them tell you about precious things that you hope will happen, or maybe will continue to happen, in your own life?

Author Q&A

**You've referred to the "curious history" of *Ultimaya 1.0*.
Tell us about it.**

I wrote an original version of the story two decades ago (1990-92), when I was still a member of the community of my primary spiritual teacher, Adi Da Samraj. Today I have only the barest recollection of when, where, and how I worked on the book back then. I do remember well the delight of discovery and just sheer joy I had writing it. Part of what made it such fun was that the story kept surprising me as I went along.

However, in the summer of 1992, around the time I finished the original manuscript, it became necessary for me to leave my teacher and his school. I had spent nearly my entire adult life there. I already had a literary agent, the now-late Oscar Collier, who loved the book and was ready to start shopping it to publishing houses. But my departure from my then-guru's work and world gave me pause. I asked Mr. Collier to hold off on presenting the book while I had to reconsider my entire take on life.

It soon became clear that subtle yet major shifts in the perspective underlying the story and its dialogues would be necessary. Until then, I couldn't be comfortable releasing the book into the public. I was not in a position at the time or even for years afterward to edit the book and make those shifts.

Part of the reason why is that, to my astonishment, later that same year (1992) I underwent an immense bio-spiritual and existential transformation—an awakening to a new, permanent, primally embodied and unitive awareness that had eluded me all those previous years. It led to the work that has consumed my life ever since, as a facilitator for many others of that same kind of transformation and ongoing evolutionary growth.

Over the years my father, Murray Bonder, consistently urged me to do whatever it took to fix up *Ultimaya 1.0* and see where it could go once published. Finally, late in 2009, I began the work. I no longer had a viable electronic version, but I did soon find the physical copy of the text that my then-copyeditor had worked on with me in 1992.

So I set about reentering the entire story into my computer from scratch. I figured as I went along I would make those subtle yet important changes I knew were needed. In the intervening years I had forgotten nearly everything in the tale except the barest plot outline. As a result, while I was reentering the text and making little edits here and there I had the bizarre—and, I have to admit, quite delicious—experience of reading the book as if for the first time myself. It was almost as though someone else had written it.

Are there any major changes between the published book and the original?

Most of the essential plot line has hardly changed at all. But at a less conspicuous level a lot has changed. Here in the back of the book, the "Acknowledgements" and "About the Author" sections have of course been updated, and the "Reading Group Guide" and this "Author Q&A" are new.

My copyeditor, Stephanie Marohn, helped me dial back the visual representation of the characters' Southern drawls, in terms of both spelling and punctuation. So the "lingo" is a bit easier to read and get a feel for. She also urged me to read the dialogue aloud in a final editorial run-through. Once I started in on that, it led me to read the whole book aloud, or at least whisper it to myself. This helped me catch a whole slew of spots where the tone inadvertently was slipping from the conversational to the obviously written, from how folks think and talk in the book's world to how I think, sometimes talk, and often write, in my own. As a very simple example, it struck me that anywhere "maybe" could replace "perhaps," that was probably a good thing to do. Never mind multi-syllabic and more intellectual words and phrases that had sneaked into the vocal tone of Ultimaya like little verbal viruses!

To go back to the story's history, the 1992 version had a bit of a dogmatic, heavy-handed message. Now there is no single message. The telling leaves things quite a bit less certain, in dramatic tension. The shifts I've made also make for key changes in the relationships between the central characters. A crucial piece of one character's development was suggested to me by fellow spiritual author and teacher Robert Augustus Masters. What I deleted and the new material I replaced it with in response to Robert's recommendation is the most substantial change from the original draft. Plus, that replacement mini-story led me to divide the two long final chapters into five shorter ones. That may make the whole third and final act more readable and satisfying. The two extra chapter titles themselves carry some heft. I hope they'll help keep readers curious and wondering right to the end, and even beyond.

Speaking of the Southern drawls, you lived in North Carolina as a boy and went to school in Tennessee—but if readers watch you on YouTube, say, they won't hear a Southern accent in your speech. How's that?

My Jewish grandparents emigrated to New York City in the early 20th century from Poland and eastern Russia. My parents and sister and I moved to small town, mostly Protestant North Carolina when I was seven. Before long my folks were teasing me about speaking two different languages—their New York accents at home, and "Southern" with my new friends. In my mid to later teens I went to Webb School, a distinguished prep school, in a village in Middle Tennessee. I spent a lot of time there studying Faulkner and other Southern literature.

So I do have an enduring love for the people, language, customs and land of the American South. And believe me, there are plenty of smart, sophisticated folks down there whose drawls can compete with Leo's, Charley's, and Nan's! But I lost mine probably in my twenties after moving to California, where I've mostly lived ever since. I only returned to the South for family visits until Linda and I also started going there to teach in 2009.

By the way, after the devastating tornadoes that struck Raleigh and nearby parts of North Carolina in mid-April 2011, Linda and I decided to donate a portion of the proceeds we get from this book and any other *Ultimaya*-related income to relief for people in my home state. Another local place we're donating to is the state-of-the-art Duke University COPD unit that did so much to help my father live a long and fulfilling life, Duke Pulmonary/Duke Geriatric.

Are any of the characters based on real people you know—including yourself?

Bits and pieces. Since some of those real people are still alive, I wouldn't want to identify who and how. Except me, of course—there are definitely elements of both Leo and Charley that resonate close to home here and can make me grin and wince at the same time. Nan, Constance, Helen, and Ernestine draw on the girls and women I knew and sometimes loved in the South when I was growing up. And little touches come from my life too—for example, when I was a kid the real version of "Paxton Folger's Best" moonshine was still being sold over the counter in Canada, though obviously under another, real Johnston County man's name!

Did you consider trying to update the story so the technology involved would be more current? The operating system MS-DOS is ancient history now. A lot of people under 25 probably have never heard of it—do you think that might turn them off?

When I started re-entering the book in my computer in late 2009, I never gave updating the story any serious thought. For one thing, I hope the book has a timelessness to it as a kind of fable about getting what we want and figuring out who we are and why we're here. This is mainly a human story; the technology is secondary, a "supporting actor."

For another thing, the back-in-the-day details make *Ultimaya 1.0* a period piece. It lets us look back at the primitive founding years that led to today's astoundingly fast hi-tech developments. I hope a lot of older people find it nostalgic to remember back to such simpler times. In effect, back then we were all driving the "Model T's" to today's computers and

283

other technology. Yet we were marveling then at how amazing they were, every bit as much as we do at the stuff we've got now. And I hope younger people might find those old-timey interactions with then-leading edge personal computer technology quaint and charming.

If you think about it, maybe precisely because the new developments have sped along so fast, there's a differential between our memories of computer technology of just twenty years ago and other aspects of our lives back then. For example, early nineties hip-hop still feels like relatively recent popular music. By contrast, DOS seems more like an operating system from the Stone Age!

Toward the end of the book the idea comes up that Ultimaya might show up in upgrades—Ultimaya 2.0, Ultimaya 3.0. Are you planning sequels, and will you ever get to more or less current time?

If Ultimaya gets traction among readers and Leopold Stokes has some enduring go-power as a protagonist, I'm game for a whole series! One day as I was finishing *Ultimaya 1.0* it occurred to me that the next book in the series will actually jump ahead an upgrade—to *Ultimaya 3.0*. I immediately thought its hi-tech element should be played out on iPhones, iPads, and Macs, which is my current platform, though I haven't yet gotten an iPad. Right away a subtitle came to mind that makes room for some "fun with fangs" (there'll always be a bit of snakebite!) without giving me much sense at all yet of a story line: *The Challenge to the Children of Leopold Stokes*.

The idea occurred to me that, circa the time of that book's writing— say, from 2012 on into 2013, most likely—we'll be tracking the later teenage adventures of Leo's son and daughter, who happen to be twins. Then just a day or two after that idea came to me, out of the blue my father suggested that maybe a sequel to *Ultimaya 1.0* could be about a son of Leopold Stokes! His independent inspiration cinched the deal. Speaking in the tantric code of my dance with the Great Feminine Muse, I got that She was saying, "This idea is a keeper. Don't bother mulling over options."

But as of today, I don't know a lot else about the challenge to Leo's kids, their characters, or the story line—even who their mother is. Details are starting to press into my mind, yes, but I'm trying to keep them at bay. I just don't have time now. *Ultimaya 1.0* still has to make its way in the world, and I've got to serve it, along with everything else I'm trying to do these days.

As for *Ultimaya 2.0* or later releases…who knows? We'll see.

You're quite a bit older than the typical debut novelist. Obviously writing fiction has not been a cornerstone of your career. You and your wife Linda have mostly worked for years as independent spiritual teachers. Why this book? Why now? And what is the relationship between *Ultimaya 1.0* and your actual teachings?

Those are big questions, so I'll respond along several lines.

First, yes, I'm certainly not your youthful novelist bursting on the scene! Technically, my book *While Jesus Weeps* is also a novel, though it's converted from and really meant to be a play. And we've only sold a very small number of copies privately to students and friends. For all intents and purposes, then, yes, *Ultimaya 1.0* is my fictional debut.

It's probably best to let each reader who's interested find out for herself or himself what might be the relation between Linda's and my spiritual teachings and the ideas presented by characters in *Ultimaya 1.0*. I will say this: none of the book's characters speak fully for me. Not even really close.

Why this book, and why now? One, and this is very fresh and tender, for my father. He was *Ultimaya 1.0*'s most constant cheerleader from early on in its first draft years ago. In late 2009, as I started re-entering and slightly revising the original 1992 manuscript, he was already a near-miraculous survivor of severe emphysema for well over three decades. But he was getting frail, he needed oxygen most of the time, and we all knew we couldn't count on his being with us too long. This became an acute issue in the fall of 2010, when he began to decline rapidly. We thought we'd have a published book in his hands early in 2011, but small yet significant ways to improve the text kept showing up. And while he longed to see it in print, I knew my dad would never have wanted us to publish it before we were satisfied we'd brought out its full potential as a story and as a piece of writing. When he died on July 2, 2011, we were just a couple of weeks from sending it to the printer and the ebook conversion specialist.

So we lost our race with my father's remaining time. But in a September 2010 printout, he was touched to see its dedication to him and my grateful acknowledgements of both his wife Carol and himself. Then, at the time of his passing, he knew we were close to having a book in hand and that I am quite intent on giving it every opportunity to reach many people. I think he felt complete with it.

Another reason is, Linda's and my work, and that of colleagues I initially trained, has always had an ahead-of-its-time quality. Whatever their background, people who get deeply into our intensive approach to healing, growth, and authentic living almost invariably notice this. They often suffer it, too, as pioneers in any field usually do. The transformation individuals go through with Linda's and my help doesn't comfortably fit under the label "spiritual." It's a bio-spiritually natural path of integrating our human, transcendent, and animal natures into a singular, grounded wholeness, springing from the roots of both body and consciousness. The result, usually in short order, is a whole new take on life and reality that you can't possibly anticipate. We don't find complete, clear precedents for it in any other traditions or schools, secular or sacred. You'd have to experience this yourself to really see what I mean.

In crucial ways, then, this path is innovative and evolutionary. It leads you to reframe how you understand just about everything in life. So it can be quite a challenge for people to understand and adapt to unless they're well primed for it.

Given all that, my writing a novel and topical non-fiction (such as a book I hope to bring out on golf's "mental game") is a creative way to do things I love that can potentially reach many more people than our advanced trainings do. The same is true for Linda's recent release of *Joy of Being,* her CD of wordless vocal toning, and *I'm Here,* her collection of original songs and jazz standards. Our offerings as creative artists allow us to touch people and help them, in Linda's words, heal their "hungry, hurting hearts." And, if these more popular communications reach, entertain, and brighten the lives of a lot of people, some of them may also become attracted to our more intensive trainings.

In that sense, we're a bit like the Indian saint I quote in this book's opening pages. We're trying to give people what they already know they want, so they'll begin to want what we most want to give them.

Also, if Linda's music and my fiction and topical non-fiction books do reach wider audiences, the proceeds can help us fund the creation of our work's full legacy, now and into the future. We're currently beginning the most challenging creative adventure of our lives in founding Human Sun Institute (www.humansuninstitute.com; its site is under construction). We want this expression of our mature work to continue to grow in close cooperation with the democratic Waking Down in Mutuality work that I founded earlier and turned over to others' mutual control. But this new expression has its own charter and calling. Linda and I look to establish Human Sun Institute as a leading edge, globally active institution for whole-being, transformational education in consciousness, character, and culture. Wish us luck and plenty of grace!

A final point about this book's relationship to our teachings has to do with the mystery of my relationship to the Feminine Divine. "Ultimaya" as the book's title character was one of Her very first forms that I encountered. But it's taken me quite a long time to grow into the fullness of this particular relationship with Her. Now, to me, Ultimaya is not just an imaginary, enigmatic computer program in a book. She is a living, mysterious, active presence and force in my world. And, if I may speak again in tantric code, well, She was getting very tired of being kept in the back room of my life and work! It's Her debutante ball, Her time to shine.

√cn

CPSIA information can be obtained at www.ICGtesting.com
Printed in the USA
LVOW080608050412

276284LV00006B/180/P

9 780975 353257